Effective Intellectual Property Management for Small to Medium Businesses and Social Enterprises

Effective Intellectual Property Management for Small to Medium Businesses and Social Enterprises

IP Branding, Licenses, Trademarks, Copyrights, Patents and Contractual Arrangements

Francina Cantatore
Elizabeth Crawford-Spencer

BrownWalker Press
Irvine • Boca Raton

Effective Intellectual Property Management for Small to Medium Businesses and Social Enterprises: IP Branding, Licenses, Trademarks, Copyrights, Patents and Contractual Arrangements

Copyright © 2018 Francina Cantatore and Elizabeth Crawford-Spencer
All rights reserved.

No part of this publication may be reproduced, distributed, or transmitted in any form or by any means, including photocopying, recording, or other electronic or mechanical methods, without the prior written permission of the publisher, except in the case of brief quotations embodied in critical reviews and certain other noncommercial uses permitted by copyright law.

BrownWalker Press/Universal Publishers, Inc.
Irvine • Boca Raton
USA • 2018
www.BrownWalkerPress.com

ISBN: 978-1-62734-699-3 (pbk.)
ISBN: 978-1-62734-700-6 (ebk.)

Typeset by Medlar Publishing Solutions Pvt Ltd, India

Cover design by Ivan Popov

Publisher's Cataloging-in-Publication Data

Names: Cantatore, Francina, author. | Crawford-Spencer, Elizabeth, author.
Title: Effective Intellectual Property Management for Small to Medium Businesses
  and Social Enterprises: IP Branding, Licenses, Trademarks, Copyrights, Patents and
  Contractual Arrangements/Francina Cantatore [and] Elizabeth Crawford-Spencer.
Description: Irvine, CA: BrownWalker, 2018.
Identifiers: LCCN 2018938421 | ISBN 978-1-62734-699-3 (pbk.)
  | ISBN 978-1-62734-700-6 (ebook)
Subjects: LCSH: Intellectual Property. | Trademarks. | Copyright. | Patents.
  | Intellectual Capital. | Branding (Marketing) | Small Business--Law and Legislation.
  | BISAC: LAW/Intellectual Property/General. | BUSINESS & ECONOMICS/
  Business Law. | BUSINESS & ECONOMICS/Small Business.
Classification: LCC K1404 .C36 2018 (print)
  | LCC K1404 (ebook) | DDC 346/.048--dc23.

TABLE OF CONTENTS

List of Figures and Tables	*ix*
Acknowledgements	*xi*
Introduction	*xiii*

1 An Overview of IP in the SME and SMSE Context — 1
  Introduction: Intellectual Property, Intellectual Capital
    and Intellectual Property Rights Management — 1
  Copyright — 2
  Trademark — 3
  Patent — 3
  Trade Secret — 3
  IP Protection and Management: General Considerations — 4
  Achieving Balance Between Reward for Work and Innovation — 11
  SMSE's and IP — 12
  Why is IP Important to SMSE's? — 13
  IP Management in Practice — 13

2 IP as a Component of Intellectual Capital — 19
  Introduction — 19
  Appropriation of IP — 22
  The Importance of IP in Brand Building — 24
  Conclusion — 28

3 IP Management, SMEs and Civil Society: Understanding the Key Factors Inhibiting the Proper Management of IP in the SME and SMSE Context — 29

Introduction — 29
The Significance of IP Management — 31
    An Evolving Landscape — 31
Contextualising IP Management — 33
    Third Sector — 33
    Social Enterprise — 36
Risks and Challenges in Managing IP in the Third Sector — 38
    Motivation — 39
    Mission and Purpose — 40
    Non-distribution of Profit — 42
    Ownership — 43
    Competence — 44
    Constraints of IP Laws and Regulation — 46
Increased Challenges for Social Enterprises — 49
Conclusion — 53

4 Case Studies in SME IP Management — 55

Introduction — 55
The Research Study — 57
    Methodology — 57
Data Analysis and Findings — 60
    Legal Structures — 60
    Importance of Branding — 60
    Registered Trademarks — 61
    Registered Patents — 61
    Copyright Protection — 62
    Regulation of IP Ownership by Agreement — 63
    Pro Bono Legal Advice — 64
Problems with Implementing an IP Management Structure — 64
Emerging Themes — 65
    Attitudes Towards IP Management — 65
    SMSEs Can Make Better Use of Pro Bono Resources — 66
    Agreements Used to Protect IP and Confidential Information to Varying Degrees — 67

Most Have IP Assets that Require Trademark and Copyright Protection	67
Disconnect Between Branding and IP Management	67
Reasons for IP Management Failure	68
Conclusions and Recommendations: A Suggested Model	68

5 IP Management in a Global Marketplace — 75

Introduction: A Tailored Approach to IP Rights Protection	75
Managing and Protecting Different Types of IP	76
Trademarks	76
Copyright	90
Patents	98
Contractual Arrangements	102
Conclusion	110

6 IP as Collateral in Security Transactions — 113

Introduction: IP as Collateral	113
IP and the PPSA	116
IP Licences	118
IP Specific Provisions	119
Maximising IP Protection	122
Priorities	122
Registration Requirements	124
Challenges for Organisations in Dealing with IP Under the PPSA	127
SMEs and SMSEs	127
Multiple IP Registers	127
Copyright	128
IP Intrinsically Associated with Collateral	133
Conclusion	134

7 Approaches to IP Management in Social Franchising — 137

Introduction	137
Models of Social Franchising: Social Franchising and Contracting Parties	143
Traditional Social Franchising: Non-profit Franchising Model with Non-profit Franchisor	143
Microfranchising: Non-profit Franchising with a Non-profit Franchisor and For-profit Franchisees	146

Social Franchise Investment: For-profit Franchisor with
   Non-profit Franchisees ... 149
The Use of Social Franchising in Australia ... 152
Traditional Non-profit Franchising and Social Franchise
   Investment: Both Under Represented in Australia ... 154
Examples of Microfranchising in the Australian Context ... 155
Mini-case Study of Microfranchising: Buffed Shoe Shine ... 156
Social Franchise: The Way Forward ... 159
Conclusion ... 161

Appendices

Appendix A: Licence of Intellectual Property ... 163
Appendix B: Deed of Assignment of Intellectual Property Rights ... 177
Appendix C: Contractor's Service Agreement With
   Confidentiality Clause ... 183
Appendix D: Confidentiality Agreement ... 191
Appendix E: Franchise Agreement ... 199

LIST OF FIGURES AND TABLES

Figure 1 – The Inter-relationship of IP with IC	22
Figure 2 – IP Management Model for SMEs	70
Figure 3 – Transferee Liability Under the *Copyright Act*	121
Figure 4 – Transferee Liability Under the PPSA	121
Figure 5 – Traditional Non-profit Franchising	144
Figure 6 – Microfranchising	146
Figure 7 – Social Franchise Investment	150
Table 1 – Legal Structures	60
Table 2 – Perceived Problems in Managing IP	64
Table 3 – Non-profit Franchising—Summary of Key Characteristics	144
Table 4 – Microfranchising with Non-profit Franchisor—Summary of Key Characteristics	147
Table 5 – Social Franchise Investment—Summary of Key Characteristics	151
Table 6 – Summary of Models of Franchising for Social Enterprise	153

ACKNOWLEDGEMENTS

We would like to sincerely thank Jeff Young of Universal Publishers for his advice, patience and attention to detail during the publishing process. We also owe a debt of gratitude to our research assistant, Marryum Kahloon, who spent countless hours editing, revising and re-editing the manuscript to shape it into its current form. Our thanks also go to colleagues and fellow professionals Professor Myles McGregor-Lowndes, Associate Professor Bobette Wolski and IP specialist lawyer Taryn Lovegrove for taking the time to read our final draft and provide us with some thoughtful and positive feedback. Your contributions are very much appreciated. And finally, we would like to thank our partners and family for their support and encouragement in helping to bring this publication to fruition.

INTRODUCTION

Intellectual property (IP) management is a topic of significant concern for all organisations, irrespective of their size and nature. It is, however, an area of corporate management that has often been neglected or overlooked by small and medium size enterprises, and even more so by smaller third sector enterprises. The reasons are varied and include a lack of money, knowledge, time, or a combination of these factors. The intrinsic value of IP is often underestimated and receives little attention from smaller organisations—yet it is an integral part of any organisation's asset portfolio. Often, effective IP management strategies can make the difference between the success and failure of an organisation. This book focuses on ways in which small and medium size enterprises—including social enterprises—can protect and manage their IP. It deals with the importance and value of IP, and the specific needs and requirements of SMEs in relation to IP management, highlighting problematic issues and providing structural guidance in relation to IP management. The book draws on qualitative research conducted in Australia in this area of the law, identifying the unique challenges faced by third sector SMEs in managing their IP, and providing practical strategies for effective IP management and protection.

CHAPTER ONE

AN OVERVIEW OF IP IN THE SME AND SMSE CONTEXT

Introduction: Intellectual Property, Intellectual Capital and Intellectual Property Rights Management

This first chapter provides an overview of intellectual property (IP) in the Small and Medium Size Enterprise (SME) and Small and Medium Size Social Enterprise (SMSE) context, and explains the nature of IP as intellectual capital (IC). It introduces the basic components of IP rights—copyright, trademark, patents, and trade secrets—and outlines the fundamentals of IP management. This chapter also considers the philosophical debate and importance of achieving a balance between protecting IP and the importance of access to IP in the interests of innovation. This chapter also outlines the particular significance of IP in the SMSE context and the challenges faced by third sector enterprise generally in the management of IP.

IP has been recognised as an element of a firm's IC. Virtually all enterprises own or use some type of IP such as logos, brand names, manuals and contracts, training materials, software, databases, sound or visual recordings, designs and even unique attributes such as sounds and colour schemes. IP is generally regarded as 'creations of the mind'[1] and includes inventions, literary and artistic works, symbols, logos and images, names

---

[1] World Intellectual Property Organization, *What is Intellectual Property?* (2016) WIPO <http://www.wipo.int/about-ip/en/>.

and brand names, designs and industrial designs, and software and sound or visual recordings. In the context of this book and research study, a high-level approach is favoured, founded on practice-based considerations, and the focus is on providing insight into sustainable IP management strategies that can be applied by stakeholders.

Some notably relevant categories of IP referred to are copyright in written materials (such as training manuals or contracts), computer software and website content, images, sound and visual recordings, trademarks (such as symbols, logos and images or business names, domain names and brand names), patents in goods, products or processes, and confidential information (including trade secrets and know-how).

From a legal perspective IP rights allow the originating creator or 'owner' to maintain control of a creation, and the enforcement of IP rights can prevent attempts to adapt or misuse the original creation for another purpose. Thus, the owner of IP may have rights to exclude others from its use, reproduction and distribution. It is important to recognise that there is no IP in an idea until such time as it's written down or made tangible. If it is only an idea, then it has no protection under the law. In the third sector context, relevant IP may typically include trademarks, patents and copyright.[2]

The three main types of IP rights that impact SMEs are examined in detail in Chapter 5. However, by way of introduction it is necessary to briefly distinguish the various concepts.

Copyright

Copyright is a statutory right which gives the owner exclusive rights over a body of work for a limited or fixed period of time dependent on the medium. It is essentially a legal right that grants the creator of an original work exclusive rights for its use and distribution. These rights are not absolute but limited by exceptions under the copyright laws of different countries and states, including the right of 'fair use'.

---

[2]In Australia, the *Trade Marks Act 1995* (Cth), *Copyright Act 1968* (Cth) and *Patents Act* 1990 (Cth) primarily regulate intellectual property. In, New Zealand the equivalent legislation is the *Trade Marks Act 2002* (NZ), *Patents Act 2013* (NZ) and *Copyright Act 1994* (NZ).

Trademark

A trademark has been defined as 'a sign used, or intended to be used, to distinguish goods or services dealt with or provided in the course of trade by a person from goods or services so dealt with or provided by any other person'.[3] A trademark may be an unregistered common law mark or a mark registered under the trademark laws of different countries. Registration gives the owner of the mark the exclusive rights listed under the legislation. Registered trademarks are the personal property of the registered owner.

Patent

Described as a set of exclusive rights granted by a country or state to an inventor for a limited period of time, patents are subject to requirements of detailed public disclosure of an invention. The invention is a solution to a specific technological problem and may consist of a product or a process of manufacture. A patent may be classified as a standard patent, innovation patent, or petty patent. Patent rights—like other IP rights—are personal property, and may be assigned, willed, sold, licensed, or otherwise dealt with by the patentee. The patented product enters the public domain after a maximum of 20 years for a normal patent; if it is an innovation patent it usually enters the public domain after eight years.

Related to these IP rights are trade secrets, which may also be protectable under the law.

Trade Secret

Trade secrets can include any formula, pattern, device, or compilation of information that is used in a person's business and that gives that person an opportunity to derive an advantage over other persons who do not know or use it. Trade secrets are a form of property and may be sold. They may also be protected against competition without infringing the general prohibition against contracts in restraint of trade. An employee is usually

---

[3] *Trade Marks Act* 1995 (Cth) s 17.

required to maintain the confidentiality of trade secrets learnt during employment, even after leaving that employment. In environmental law, for example, persons who gain knowledge of trade secrets in the course of considering applications for permits to emit pollution, or otherwise in the course of administering legislation, may commit an offence if details are improperly disclosed.

IP Protection and Management: General Considerations

As with other types of property rights, an owner of IP has certain rights to exclude others from its use—IP rights have value and can create new value both financially and in terms of social welfare benefits, during operation and expansion as well as upon disposition.[4] For these reasons organisations have an interest in ensuring that IP is managed effectively; a firm 'must use IP rights in combination with other strategies, while being fully cognisant of the strengths and weaknesses of the various IP regimes'.[5]

Due to the importance and value of IP, commercial success in the information age is inextricably linked to the effective management of IP.[6] Philips Electronics, for example, reportedly employs over 300 IP staff, while Toshiba has a dedicated IP group that handles all the activities surrounding filing and enforcing IP rights; it also hosts an information centre dedicated to supporting IP management. Case studies of blue chip corporations

---

[4] Gollin argues that copyright balance is the free global flow of creative expression with incentive to express new ideas; patent systems balance access to existing inventions with incentives to invent new ones; trade secret balances benefits of sharing personal knowledge publicly with the possibility of keeping the secrets safe within a limited group; trademarks systems balance the benefits of merchant creativity in marketing goods and services and consumers' need to know the source of goods. See Michael A. Gollin, *Driving Innovation: Intellectual Property Strategies for a Dynamic World* (Cambridge University Press, 2008) 51–52, 59.

[5] William van Caenegem, 'Intellectual Property and Intellectual Capital' (2002) *Intellectual Property Forum* 10.

[6] Wuryan Andayani et al, 'Corporate Social Responsibility, Good Corporate Governance and the Intellectual Property: An External Strategy of the Management to Increase the Company's Value' (Paper presented at National Conference on Management Research, Makassar, 27 November 2008). The authors conclude that 'intellectual property had important role towards the values of the company. The intellectual property could improve the values of the company and investors considered the variable of intellectual property as an important thing'. See also Although it has been recognized that economic wealth comes from knowledge assets-intellectual capital- and its useful application, replacing or perhaps supplementing land, labour, and capital (Dean and Kretschmer, 2007).

have documented a range of IP management strategies.⁷ Indeed it is not hard to think of the current era in the progression of capitalist economic systems as an era of 'intellectual capitalism,' in which building effective strategies around IP provides a major, sustainable advantage.⁸

What is clear is that, in order to manage them, IP assets must first be identified; second, the value of trademarks, patents, copyright and trade secrets held by the organisation must be quantified; and third, the level of risk associated with IP rights protection, or failure to protect, must be assessed. These processes should incorporate planning and strategies for protecting against threats and vulnerability, and establishing controls with both offensive and defensive efforts.⁹

IP rights are viewed as a valuable asset to any organisation, including third sector organisations. IP is considered by many to be instrumental in the ongoing viability and innovative capacity of an organisation, namely 'the invisible infrastructure of innovation'.¹⁰ The value of IP rights is increasingly recognised in commercial dealings.¹¹ Organisations are more frequently offering intangible property as collateral, and creditors are more readily accepting such assets as security for loans.¹² In this way commercial organisations have been increasing their ability to obtain funding by offering intangible property, for example copyright in a film or in musical works,¹³ as collateral. It has been said that the importance of tangible property such as real estate, machinery, and inventory has reduced, and intangible property has gained greater significance,¹⁴ causing a 'paradigm shift'.¹⁵ Moreover, the inclusion of IP rights is often incidental

---

⁷Scott Wilson, 'Value, Protect, Exploit: How Managing Intellectual Property Can Build and Sustain Competitive Advantage' (Research Study, Deloitte Research, Deloitte Services LP, 2007) <http://www.deloitte.com/assets/Dcom-Bulgaria/Local%20Assets/Documents/BG_tmt_ManagingIP_160807.pdf>.

⁸Ove Granstrand, *The Economics and Management of Intellectual Property* (Edward Elgar, 1999).

⁹Ibid.

¹⁰Gollin, above n 4, 51–59; see also Francina Cantatore and Elizabeth Crawford-Spencer, 'Yours, Mine, and Ours: The Development, Management and Protection of Intellectual Property in Third Sector Enterprise' (2014) 3 *Intellectual Property Quarterly* 210, 210–226.

¹¹Francina Cantatore 'Intellectual Property Rights and the PPSA: Challenges for Interest holders, Creditors and Practitioners' (2015) 25(3) *Australian Intellectual Property Journal* 141.

¹²Andrea Tosato, 'Security Interests Over Intellectual Property' (2011) 6(2) *Journal of Intellectual Property Law & Practice* 93, 93.

¹³Judy Lam, 'Banking on a Dream: Perfecting Security Interests in Copyright—An International Survey' (1993) 13 *Loyola of Los Angeles Entertainment Law Journal* 319.

¹⁴Tosato, above n 12, 93.

¹⁵Gordon V. Smith and Russell L. Parr, *Valuation of Intellectual Property and Intangible Assets* (Wiley, 3rd ed, 2000) 1.

in transactions where security is taken over the assets of an organisation obtaining funding.[16]

The ability of any enterprise to manage its IP effectively is seen by IP protection advocates as a significant factor in achieving goals and maximising the benefits of assets. IP management is important to any business structure that creates, innovates, expands or advances pre-existing ideas. As IP owners have certain rights to exclude others from its use, reproduction and/or distribution,[17] organisations have an interest in ensuring that IP is managed effectively. A firm 'must use IP rights in combination with other strategies, while being fully cognisant of the strengths and weaknesses of the various IP regimes'.[18]

Thus, engaging effectively with IP rights allows creators to maintain control over the use of their ideas, developments or innovations which then protect the organisation's core values and social causes from misuse by others. By protecting its core values, the organisation will maintain accountability to stakeholders, its target audience and the general public.[19] Consequently, the failure to adequately manage IP is thought to have adverse consequences for organisations in relation to economic sustainability, growth and public image.

Of course, the benefits of protecting IP are regarded as more than just economic:[20]

> social welfare should not be assessed by reference only to the price of access to copyright material, but also by reference to non-economic benefits such as being part of a community in which creative activity is encouraged and fostered.[21]

There is, of course, a healthy debate surrounding the underlying values of IP ownership and protection. The politics of IP can be polarising.

---

[16] Tosato, above n 12, 93.

[17] World Intellectual Property Organization, above n 1.

[18] Nick Bontis, 'Managing Organisational Knowledge by Diagnosing Intellectual Capital: Framing and Advancing the State of the Field' in Chun Wei Choo and Nick Bontis (eds) *The Strategic Management of Intellectual Capital and Organisational Knowledge* (Oxford University Press, 2002) 621, 642.

[19] Francina Cantatore and Elizabeth Crawford-Spencer 'Intellectual Property Rights Management in Small and Medium Size Social Enterprise in Australia' (2015) 4 *Intellectual Property Quarterly* 328, 331.

[20] Cantatore and Crawford-Spencer, above n 10, 210.

[21] Australian Copyright Council, Submission to the Intellectual Property & Competition Review Committee (IPCRC), *Effects On Competition Of Australia's Intellectual Property Laws*, 17 December 1999, 3.

Proponents espouse a range of benefits of IP management and protective measures, while critics advocate abolishing them. Advocates of IP rights emphasise their value and potential to create new value, both financially and in terms of social welfare, during operation and expansion of an organisation as well as upon its disposition. It is claimed that the active management and protection of IP rights aids organisations to compete on the basis of reputation associated with a product rather than price alone. For this reason, SMSEs have an interest in ensuring that IP is managed effectively, including measures for protection of IP. Advocates of IP legal regimes argue that IP laws provide incentives for people to be creative, promote public disclosure of new information, facilitate the transfer of (and investment in) innovation, and implement industrial policy.[22] They credit IP rights with driving innovation, which in turn improves standards of living.[23] For them the key to progress is balance; 'the right combination of access and exclusivity can drive the innovation cycle.'[24]

Critics, however, argue that IP regimes facilitate the withholding or restricting of information from others. They suggest that IP protection keeps innovations out of the public domain; increases the cost of technology; creates monopolies; concentrates industry on what can be protected, not what is best; is expensive to obtain and maintain; and requires burdensome and costly legal and regulatory institutions.[25] They say there is no conclusive evidence that IP regimes create value, and there is also uncertainty with respect to valuation of IP rights. Critics also point out that accounting standards and methods vary, and that there is generally little co-ordination among diverse professionals dealing with an organisation's IP rights.[26] The nature of IP is constantly changing in response to technology, which means that it can be difficult to maintain consistent and fair rules around IP.

While protection of IP may benefit an organisation, there are risks. Every enterprise needs to find the balance and approach that is appropriate,

---

[22]Gollin, above n 4, 51–59. Gollin further argues that IP is a means of balancing public access and private exclusivity and that exclusivity and access are part of a dynamic system of creativity, '[s]uccessful IP management involves finding the right balance of exclusivity and access in any given situation'.
[23]Ibid 104–109.
[24]Ibid 299.
[25]Cantatore and Crawford-Spencer, above n 10, 225.
[26]Jason Sacha, 'Virtual Advantages for Charities' (2012) 25(1) *Intellectual Property Journal* 75, 75–95.

8   Effective Intellectual Property Management

'the right combination of access and exclusivity can drive the innovation cycle.'[27] The underlying question of whether the cost-benefit considerations of commercial organisations translate to the SMSEs context (where the emphasis is on collaboration rather than competition) is further explored and discussed in a future chapter.

While it is true that an organisation without an IP strategy can save short-term costs and the effort involved in reporting, tracking and protecting their trade secrets, inventions, copyright, and trademark risks, such an organisation may also miss opportunities to build assets, may be more vulnerable to competitors' activities, and can incur liability for infringement.[28] An organisation without an IP strategy is likely to fail to acknowledge the return on its investments in innovation (even though it may have a duty to shareholders) and is likely to miss opportunities to use IP tools to help fulfill its mission.[29] Furthermore, if an organisation permits others to use its IP—such as logos, name or copyrighted works—the terms and conditions of use should be contained in a written licensing agreement, to prevent trademark infringement and damage to the organisation's reputation and goodwill.[30]

While copyright in work undertaken by employees within the scope of their employment will generally be owned by the organisation,[31] written

---

[27] Gollin, above n 4, 29–40.

[28] Ibid 132. Gollin describes the risks for an organization with 'nonstrategy': It may lose technical information, control over processes, specifications and other operations information. Software and graphic designs in reports, packaging, and webpages are at risk and the value of copyrights can be lost or diminished due to non-marking of works and nonregistration. And a zero level organization is likely to violate software user licenses. There may be also issues with respect to patent protection and exposure to damages for infringement.

[29] Though in many cases the common law will confirm rights to trademarks in use by an organization, employees and consultants may be free to register and use trademarks in foreign jurisdictions. Independent contractors and consultants who create logos and marketing copy may secure copyrights, and trade secrets such as formulas, contact lists, organizational policies may be appropriated by employees and others. It depends on insurance coverage in case of liability for mismanagement of IP, permits competitors to use its IP without sharing of benefits, and ignores legal avenues available to expand its IP portfolio. Such an organization allows others to use its IP without any charge, recognition, or obligation and may similarly fail to respect IP rights of others, and therefore faces exposure to liability for infringement. For these and other reasons Gollin suggests that 'nonstrategy' is the worst alternative for most organizations. See ibid 361–363.

[30] Jeffrey S. Tenenbaum, *Licensing your Association's Logo to Others*, Venables News and Insights <http://www.venable.com/licensing-your-associations-logo-to-others-01-01-1999/>.

[31] Jeffrey S. Tenenbaum, *Does Your Association Own the Work Product of Your Contractors, Authors, Speakers, Officers, Directors and Committee Members?* Venables News and Insights <http://www.venable.com/does-your-association-own-the-work-product-of-your-contractors-authors-speakers-officers-directors-and-committee-members-03-01-2002/>.

copyright assignments should be obtained for work done by external contractors including work such as written copy, graphics or videos. Computer programs commissioned by a firm are also not protected unless covered by a written assignment.[32] Under Australian law, inventions will be owned by the employing organisation only if they were invented in the course and scope of an employee's duties.[33] Using an employer's resources will not automatically entitle the organisation to the assignment of an invention,[34] thus a written contract should be concluded to protect both parties' interests.

Licensing of IP can play an important role in creating functional structures within an organisation or entity. For organisations reliant on the use of patents, the concept of patent pools has become a relevant consideration. Evidence suggests that companies are acknowledging the benefits of participating in IP collaborations. In 2001, for example, sales of devices in the US based in whole or in part on pooled patents were estimated to be at least US$100 billion.[35] Patent pools provide collaborative advantages such as cost sharing and obtaining the benefit of others' experience,[36] as well as opportunities to obtain IP rights at a reasonable cost 'without having to negotiate at their own expense for months or years.'[37]

These types of arrangements have been a viable option for large corporations holding patents to consumer electronics such as Dell and Apple over recent years.[38] The biomedical research community has also embraced development of patent pools for cancer, HIV/AIDS, severe acute respiratory syndrome (SARS), and agricultural biotechnologies research.[39] Patent pool arrangements do, however, raise some concerns, such as the potential for anti-competitive behaviour and the difficulties associated with

---

[32]Michael L. Gollin and Ronald W. Taylor, *Protecting Your Company's Intellectual Property*, Venables News and Insights <http://www.venable.com/protecting-your-companys-intellectual-property-04-01-1999/> 8.

[33]William van Caenegem, *Intellectual Property Law and Innovation* (Cambridge University Press, 2007), 97.

[34]Ibid; *Victoria University of Technology v Wilson* [2004] VSC 33.

[35]Josh Lerner and Eric Lin, 'Collaboration in Intellectual Property: An Overview', *WIPO Magazine* (online), November 2012 <http://www.wipo.int/wipo_magazine/en/2012/06/article_0008.html>.

[36]Ibid.

[37]Cameron Gray, 'A New Era in IP licensing: The Unit Licence Right™ Program' (2008) 28(10) *The Licensing Journal* 5.

[38]Ibid.

[39]Lerner and Lin, above n 35.

monitoring a partner's actions.⁴⁰ For larger third sector organisations patent pools may provide long term IP solutions, as the sharing of inventions and innovative research also provides the opportunity for the development of strategic and collaborative relationships.

The issue of trade secrets merits consideration as organisations may rely on confidential information or trade secrets in their activities, which should be protected. The form of protection will differ depending on where the organisation is situated. For example, Japan and some US states provide statutory protection for trade secrets,⁴¹ but Australia relies on its common law and remedies for the unauthorised use of trade secrets or confidential information are limited to contract or equity.⁴² While trade secrets do not require registration in order to be protected, adequate security measures should be in place to demonstrate that reasonable measures have been taken to maintain the secrecy of the information.⁴³ Gollin and Taylor suggest that confidential information should be provided to employees on a 'need-to-know' basis only, and that passwords should be used for computer files and email. Furthermore, they propose that confidentiality clauses should be inserted into all employment agreements.⁴⁴ In theory, these steps are basic protection standards that should be applied in all organisations, and need not be costly.

In practice, protection measures may impact upon the organisation's IC, as discussed in greater detail in Chapter 2. For example, they may impact upon flexibility to work collaboratively with others and to effectively harness human capital. Employees and stakeholders in the organisation comprise the human capital of the organisation, including their competences, skills and innovative talents.⁴⁵ It may be difficult to impose stringent protection strategies where such individuals are closely involved with the organisation's day-to-day operations. In Australia an action for breach of confidence requires the information to be 'secret'.⁴⁶ Although absolute

---

⁴⁰Ibid. The authors provide an example of the recent lawsuits between Apple and Samsung, a key supplier of Apple's processor chips, which 'provide a cautionary tale about the pitfalls of contractual joint collaborations and the disputes that can arise between market rivals operating within a complex strategic context.'

⁴¹For example, *The Uniform Trade Secrets Act* (UTSA) applies in Maryland, Virginia and the District of Columbia. See also Gollin and Taylor, above n 36, 6.

⁴²William Van Caenegem, Intellectual Property in Australia, (Wolters Kluwer 2010), p. 184.

⁴³Gollin and Taylor, above n 36, 5.

⁴⁴Gollin and Taylor, above n 36, 5–6.

⁴⁵Bontis, above n 18.

⁴⁶*Coco v AN Clark (Engineers) Ltd* (1986) 1A IPR 587, 590.

secrecy is not required, the information must not be available in the public domain or known to those 'amongst whom such information normally circulates.'[47] This requires careful monitoring on the part of management and is a consideration in deciding whether or not to register an innovation or share knowledge with collaborators. IP protection may also impact upon relational capital, including relationships with customers, suppliers and other partners and to the public, as well as strategic alliances, licenses and agreements.[48] Implementing adequate protection measures for confidential information and trade secrets, while maintaining strategic alliances and collaboration, can present significant challenges.

Achieving Balance Between Reward for Work and Innovation

IP can serve as an instrument for innovation if there is a balance between exclusion and access to ideas. The International Commission on Intellectual Property Rights has stated that the crucial issue is to reconcile the public interest in accessing new knowledge and the products of new knowledge and products on which material and cultural progress may depend.

People who wish to cite and learn from others' patented ideas can search the public domain, which contains publicly accessible published and recorded information. There should be a balance between protecting the rights and interests of the IP rights owners (rewarding them for their efforts) and opportunities for the public to innovate and develop new ideas.

This balance of interests in IP protection can be characterised according to the four basic categories of IP: (1) Copyright, balances the free global flow of creative expression with incentive to express new ideas; (2) Patents, balances access to existing inventions with incentives to invent new ones; (3) Trade secrets, balances the benefits of sharing personal knowledge publicly with the possibility of keeping the secret safe within a limited group; and (4) Trademarks, balances the benefits of merchant creativity in marketing goods and services through commercial channels of trade with the consumer's need to know the source of goods.

---

[47]William Van Caenegem, *Intellectual Property in Australia* (Wolters Kluwer 2010), 186. For example, in the case of *Franchi v Franchi* [1967] RPC 149 an invention which was made public in a patent application in Belgium, was held not to be sufficiently secret in the United Kingdom as patent agents could be expected to monitor such publications.
[48]Bontis, above n 18.

The economic development and human rights benefits of IP systems are also factors in this equation. To be of benefit to poor countries, IP systems should contribute to sustainable development by stimulating local innovation, and making more technology and cultural innovation available locally at competitive prices. In a balanced system, innovators have sufficient exclusivity to achieve their goals, while people wanting to use innovative information, material, or products have sufficient access to reach their own goals.

IP laws are designed to strike a balance between development of new ideas and reward for effort in creating new IP. Laws such as time limitations on how long patents last allow others to develop and use ideas and encourage the patent owners to create new and continue to develop their own patented ideas.

SMSE's and IP

This book is principally focused on SMEs, and includes consideration of SMSEs. 'Third sector' is a term that has come into increasing use over the past 20 years as an alternative to the term 'non-profit' or 'not-for-profit' to describe the sector of the economy that is neither public/government nor private/for profit. 'Third sector enterprise' is often used to refer to enterprise with an overriding social purpose that may be public or private, involving diverse models of ownership, and that *may or may not distribute profit* (hence the need for an alternative to the 'non-profit' designation). Other terms that continue to have related meanings include 'not-for-profit enterprise' and 'social enterprise'. Because there is still a need for clarification of the meanings of these terms, the 'third sector' is used in the context of this book as an umbrella term for SMSEs and other non-profit organisations.

Due to an increasing tendency of government to turn to third sector organisations to assist in carrying out a wide variety of functions, from the provision of social welfare to the promotion of economic development, the sector is expected to continue to play an important role, not only in developed countries such as the United Kingdom and Australia, but also more globally. In 2002 a Social Enterprise Unit was established within the British Department of Trade and Industry as a centrepiece of social reform policy; and social enterprise has been reported to be the fastest growing sector in the UK. As one researcher has put it, 'As "Big Society" tends to cut funding and discredit business, both for-profit (FP) and not-for-profit (NFP) activity gravitate toward social enterprise."

Why is IP Important to SMSE's?

By enforcing IP rights, competitors in a commercial workplace will be unable to access and benefit from the creator's ideas. IP protection thus provides a reward for effort; and in the third sector, enforcement of IP rights may prevent attempts to adapt or misuse the original ideas for another purpose. The different types of creations or innovations consequently affect the processes of application, length of time the creation is protected, and the enforcement mechanisms for the IP.

Because protected IP rights are a valuable asset, they can be sold for financial gain. The active protection of these rights can aid businesses in competing on the basis of reputation associated with a product rather than on price alone. Critical to the protection of IP is allowing the owner the right to determine *who* can use their intellectual property and *how* it can be used. As the World Intellectual Property Organization states:

> Protection of intellectual property is not an end in itself: it is a means to encourage creative activity, industrialization, investment, and honest trade. All this is designed to contribute more safety and comfort, less poverty and more beauty, in the lives of men.

IP Management in Practice

Managing IP is critical to any business structure that creates, innovates, expands, or evolves pre-existing ideas. Rather than viewing IP as withholding or restricting information from others; engaging with IP allows the creator to maintain control over the use of their ideas, developments or innovations which then protects the organisation's core values and social causes from misuse by others. SMSE's risk missing a key component of success if they neglect to attend to the strategic management of IP.

In their 2013 Report,[49] Brant and Lohse noted that SMEs develop IP management strategies for four purposes, namely to appropriate interests; to protect interests when collaborating; to ensure freedom to operate and to avoid infringement of third party IP rights; and to signal value. They noted that IP management may represent a particular challenge for smaller firms that are active in several markets, as global activities require a more sophisticated approach that can be harder to develop. In order to secure the firm's competitive position and manage IP-related risks, an SME's leadership needs to know whether the company's inventions are properly protected in each strategic jurisdiction—for instance, whether a patent claim has been appropriately drafted so as to protect the most valuable features of an invention—and whether it has a freedom to operate in relation to its most important products or processes. Training programs to inform managers of innovative SMEs about the importance of IP management while coaching them on the practical aspects are useful in this regard.[50]

Apart from formal IP rights registration, some of the alternative 'complementary' IP protection methods may focus on secrecy; capitalising on first mover advantages and innovating faster than competitors; building complexity into products and processes, making them difficult to imitate; defensive publishing (destroying novelty so that a competitor cannot patent a product or process); focusing on achieving a large market share in niche markets; building strong brand recognition; and creating strong commercial channels and relationships with customers. In addition Brant and Lohse recognise the value of hybrid strategies combining formal and complementary methods, which usually combine formal registration with secrecy:[51]

> Recent research has revealed that the most successful innovative SMEs strategically blend formal and alternative mechanisms, according to their specific resources, needs, and business environment … These results, at least partially, refute studies claiming that SMEs use fewer formal IP rights solely due to resource constraints and lack of knowledge, as well as the work of certain authors equating relatively lower use of formal IP rights with ineffective appropriation.

---

[49]Jennifer Brant and Sebastien Lohse, 'Enhancing Intellectual Property Management and Appropriation by Innovative SMEs' (Innovation and Intellectual Property Series Research Paper No 1, International Chamber of Commerce, 2013) 5.
[50]Ibid 10.
[51]Brant and Lohse, above n 51, 15.

They make several useful recommendations regarding IP management, namely: SMEs can take steps to improve patent quality, which can increase legal certainty and help to ensure that IP rights can be used to signal value to potential investors, partners, and competitors. Government can ensure that IP rights are available and enforceable at reasonable cost, including by reducing official fees for patent filing, prosecution, and maintenance by SMEs. There should be ease of access to patent filing and prosecution by SMEs, including by providing for expedited review of applications from SMEs. They also recommend instituting outreach and training programs for SME business leaders. This will raise awareness about the importance of sound IP management, improve SMEs' intellectual asset management, and increase opportunities for them to engage with IP officials. Government should consider enacting policies that support the provision of insurance for SMEs to offset the costs associated with defending their IP positions in litigation, which represents a significant risk for smaller firms; and enacting modern trade secrets laws to bolster the protection afforded by resource-effective secrecy strategies, which are often the default protection mode adopted by innovative SMEs.[52]

In addition, to encourage innovation and partnerships, government can support the establishment of clusters and innovation networks, on their own or together with industry groups, whether directly or indirectly through incentives; develop frameworks that enable patenting and subsequent licensing of publicly-funded research, and that enhance collaboration in general between the private sector and public research institutes; and support the creation of incubators, whether government-run or for profit, which can deliver access to services that innovative SMEs need, such as coaching on business skills and IP management strategies.[53]

The next chapters in this book explore some of the many reasons why organisations in the third sector may fail to adequately manage and protect their IP, and suggest that many face greater challenges than for profit organisations. For example, they may lack the 'eyes and ears' to sufficiently understand and effectively identify, evaluate, and manage IP in business. This is because of a deficiency of infrastructure, management skills and funds. Also, they depend greatly on sustaining industry relationships and cultivating partnerships, which can create tension between IP protection

---

[52]Ibid 17.
[53]Ibid 18.

and collaboration. An example of this is naked licensing—where a trademark owner can lose the right to enforce a trademark against a licensee. In the US case of *Freecycle Sunnyvale v Freecycle Network* (2010) the Court of Appeals found that a non-profit organisation, Freecycle Network, had abandoned its trademarks by allowing another party to use them without sufficient quality control.

The best approach to managing IP is to create a strategy, i.e. a process of establishing goals and priorities and then achieving them. Strategic management takes place when a leader sets simple, long-term consistent goals based on an objective appraisal of available resources and a profound understanding of the competitive environment, and then follows up with effective implementation.

The chapters in this volume help to illuminate this rather neglected aspect of governance of SMEs and SMSE's. Building on the fundamentals set out in this first chapter, the second chapter explains the nature of IP in the broader context of the IC of an organisation and the fundamental importance of IP in maintaining and building brand awareness, recognition and value, all of which are of increasing importance in the modern economic era.

The third chapter considers IP management in SMEs and civil society with a focus on the key factors that may inhibit the proper management of IP in the SME and SMSE context, factors such as motivation, the nature of the mission and purpose of the organisation, the non-distribution of profit, ownership interests, competence of personnel, constraints of electoral property laws and regulation. The fourth chapter moves into case studies in SME IP management in Australia. It reports on an examination of a collection of SMSEs and their attitudes towards IP management, their use of pro bono resources with respect to IP management, their approaches to agreements to protect IP and confidential information and the nature of their IP assets. It also considers the lack of recognition of the connection between branding and IP management. This chapter concludes with a suggested model for managing IP in the social enterprise context. Chapter 5 posits a tailored approach to IP rights protection and suggest strategies for managing and protecting trademarks, copyright, and patents and ways of approaching contractual arrangements to maximise the benefits of IP protection for social enterprise.

The last two chapters deal with special topics in IP management. Chapter 6 deals specifically with the role of IP as collateral in security transactions, the significance of the *Personal Property Securities Act* (PPSA), approaches to maximising IP protection, and challenges for organisations in their management of IP under the PPSA. Chapter 7 looks at structuring social enterprise according to models of franchising and examines the nature of IP protection and management as it varies under emerging models of social franchising.

CHAPTER TWO

IP AS A COMPONENT OF INTELLECTUAL CAPITAL

Introduction

IC includes knowledge, information, IP, and the experience base that can be put to use to create wealth.[1] IP is a significant component of the IC of a business.[2] IC has been defined as 'the sum of all knowledge an organisation is able to leverage in the process of conducting business to gain competitive advantage'.[3] It has also been characterised as, 'the pursuit of effective use of knowledge as opposed to information.'[4]

Conceptually, IC can be divided into the subcategories of human capital, structural capital, and relational capital.[5] Human capital inheres in the workers of the organisation; it includes competences, skills and innovative talents of people in the operation.[6] While it is not owned by the organisation, IC can be managed by the organisation and its value can be transferred or transformed to structural capital, which is owned

---

[1] Thomas A. Stewart, *Intellectual Capital: The New Wealth of Organizations* (Doubleday/Currency, 1997).
[2] Van Caenegem, above n 5.
[3] Mark A. Youndt, Mohan Subramaniam and Scott A. Snell, 'Intellectual Capital Profiles: An Examination of Investments and Returns' (2004) 41(2) *Journal of Management Studies* 335, 337.
[4] Bontis, above n 18.
[5] Leif Edvinsson, and Michael Malone, *Intellectual Capital: Realizing Your Company's True Value by Finding its Hidden Brainpower* (HarperBusiness, 1997). IC can be broadly broken down into two subcategories, human and structural capital.
[6] Bontis, above n 18.

by the organisation. Human capital has been regarded as embodying attitude, competence, and intellectual agility. Attitude in this context refers to the behavioural dimension of people-embodied knowledge including motivation and mindset. Competence refers to human capabilities, the firm's strategically relevant knowledge and its skillsets. Intellectual agility encompasses the firm's predisposition to adapt in the face of changing competitive environments.

Structural capital is comprised of all organisational and infrastructural instruments that support the management and carrying out of efficient business processes, including systems and programs, research and development, and IP rights. Additionally, it encompasses databases, process manuals, strategies, routines, organisational culture, publications, and copyrights, all of which may add significant value to the organisation.[7] 'Structural capital is the Holy Grail of knowledge economy. It is the way that [an] organisation captures knowledge and makes it re-usable ... structural capital makes an enterprise scalable.'[8] Relational capital is comprised of the relationships to customers, suppliers and other partners as well as to the public,[9] and also includes strategic alliances, licences and agreements.[10]

Clearly, the value of IC can be significant; it is 'recognised as the most important asset of many of the world's largest and most powerful companies ... the foundation for the market dominance and continuing profitability of leading corporations'.[11] An organisation's competitive position and its innovative capacity are highly dependent on its IC and its ability to deploy IC through its knowledge management processes.[12] Managers need to appreciate the influence knowledge management can have on an organisation's performance, as measuring and strategically managing knowledge can make the difference between mediocrity and excellence.[13]

---

[7] Nick Bontis, William Chua Chong Keow and Stanley Richardson, 'Intellectual Capital and Business Performance in Malaysian Industries' (2000) 1(1) *Journal of Intellectual Capital* 85.

[8] Mary Adams and Michael Oleksak, Intangible Capital: Putting Knowledge to Work in the 21st Century Organization (Praeger, 2010).

[9] Bontis, above n 18.

[10] Bontis, above n 18.

[11] Kelvin King, *The Value of Intellectual Property, Intangible Assets and Goodwill* (June 2003) World Intellectual Property Organization <http://www.wipo.int/sme/en/documents/value_ip_intangible_assets.htm>.

[12] Ikujiro Nonaka and Hirotaka Takeuchi, *The Knowledge-Creating Company: How Japanese Companies Create the Dynamics of Innovation* (Oxford University Press, 1995).

[13] Bontis, above n 18.

Each category of IC involves some aspects of IP. IP as a part of human capital includes, for example, know-how, confidential information, and personal goodwill. Structural capital involves IP such as copyright in policies and procedures manuals, and other documentation. Relational capital involves IP such as trademarks and brand and the overall goodwill of the business. Each category of IC also pertains to particular constituencies and components of the business (Figure 1).

Unfortunately, the effective identification, valuation, and management of IP in business remains insufficiently understood.[14] In SMSEs this situation is amplified significantly, due to the lack of infrastructure, management skills and funds typically experienced by these organisations. In addition, third sector organisations are often highly dependent on sustaining industry relationships and cultivating partnerships, which creates a tension between IP protection and collaboration, as discussed below.

The diagram below illustrates a graphic depiction of the inter-related nature of all aspects of IC, and denotes how IP rights are central to the optimisation of a business' IC. How an enterprise manages its IP can impact significantly on its ability to regulate business relationships, manage employees, innovate and create protective structures for its intellectual assets.

The considerations in respect of each branch impact on the other branches, for example, the use of structural capital for brand building also requires the cooperation of employees, volunteers and stakeholders. Similarly, in order to build trust with stakeholders, relationships which promote trust and credibility are important. All of these components impact on IP rights management, and are regulated or affected by the way in which an organisation manages its IP. For example, in relation to partnerships and stakeholders, the availability of IP rights use through licensing agreements and confidentiality agreements may be a significant consideration.

As a subset of IC, IP is instrumental in the ongoing viability and innovative capacity of an organisation, 'the invisible infrastructure of innovation'.[15] The ability of any enterprise to manage its IP effectively

---

[14]King, above n 68. Although intellectual capital may be a source of competitive advantage, generally speaking, most organizations do not understand its nature and value (Collis, 1996). Nevertheless, one of the first firms ever to report on their invisible assets was Skandia (Bontis, 1998). The field has since exploded with dozens of dedicated publications and academic researchers.

[15]Gollin, above n 4, 1.

22 Effective Intellectual Property Management

within the broader context of its IC is a significant factor in achieving its goals and in maximising the benefits of these assets.

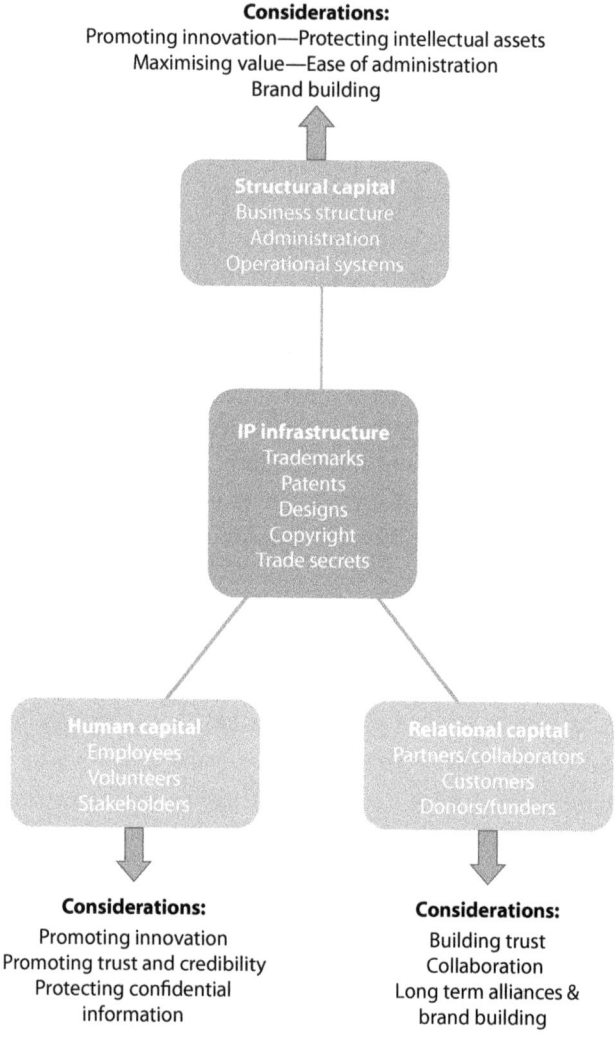

Figure 1 The Inter-relationship of IP with IC.

Appropriation of IP

'Appropriation', a term that is widely used in literature on innovation, refers to the act of capturing the value of one's ideas and investments in developing and bringing them to market. If a firm is unable to appropriate, or capture the value of, its IP, competitors may imitate its offerings without significant investment. This could eliminate its competitive edge, together with the incentive to continue to engage in risky innovative ventures.[16]

Brant and Lohse contend that SMEs tend to work to a significant degree with external partners, in order to fill gaps in their own resources and expertise and also because their niche expertise is attractive to established players. However, collaboration carries the risk of knowledge leakage to rivals and thus requires judicious management of intellectual assets.[17] In the case of SMSEs this danger is exemplified given the collaborative approach favoured by SMSEs in general. It follows that, given their limited resources, innovative SMEs as well as SMSEs need to develop strategies that are resource-effective to protect and manage their IP.[18] As an important purpose of IP management strategy is appropriation, a creative approach is needed, especially where SMSEs need to accommodate lucrative partnerships. Often this objective can be addressed through appropriate contractual arrangements, as will be discussed below.

It may be said that SMEs have a particular advantage in areas where there is rapid technological advancement because reaction time is much faster; however, in contrast, larger firms can spread research and development costs over a more extensive and diversified sales base.[19] Brant and Lohse suggest greater collaboration to 'intensify innovation and fill resource gaps' through partnerships between large firms and SMEs or SME networks, as well as licensing or working with universities and research institutes.[20] SMEs often work to a significant degree with external partners, in order to fill gaps in their own resources and expertise and also because their niche expertise is attractive to established players. However, collaboration carries the risk of knowledge leakage to rivals and thus requires judicious management of intellectual assets. Given their limited resources, innovative SMEs need to develop strategies that are resource-effective to protect and manage their IP.

Brant and Lohse refer to 'innovative SMEs which represent a particularly impactful category of SMEs, and point out that these firms have a high propensity to experiment and to generate new inventions

---

[16] Brant and Lohse, above n 51, 5.
[17] Ibid.
[18] Ibid.
[19] Ibid.
[20] Ibid.

and processes.[21] Innovative SMEs have the potential over the long-term to contribute substantially to improvements in productivity, competitiveness, and technological progress in their sector and the economy as a whole.[22] Quality patents and a strong IP position can help innovative SMEs signal the value of their invention to the market in general and, specifically, to potential funders and partners.[23] However, SMEs are unlikely to invest in creating a strong IP position unless they are aware of the value of managing their intellectual assets and of the appropriate tools that can be deployed to this end. However, they recognise that crucial to this is the development of sound IP management processes to ensure that both parties benefit.[24] In a similar way in the case of SMSEs it could be useful to partner with commercial SMEs where the outcomes are mutually beneficial.

The Importance of IP in Brand Building

The concept of 'brand building' is closely associated with an organisation's IP, specifically in relation to identifying trademarks and logos. Large non-profit organisations are known to have detailed policies to manage the use of their names and logos,[25] and many non-profits use brand management as a tool for fundraising.[26] 'Brand' can be defined as a 'name, term, design, symbol, or any other feature that identifies one seller's good or service as distinct from those of other sellers.'[27] Brand is also 'a set of mental associations, held by the consumer, which add to the perceived value of the product or service.'[28] The value of brand is notoriously difficult to

---

[21]Brant and Lohse, above n 51, 5.
[22](Ohler et al. 2007; OECD 2010; Pederzoli et al. 2011).
[23](Pederzoli et al. 2011).
[24]Brant and Lohse, above n 51, 6.
[25]Examples include the American Cancer Society and American Red Cross: Nathalie Kylander and Christopher Stone, 'The Role of Brand in the Nonprofit Sector' (2012) 29 *Stanford Social Innovation Review* 1.
[26]Ibid.
[27]K. L. Keller, *Strategic Brand Management: Building, Measuring And Managing Brand Equity* (Pearson Prentice Hall, 2nd ed, 2000) 10. Keller identifies the balance between continuity and change as critical to brand development: K. L. Keller, 'The brand report card' (2000) 78(1) *Harvard Business Review* 147.
[28]Ibid. Keller identifies the balance between continuity and change as critical to brand development: K. L. Keller, 'The brand report card' (2000) 78(1) *Harvard Business Review* 147–157.

determine with accuracy,[29] but it has been estimated that brands can drive up to 70% of a company's market capitalisation.[30]

The development and management of a strong brand—which is closely interlinked with the management of IP assets—also encounters certain obstacles in the global market, and as 'language and symbols vary from country to country, equating brands with specific words or images can be perilous for global organisations.'[31] For example, the name might be hard to pronounce or may have undesirable associations in the local language. Soft drinks like the Japanese brew Pocari Sweat and the Dutch beverage Sisi would be difficult to sell, using the same names, in Anglo-Saxon countries. Similarly, brand names like 'Snuggle,' 'Healthy Choice,' 'Weight Watchers', or 'I Can't Believe It's Not Butter' may not be very effective in non-English-speaking foreign markets.[32]

The concept of 'brand' incorporates several elements of IP.[33] Given that part of what distinguishes a social from a commercial enterprise is where it falls on the motivation spectrum (profit versus social welfare), brand for an organisation is worth more than its monetary value. Whatever its quantitative value, brand is significant to any enterprise, not only in financial terms, but in social and political terms as well.

The case of *WWP Inc v Wounded Warriors Family Support Inc*[34] involved two distinct charities for injured veterans and their families. The plaintiff alleged that the defendant had sowed confusion on the Internet by using a website to solicit donations, had failed to advertise or promote its own

---

[29]Estimates vary, but a widely acknowledged leading source for brand values is the Interbrand annual survey, which estimates the highest valued brands of 2011 to be Coca Cola at $72 billion and IBM at $69 billion. Microsoft's brand value was estimated to be around $59 billion, Google's about $55 billion; and McDonald's $36 billion: Interbrand, *Best Global Brands 2011 Rankings* <http://interbrand.com/best-brands/best-global-brands/2011/ranking/>. The methodology for arriving at these estimates is also provided at the website and is open to debate. Other sources assign very different values. See, for example, Will Ashworth, *What's Your Brand Worth?*, Investopedia (9 July 2009) <http://stocks.investopedia.com/stock-analysis/2009/Whats-Your-Brand-Worth-WPPGY-RIMM-AMZN-T-VOD0709.aspx>. Note that according to these figures McDonald's brand value is higher than its current market cap, and that the world's number one brand, Google, is worth over $100 billion.
[30]Elsie Maio, 'Managing Brand in the New Stakeholder Environment' (2003) 44(2–3) *Journal of Business Ethics* 235.
[31]Kylander and Stone, above n 82, 10.
[32]A.V. Vedpuriswar, Taking your Business Global <http://www.vedpuriswar.org/BookWritten.htm> chp 8, p 3.
[33]Keller, above n 84, 10. Keller identifies the balance between continuity and change as critical to brand development. K. L. Keller, 'The brand report card' (2000) 78(1) *Harvard Business Review* 147–157.
[34]628 F 3d 1032 (2011).

charitable work, and had instead relied on the reputation of the plaintiff to raise funds, thus engaging in deceptive and unfair trade practices. The Eighth Circuit Court of Appeals held that 'reputation and good will are as important to eleemosynary institutions as they are to business organisations financial credit—its ability to raise funds, its general reputation, the reputation of those managing and supporting it, are all at stake if its name is used by some other organisation and the two become confused in the minds of the public.'[35]

Similarly, in *Deborah Heart & Lung Centre v Children of the World Foundation*[36] in which two distinct non-profit programs used the same name, a US District Court granted an injunction to prevent infringement and dilution of the plaintiff's trademark, noting that, 'the public has a right to know to whom they are giving their money and who is administering these services.'[37] To a large extent an organisation's brand will be closely associated with or determinative of its reputation. For example, trademarks can serve as a disincentive against producing low quality, defective or harmful products; and help the public to identify the source of high quality products.[38]

While branding is reflected in the use of trademarks,[39] a strong brand has also been associated with 'strong cohesion and high levels of trust',[40] thus extending its reach and perceived value beyond the scope of the organisation's trademarks and logos. To ensure its reputation remains strong, an organisation must engage with best practice in risk management, and manage its IP effectively. It needs to consider, *inter alia*, property risks, both tangible and intangible; income risks; liability risks; reputation and mission risks; managing volunteer risks; governance and fiduciary risks; collaboration risks; and insurance.[41] The ability of an organisation to capitalise on its brand is inevitably influenced by its ability to effectively manage and maximise its IC and, in particular, its IP. Very often an organisation is instantly recognizable by its trademark or trade name,[42] which reflects

---

[35]Ibid.
[36]99 F Supp 2d 481 (2000).
[37]Ibid.
[38]Ibid.
[39]Gollin, above n 4, 179–180.
[40]Kylander and Stone, above n 82, 6.
[41](Based on table of contents)
[42]Above n 55.

its brand. It follows that deficiencies in the management of its IP rights may translate into a loss of confidence, internally and publicly.

The failure to manage IP can have serious negative consequences for non-profit organisations and their branding.[43] Consider, for example, naked licensing, where a trademark owner can lose the right to enforce a trademark against a licensee. As noted in Chapter 1, in the US case of *Freecycle Sunnyvale v Freecycle Network*[44] the US Ninth Circuit Court of Appeals found that a non-profit organisation, Freecycle Network, had abandoned its trademarks by allowing another party to use them without sufficient quality control.[45] A Freecycle Network representative had responded to a licensee's query, 'You can get the neutral logo from www.freecycle.org, just don't use it for commercial purposes ... [maybe one of our people] can help you to do your own fancy schmancy logo!' The licensee was added to The Freecycle Network's list of online recycling groups displayed on The Freecycle Network's Web site and received an 'all members' e-mail from The Freecycle Network welcoming it to the network. The message came without any restrictions or guidance on the use of the trademarks and there was no express licence agreement. Despite the Freecycle Network's argument that the 1993 case *Birthright v Birthright Inc*[46] had confirmed the principle that non-profits which shared 'the common goals of a public service organisation' should be subjected to less stringent control requirements,[47] the Court found that there was no implied licence. Instead, the Court found that what had occurred was 'naked licensing.'

Naked licensing occurs when a licensor fails to retain or exercise adequate quality control over a licensee's use of its licensed trademark, resulting in the trademark no longer representing the quality of the licensor's product or service. The Court in *Freecycle* opined that even if it were to apply 'less stringent quality control requirements for trademark purposes', the trademark owner would not meet the lower standard applied in

---

[43] Andrew Price, *Non-profits: Don't Get Caught Naked (Licensing)* (2011) Venables News and Insights <https://www.venable.com/non-profits--dont-get-caught-naked-licensing-03-01-2011>.
[44] 626 F 3d 509 (9th Cir, 2010).
[45] In this case the traditional trademark used to identify the source of the goods was 'FREECYCLE'. The Court found that the owner had failed to retain express contractual control, failed to exercise actual control over its use by the members of the organisation, and was unreasonable in relying on the quality control measures of its members.
[46] 827 F Supp 1114 (D NJ, 1993). The trademark owner in this case provided charitable emergency services for pregnant women in crisis.
[47] Price, above n 100.

Birthright, in respect of monitoring and control.[48] It is arguable that courts today might not apply the 'lower standard' applied in *Birthright*, due to technological advances and greater resulting possibilities of infringement. Furthermore, the application of lower standards may have been limited to non-profits with charitable missions.[49]

The *Freecycle* judgment puts non-profits in the US on notice that they do need to comply with trademark laws in the same way as commercial enterprises. The importance of IP protection in a non-profit organisation was also illustrated in the United Kingdom in 2012 by the removal of ShelterBox founder Sir Tom Henderson as the disaster relief charity's chief executive. Henderson was relieved for gross misconduct, including trying to place a contract worth £650,000 with a company connected with his son and 'neglecting the charity's intellectual property rights'.[50]

Conclusion

It is evident that IP rights management is central to the optimisation of the IC in an enterprise. Effective IP management can significantly increase an enterprise's ability to regulate partner and contractual relationships, manage employees, create innovations and provide protective structures for its intellectual assets. Furthermore, a proactive IP management strategy will enable an organisation to enhance its brand, specifically in relation to trademark protections of names and logos, and protect it from infringements of its IP rights. Brand building has become an important consideration for all SMEs, including SMSEs, not only in relation to its reputation and general standing in the public arena, but also as a valuable commodity which can be increased and protected through efficient IP management.

---

[48]Ibid.
[49]Price, above n 100.
[50]Andy Hillier and Ian Griggs, "ShelterBox Boss 'Misconduct'" (2012) 731 *Third Sector* 4.

CHAPTER THREE

IP MANAGEMENT, SMES AND CIVIL SOCIETY: UNDERSTANDING THE KEY FACTORS INHIBITING THE PROPER MANAGEMENT OF IP IN THE SME AND SMSE CONTEXT

Introduction

Businesses today operate in an era of information overload, as consumers are targeted by electronic advertising and social media marketing that have become accepted as part of daily living. Advertisements for global charities proliferate on television and non-profit organisations face increased challenges to obtain funding and secure contributions in this competitive marketplace. Although it can be argued that non-profits—including social enterprises—have at their core a collective focus on community interest and collaboration, there is also the incontrovertible reality of sustainability to consider.

Without funding or other forms of financial support, a social enterprise will—however worthy its cause—be doomed to failure. In pursuing their philanthropic purpose, it is not always immediately apparent to the parties involved why they should be concerned about their IP rights. The dynamics of commercially motivated practices such as trademark protection may be seen to fly directly in the face of philanthropic pursuits. Yet, in order to be sustainable and to foster longevity, non-profits need to acknowledge the importance of brand building and the attendant necessities of protecting an organisation's IP.

However, while it may be self-evident that a *business* must comprehensively protect IP, protection of IP in social enterprise may require different approaches to those of their commercial counterparts. Understanding how to structure IP management to cater to particular conditions and needs can help businesses and social enterprises more effectively engage with the status quo of legal protection for IP in the commercial context. It can also ensure that civil society plays an appropriate role in informing policy and the structure of legal regimes for the protection of IP. With this in mind this chapter introduces considerations for establishing the IP protection requirements of SMEs—including SMSEs. It is proposed that a tailored approach will best serve the needs of SMEs and SMSEs alike. While an SME generally requires a more commercially focused approach, cognisant of revenue streams, an SMSE may seek or enforce IP rights only to the extent that identification or enforcement is consistent with the needs or welfare of the organisation. In both commercial and social enterprises appropriate protective measures may be achieved effectively through streamlined IP regulation by emphasising brand protection and contractual arrangements. In addition to commercial considerations, perspectives and interests of civil society may well help to mould the future of IP regimes in a way that is beneficial, not only to social enterprise but also to its commercial counterparts.

Civil society has an important role to play in informing the structure and politics of the law of IP. Justice L.T.C. Harms argued that, 'there is no such thing as an intellectually sustainable concept of IP law ...' and that 'we lack a politics, or perhaps a political economic theory, of IP.'[1] Whatever the concepts and theories of IP law are to become, they should be widely informed by those who are affected by them, and that includes enterprises focussed on philanthropic purposes rather than financial gain. IP law, as analysed through theorists, yields some interesting perspectives.[2] More fundamentally, because civil society plays an important role in municipal economies and in the global economy, management and protection of IP must not be overlooked. Whatever direction the politics of IP may lead, civil society can only have a voice if it is fully engaged with, participates in, and comprehends IP law.

There are indications that some sectors of civil society lack engagement with the concepts and practices of IP protection. The research examined in a later chapter of this book indicates that there are particular attitudes and conditions in social enterprise in respect of IP rights protection that are

---

[1] LTC Harms, 'The Politics of Intellectual Property Laws' (Paper presented at the Intellectual Property 2012: Topical Issues seminar, University of Johannesburg, 23 March 2012).

[2] Dan L. Burk, 'Intellectual Property and the Firm' (2004) 71(1) *The University of Chicago Law Review* 1, 3–20.

separate to that of commercial enterprise. Contextually this book examines the approach to IP management and protection in social enterprise with a focus on patent, copyright and trademark law and contractual arrangements. We attempt to isolate the IP protection requirements of SMSEs and suggest a nuanced approach to management and protection of IP.

The Significance of IP Management

An Evolving Landscape

Constant advances in technology demand that organisations remain vigilant in reviewing their IP strategies on a regular basis, or face risk of serious IP infringements, especially online. For example, with the advent of social media and online marketing the risk has increased that businesses' logos and trademarks may be misappropriated, and organisations need to monitor their online presence very carefully. In addition to IP management issues there are consumer law issues to consider and as a result many businesses devote considerable resources to attaining and maintaining a high profile and credible online presence. In the case of SMSEs there may be less incentive and more barriers to attaining a high standard of IP management, as we shall see. Johnston, Wade, and McClean, when investigating SMEs adopting Internet Business Solutions across five OECD nations from Europe and North America, concluded that e-business adoption resulted in tangible financial benefits for SMEs in customer development and e-marketing.[3] The same can be said for SMSEs—however, these organisations are generally less attuned to potential risks in e-marketing, and particularly oblivious to possible risks of IP infringement. In a study by Grant and Edgar of 600 SMEs in the UK,[4] they reported that most viewed threats relating to IP as a medium risk when considering e-business deployment. Perceptions of legal and compliance risks associated with implementing e-business directly contrasted with perceptions of

---

[3] David A. Johnston, Michael Wade, and Ron McClean, 'Does E-Business Matter To SMEs? A Comparison of the Financial Impacts of Internet Business Solutions on European and North American SMEs' (2007) 45(3) *Journal of Small Business Management* 354.

[4] K Grant, D Edgar, A Sukumar and M Meyer, '"Risky business": Perceptions of E-Business Risk by UK Small and Medium Sized Enterprises (SMEs)' (2014) 34 *International Journal of Information Management* 99, 105.

dependency risks. Younger enterprises rated legal and compliance threats as lower risk than those with more e-business experience. The explanation for that finding reflected personal exposure and knowledge of risks that come with experience. Legal and compliance risks associated with e-business environments have been discussed previously.[5] Geist found the existence of 'grey areas' in e-business environments stemming from complicated legal domains (such as IP, digital contracts, licensing and copyright, etc.). Grant and Edgar's findings are consistent with those of Geist, namely that experience of e-business influences perceptions of online/e-business risk.[6] In general, mature firms were more cautious, identifying and rating legal and compliance risks higher. In the case of SMSEs, we found that there is generally a lack of maturity and sophistication in the online business environment, as evidenced by the research findings discussed in Chapter 5.

On digital platforms, 'Terms of Use' have become very important in determining the allocation of rights. For example, whether tweets are copyrighted in the context of usage can be determined by a website's 'Terms of Use'. In this sense digital platforms (such as 'virtual worlds'[7] and other games based platforms) may create IP rights,[8] which need to be observed and could benefit commercial businesses and SMSEs alike. All e-businesses are potentially subject to copyright and trademark infringements, which could adversely affect their brand, image and revenue streams.

Companies engaging in television advertising and programming similarly need to heed the importance of IP management. In an article[9] related to the food industry and television viewers' obsession with food programmes, Logan and Lau write about some pressing issues these organisations need to consider. They propose, for example, restaurateur celebrity chefs should ensure their staff and contractors are required contractually to keep recipes and plating instructions that are key to their business confidential, and if

---

[5] Michael A. Geist, 'Is There a There? Towards Greater Certainty for Internet Jurisdiction' (2001) 16(3) *Berkley Technology Law Journal* 1345.

[6] Grant, Edgar, Sukumar and Meyer, above n 111, 105.

[7] K Hallenstein and J Perrier, '10 tips for trade mark owners in virtual worlds' (2009) X *Australian Intellectual Property Law Bulletin* 6, 6. Virtual worlds (VW) are computer-based simulated environments designed for users to inhabit and interact through character representations called avatars. Participation in VWs is widespread and growing. Garner, Inc., a technology analyst group, has predicted that by the end of 2011, 80% of active internet users will have some sort of presence in a VW.

[8] B Fitzgerald, C Foong and M Tucker, 'Wed 2.0, Social Networking and the Courts' (2011) 35 *Australian Bar Review* 281.

[9] C Logan and C Lau, 'First World Fine Food Frenzy—IP Tricks and Traps' (2014) 27(9) *Australian Intellectual Property Law Bulletin* 249, 249.

they have not, should consider trademarking their names and logos and the look and feel of their restaurants. They also suggest that staff should sign confidentiality or non-disclosure agreements to maintain secrecy of recipes, that manufacturers and importers of gourmet food and ingredients should review their trademark portfolios and supply agreements, as well as their employee and contractor terms with regards to confidential information. Additionally, if their product has a distinctive shape, then design or possibly shape trademark registration should be considered.[10] This example illustrates the potential pitfalls for organisations which rely on their unique attributes for success in the marketplace. In many instances SMSEs may face the same issues where they are reliant on sponsorships, patronage and other external funding—an example is Lentil as Anything, discussed later in book.[11]

Contextualising IP Management

In discussing the pivotal role of IP management in modern day businesses and social enterprises, it would be useful to contextualise our discussion with a definition of some of the key concepts referred to in this book, namely what is regarded as a 'social enterprise' and what type of interests do we refer to when we discuss 'intellectual property' or 'IP' in the realms of social enterprise activities. It is also useful to define what is regarded as the 'third sector'.

Third Sector

As noted in a previous chapter the term 'third sector' describes an additional sector of the economy distinct from the public/government and private/for profit sectors.[12] As such it denotes a very diverse range of

---

[10]Ibid, 249.

[11]See *Lentil as Anything*, <https://lentilasanything.com>.

[12]Lyons defines the term 'third sector' a distinguished from other terminology in some detail at 5–7. Noting a need for clarification of the meanings of these terms, he settles on the term 'third sector' as having 'the greatest potential to avert misunderstanding.' 'Third sector' is also distinguishable from non-government organisations (NGOs), a term often used in development literature to describe non-profit organisations, and is also distinguishable from other terms that can be similarly freighted with particular and sometimes politically sensitive meanings: Mark Lyons, *Third Sector: the Contribution of Nonprofit and Cooperative Enterprise in Australia* (Allen & Urwin, 2001); See, eg, Jon Van Til, *Mapping the Third Sector* (Foundation Center, 1988); Peter Hall, *Inventing the Nonprofit Sector* (1992); Kim Alter, *Social Enterprise Typology* (Virtue Ventures LLC, 2010); The Four Lenses Strategic Framework.

structures and purposes.[13] Third sector enterprises combine 'strong public service ethos with business acumen ... highly responsive to customers and with the freedom of the private sector—but ... driven by a commitment to public benefit rather than purely maximising profits for shareholders.'[14]

The third sector in Australia has grown rapidly over the past decade, representing over 4 per cent of GDP—just under $43 billion—with nearly 5 million volunteers contributing an additional $14.6 billion in unpaid work.[15] The era of non-profit managementhas also seen efforts to change the formal character of non-profit enterprise and a related growth in the importance of alternative service delivery and 'partnerships'. The third sector's role in new governance models has broadened not only in the delivery of 'public' services but also in a restructured state-societal relationship worldwide.[16] For example, in 2002 a Social Enterprise Unit was established within the British Department of Trade and Industry as a centrepiece of social reform policy, and social enterprise has been reported to be the fastest growing sector in the UK.[17] With this growth and ever widening and more complex relationships, there are also interesting new interactions. Clear distinctions between third sector and commercial enterprise are increasingly difficult to identify, as

> the stakes are now higher ... for successful relationships between nonprofits and business. Nonprofits are coming to depend more on corporations for their material support, and corporations are becoming more reliant on nonprofits for the patina of credibility and public trust they can bring to efforts for gaining visibility and market share and for the benefits they can offer to improve the business environment, including community attitudes and the morale of the labour force.[18]

---

[13]See (Salamon and Anheier 1997; Kong, Lyons, 2001; Sheppard et al., 2001).

[14]David Billis, *Hybrid Organizations and the Third Sector* (Palgrave Macmillan, 2010) 154. A typology of social enterprise can be found at <http://www.4lenses.org/setypology>.

[15]Productivity Commission, *Contribution of the Not-for-Profit Sector* Report (2010) http://www.pc.gov.au/__data/assets/pdf_file/0004/94549/01-preliminaries.pdf

[16]B. Mitchell Evans and John Shields, 'Neoliberal Restructuring and the Third Sector: Reshaping Governance, Civil Society and Local Relations' (Working Paper Series No 13, Ryerson University, July 2000) <http://www.ryerson.ca/~cvss/WP13.pdf>.

[17]Alter, above n 119; The Four Lenses Strategic Framework, above n 119.

[18]Dennis R. Young, 'The Influence of Business on Nonprofit Organizations and the Complexity of Nonprofit Accountability Looking Inside As Well As Outside' (2002) 32(1) *American Review of Public Administration* 3.

To succeed in these interactions third sector organisations must be competitive and must speak the languages of their counterparts in business to take advantage of corporate partnerships. There are parallels between commercial and third sector management; indeed convergence and hybridisation are blurring in many ways the distinctions between them. Inevitably, commercial considerations apply:

> 'The work of social entrepreneurship and the creation of social enterprise is also the work of a for-profit manager striving to drive the practice of corporate social responsibility into her firm; and, in truth, the approach of a venture philanthropist is not six degrees removed from that of a socially responsible investor or manager of a community loan fund. ... it is all the same and we are all part of a common effort to create more effective tools to maximize total value for our entire global community'.[19]

Third sector organisations, however, can be prone to unique challenges because of their special characteristics, such as their purposes and motivations; their particular ownership and stakeholder structures; non-distribution of profit to members. Moreover, third sector entities are unique on account of governance, management and workforce issues, including their reliance on volunteers, the complexity of resource generation,[20] legal and regulatory considerations, and the increasing prevalence of hybrid forms. Such special characteristics can lead to difficulties in setting and maintaining consistent goals and judging organisational performance. They may also contribute to problems with accountability, and to conflict between board and staff.[21]

The approach to the management of IP in the third sector may be very different from that of organisations that are characterised principally by their profit-making orientation. There is a growing recognition of the value of intellectual innovation in these organisations; 'the increasingly competitive environment has forced traditional non-profit organisations to place

---

[19] Jed Emerson, *Introduction to The Four Lenses Strategic Framework: Toward an Integrated Social Enterprise Methodology*, The Four Lenses Strategic Framework (2010) <http://www.4lenses.org/setypology/foreword>.

[20] Lyons, above n 119, 5–7.

[21] See Lyons, above n 119, 22. See also Alter, above n 119. The UK-based Social Enterprise Coalition, <http://www.socialenterprise.org.uk> in which common characteristics of social enterprises have been identified as social aims, social ownership, and enterprise orientation.

great emphasis on innovation in all their social value creating activities.'[22] At the same time, however, third sector organisations may be resistant to IP management or lack a coherent strategy, as they 'are more focused on disseminating knowledge than profiting from it'.[23]

Social Enterprise

Social enterprise (SE) is a subset of the third sector and the term is often used to distinguish less formal or more loosely regulated structures and initiatives from registered charities. As is often the case with scholarship in a new area of inquiry, the boundaries of SE are indefinite and the terminology is inconsistent.[24] In academic literature SE has been characterised as the use of nongovernmental, market-based approaches to address social issues.[25] It is generally regarded as part of the 'third sector'.[26] The UK-based Social Enterprise Coalition identifies the common characteristics of a SE

---

[22]Eric Kong, 'Innovation Processes in Social Enterprises: An IC Perspective' (2010) 11(2) *Journal of Intellectual Capital* 158, 160.

[23]Gollin, above n 4, 104.

[24]'A distinguishing feature of the SE literature is controversy over definitions and classifications is a recurring theme in the SE research literature': Kenneth Peattie and Adrian Morley, *Social Enterprises: Diversity and Dynamics, Contexts and Contributions* (Social Enterprise Coalition, 2008), 6. Noting that, '[s]cholars have yet to agree a universal and distinctive definition', Haugh suggests several challenges for theoretical developments in the field, such as the context-bound nature of social enterprise, the tautology of using 'social' in both the article and the definition, the prevalence of actor-centred perspectives, and the paucity of theory development concerning the generalisability of findings from individual case studies: Helen Haugh 'The Importance of Theory in Social Enterprise Research' (2012) 8(1) *Social Enterprise Journal* 7, 9. Another challenge is to reconcile and harmonise approaches across jurisdictions. The United States and Europe, for example, have in their different contexts developed disparate conceptions and theoretical approaches to the phenomenon: See Matthew Doeringer, 'Fostering Social Enterprise: A Historical and International Analysis' (2010) 20(2) *Duke Journal of Comparative & International Law*, 291; Marthe Nyssens and Jacques Defourny 'Conceptions of Social Enterprise in Europe: Comparative Perspective with the United States' in Benjamin Gidron and Yeheskel Hasenfeld (eds), *Social Enterprises: An Organisational Perspective* (Palgrave-Macmillan UK, 2012) 71–90.

[25]Paul Charles Light, *The Search for Social Entrepreneurship* (Brookings Institution Press, 2008); Johanna Mair, Jeffrey Robinson and Kai Hockerts (eds), *Social Entrepreneurship* (Palgrave Macmillan, 2006); Alex Nicholls, *Social Entrepreneurship: New Models of Sustainable Change* (Oxford University Press, 2006).

[26]Lyons, above n 119. Lyons defines the term 'third sector' a distinguished from other terminology in some detail at 5–7. Noting a need for clarification of the meanings of these terms, he settles on the term 'third sector' as having 'the greatest potential to avert misunderstanding.' 'Third sector' is also distinguishable from non-government organisations (NGOs), a term often used in development literature to describe non-profit organisations, and is also distinguishable from other terms that can be similarly freighted with particular and sometimes politically sensitive meanings.

as a firm with social aims and ownership with an enterprise orientation. SE organisations have been identified as having:

> an explicit aim to benefit the community, initiated by a group of citizens and in which the material interest of capital investors is subject to limits. They place a high value on their independence and on economic risk-taking related to ongoing socio-economic activity.[27]

Raz cites the social enterprise alliance definition of SE as, 'an organisation or venture that achieves its primary social or environmental mission using business methods'.[28] Defourny and Nyssens prefer 'the identification and clarification of indicators over concise and elegant definition'; their work 'classifies' SE as an alternative to definition.[29] In the absence of a globally accepted single definition of the phenomenon, and because the focus of this research is on SEs in Australia, an Australian approach to classifying the phenomenon is employed here. As Defourny and Nyssens have proposed, selection is based on 'indicators' of SE, but the indicators are derived from Australian data about the sector.

SEs in Australia are defined as organisations that:

- are led by an economic, social, cultural, or environmental mission consistent with a public or community benefit;[30]
- trade to fulfil their mission;[31]
- derive a substantial portion of their income from trade;[32] and
- reinvest the majority of their profit/surplus in the fulfilment of their mission.[33]

---

[27] EMES, *Focus Areas*, International Research Network (2011) <http://emes.net/focus-areas>.

[28] Keren Raz, 'Toward an Improved Legal Form for Social Enterprise,' (2012) 36 *New York University Review of Law and Social Change* 283.

[29] Nyssens and Defourny, above n 132.

[30] 'This may include member benefits where membership is open and voluntary and/or benefits that accrue to a subsection of the public that experiences structural or systemic disadvantage': Jo Barraket, Nick Collyer, Matt O'Connor and Heather Anderson, *Finding Australia's Social Enterprise Sector: Final Report* (Australian Centre for Philanthropy and Non-Profit Studies, 2010) 16 n 1.

[31] 'Where trade is defined as the organised exchange of goods and services, including: monetary, non-monetary and alternative currency transactions, where these are sustained activities of an enterprise; contractual sales to governments, where there has been an open tender process; and trade within member-based organisations, where membership is open and voluntary or where membership serves a traditionally marginalised social group': Ibid 16 n 2.

[32] 'Operationalised as 50% or more for ventures that are more than five years from start-up, 25% or more for ventures that are three to five years from start-up, and demonstrable intention to trade for ventures that are less than two years from start-up': Ibid.

[33] Ibid 16.

SMSEs are a subcategory of SEs. Barraket et al estimate that there are up to 20,000 Australian SEs.[34] This estimate takes into account the fact that that some non-profit organisations have multiple business ventures, and that not all SEs are incorporated as non-profits.[35] For the purposes of the research discussed in this book, the Australian Bureau of Statistic's definition for SMEs has been adopted, that is organisations with fewer than 200 staff.[36]

SMSEs are not purely commercial and philanthropic; they represent a hybrid form of organisation that involves taking business-like innovative approaches to deliver public services; however, '[i]n contrast to for-profit organisations in which profits are often distributed to their owners and shareholders, economic value creation in social enterprises is perceived as a by-product which allows the organisations to achieve sustainability and self-sufficiency.'[37]

Risks and Challenges in Managing IP in the Third Sector

The expansion and diversification of the third sector brings the issue of good governance practices to the fore. It is an issue not only for individual organisations but to the sector as a whole: 'It is only a small exaggeration to suggest that unless capacity for good governance is considerably enhanced, *the reputational risk* to the sector could transform into substantial *reputation damage.*'[38] An important aspect of good governance is the question of how IP in diverse third sector organisations is developed, managed, and protected. In an era when intangible assets have become the most valuable asset of many commercial enterprises, the efficient management of IP is a critical part of good governance. However, just as the role of IP in business remains insufficiently understood, so, too, the implications for IP with respect to the third sector in an era of intellectual capitalism are unclear.

---

[34]Ibid 4.

[35]While some of Barraket et al's data includes NFPs, charities and non-NFPs, most of their responses were obtained from small enterprises: Ibid 4.

[36]Other definitions of 'small business' under Australian law include: the *Australian Securities and Investment Commission Act 2001* (Cth) s 12BC: 'small business means a business employing less than: (a) if the business is or includes the manufacture of goods—100 people; or (b) otherwise—20 people'; and the *Corporations Act 2001* (Cth) s 761G: 'small business means a business employing less than: (a) if the business is or includes the manufacture of goods—100 people; or (b) otherwise—20 people'.

[37]Kong, above n 130, 160.

[38]Roger Spear, Chris Cornforth and Mike Aiken, 'For Love and Money: Governance and Social Enterprise' (National Council for Voluntary Organisations, 2007) 58.

If a key determinant of success for business is how effectively it manages its intellectual assets, there is no reason to expect that this would be different for third sector enterprise.

Their continuing success and survival require that they maintain and protect their IP. An effective and interactive IP management strategy, as a minimum, is likely to be as essential, or even more so, for third sector enterprise, where the balance between exploiting and sharing knowledge is arguably even more delicate.[39] The key for third sector organisations is to formulate IP management strategies that are consistent not only with their operational needs but also with their philosophical orientations.

Despite the likelihood that IP is also crucial to successful SEs, there is evidence that third sector enterprise is not maximising this important resource.[40] The founder of Public Interest Intellectual Property Advisors (PIIPA), Michael Gollin, identifies a strong and growing need for advice about IP law and practice across many applications including housing, health care programs, education, training, environmental protection, and local knowledge, particularly in developing countries. He suggests that though IP laws and practices are complex and require expertise to fully understand and apply, the basic skills required to manage IP can be learned by most people.[41] Though the necessary capabilities may be accessible, however, other factors persist in inhibiting good management of IP. This paper highlights some of the theoretical and practical tensions in non-profit organisations' management of IP.

Motivation

Critics argue that policies of IP protection may keep innovation out of the public domain, increase costs, and create monopolies. Further, a focus on IP protection may cause industry to prioritise what can be protected, not what is best; and requires burdensome and costly legal and regulatory institutions.[42] Such opinions and attitudes can undermine even the most

---

[39] Interview with Professor William van Caenegem (Bond University, xx August 2011).
[40] Deatherage reports that in her recent work "with a fairly large and long-established (nonprofit) organization," that only a few people within the organization understood what a brand is and what it can do for a nonprofit (Deatherage, 2009).
[41] Gollin, above n 4, 345.
[42] Ibid.

preliminary attempts to ensure that IP is maximised for an organisation. Social and cultural attitudes may also come into play; in many Asian cultures, for example, copying is heavily imbued with connotations of flattery.

Third sector organisations, in particular, can lack the will to strategically manage IP for many reasons. These relate to philosophical issues of ownership versus sharing and disseminating, and protection of ownership of the assets of the organisation; exclusivity versus access; competition versus cooperation; and the tensions between value placed on imitation and replication versus innovation and adaptation. All of these factors can constrain an organisation's ability to formulate and execute a coherent and effective IP management strategy. These factors have been recognised in practice—there are the 'hawks' on the one hand, who argue that charities should treat their IP with the same commercial value that a private sector company would, and trade it accordingly, and the 'doves' on the other, who point to the broader social impact and wider responsibility of charities to contribute to society as a whole.[43]

There are not only philosophical issues attached to this issue. Practical considerations include the significance of the organisation's mission both as a part of IP and as a factor that affects the management of IP. Closely related to this is the non-distribution of profit, which leads to difficulties of accountability to a complex mix of stakeholder interests rather than the principal obligation of management to return profit to owners. The need for third sector enterprise to address a multiplicity of audiences requires flexibility.[44] In a landscape of relationships characterised by diverse motivations: 'There are problems managing the often competing *demands of different stakeholders are* particularly around public service contracts, and with multi-stakeholder boards.'[45]

Mission and Purpose

Third sector enterprises may be vulnerable with respect to mission and purpose where these conflict with commercial considerations. As a factor

---

[43]Javed Kahn, 'Our Intellectual Property is a Goldmine—So How to Exploit It?', *Third Sector* (29 October 2013) <http://javedkhan.thirdsector.co.uk/2013/10/29/our-intellectual-property-is-a-goldmine-so-how-to-exploit-it/>.
[44]Kylander and Stone, above n 82, 4.
[45]Spear, Cornforth and Aiken, above n 146, 59.

that affects management of IC, a distinguishing feature of third sector enterprise is social purpose; such enterprise is directed first and foremost toward advancing a purpose, rather than being motivated strictly by profit.[46] In their work on governance and social enterprise Spear, Cornforth and Aiken note, 'problems managing the tension between social and business goals.'[47] When it comes to the concept of 'blended value', i.e. economic, social, and environmental,[48] third sector enterprise may derive its value differently. The issue for management is that multiple, often inconsistent, objectives combined with a social welfare philosophical orientation, may detract from motivation to protect IP, which may be perceived primarily as a commercial objective.

One example of this is the frequent association of 'branding'—which includes trademarks and logos—with commercial pursuit of monetary gain, when in fact brand is also critical to the success of non-profit enterprise.[49] A reputable brand empowers a non-profit to perform all its normal activities in pursuing its central mission; 'a non profit's reputation–its status in the eyes of its clients, staff, contributors, regulators, and the general public– is often said to be the organisation's most valuable asset.'[50] As such '[a] good reputation is the ultimate source of the non profit's net income flow. A loss of that reputation halts the flow.'[51]

Many non-profit enterprises, however, are ambivalent about the concept of branding and/or may view it with some suspicion in collaborations and partnerships where a stronger brand may overshadow a weaker brand.[52] Third sector organisations are often highly dependent on sustaining industry relationships and cultivating partnerships. This creates a tension between IP protection and collaboration. Kylander suggests two kinds of brand management activities for non-profit organisations: those that focus on growing brand equity through alignment and mission implementation in partnership and cooperation with other organisations, and those aimed

---

[46] See Farrar, 442–443.
[47] Spear, Cornforth and Aiken, above n 146, 59.
[48] Jed Emerson and Sheila Bonni, 'Mapping the Blending Value Proposition: Integrating Social and Financial Returns' (2003) 45(4) *California Management Review* 35.
[49] Kylander and Stone, above n 82, 4–5. Examples are the American Cancer Society and American Red Cross.
[50] Melanie L. Herman, George L. Head, Peggy M. Jackson, Toni E. Fogarty, *Managing Risk in Non-Profit Organizations: A Comprehensive Guide* (Wiley, 2003).
[51] Ibid 78–79.
[52] Kylander and Stone, above n 82, 4–5. Examples are the American Cancer Society and American Red Cross.

toward protecting brand equity, put at risk in part by the very partnerships and cooperation that grow the brand.[53] Within this dichotomy, between the need to create partnerships and the converse requirement for protection of intellectual assets such as an organisation's identifying trademarks, IP rights can play a central role. This was clearly an important aspect of the *Freecycle* dispute; the email, 'You can get the neutral logo from www.freecycle.org, just don't use it for commercial purposes ... [maybe one of our people] can help you to do your own fancy schmancy logo!', suggests that a spirit of cooperation took precedence over any concern for protection of the Freecycle trademark, if indeed such a concern existed at all. The necessity for third sector organisations to create partnerships and attract funders means that a collaborative framework is essential to promote the sharing of ideas and enhancement of social impact.[54] These objectives need to be balanced with a strategy that encourages creativity and protects its intellectual assets.

Non-distribution of Profit

Attitude and motivation with respect to maximising the value of IP are also vulnerable to the condition of non-distribution of profit to members. Traditional distinctions between third sector enterprise and commercial enterprise have been driven to a large extent by the non-distribution constraint,[55] concomitant with tax status and funding considerations. Such distinctions are becoming blurred with the diversification and growth of alternative styles and structures for third sector enterprise initiatives, and the proliferation of SEs.[56] Nevertheless, non-distribution of profit to members has been a traditional feature of non-profit enterprise, one that can detract from the motivation to effectively manage the asset. Because profit is not distributed to members, there is less direct financial accountability for the management of IP.

---

[53] Do the brand protecting activities impose limits a nonprofit's ability to take risk and stretch the organization? What are the other potential downsides or detrimental aspects of traditional brand management activities? (Kylander chapter/Book).

[54] Kylander and Stone, above n 82, 4.

[55] R. Hirshhorn, 'The Governance of Nonprofits' in R. J. Daniels and R. Morck (eds), *Corporate Decision-Making in Canada*, (University of Calgary Press, 1995) vol 5.

[56] Kong, above n 130, 160.

Ownership

Ownership is another important influencer on attitudes toward maximising the value of IP. Third sector enterprise is characterised by social ownership, i.e. autonomous organisations, governance and ownership structures normally based on participation by stakeholder groups or by trustees or directors on behalf of a wider group of stakeholders. The concept of ownership of knowledge is critical and can be complex. In many third sector applications owners are not clearly defined, and so the rights of ownership are not exercised. These practical issues of ownership of course arise out of philosophical considerations, and there are many other aspects of the exploitation of IP that present challenging political and philosophical problems. In the case of Traditional Knowledge (TK), for example, ownership often does not inhere in one person or even in one organisation.[57] The owners of TK may include an entire community, if the concept of ownership is acknowledged at all.[58] Creative individuals may also 'share their ideas openly with the rest of the community, allowing the ideas to move directly into broader use, without asserting intellectual property rights.'[59]

Even where ownership can be established, the managers of third sector programs may feel uncomfortable with the exploitation of IP due to a moral commitment to the concept of a commons, that the ownership of IP should be shared for the collective benefit, and should not be enclosed. They may oppose on a political or philosophical basis the exploitation of IP because they believe that protecting and exploiting IP rights leads to excessive privatisation of creative activity, limits access, supports monopoly

---

[57] Heather Forrest notes that 'Even before you get to the ownership problem, there is a serious challenge to even defining TK–what sorts of things fall within the scope of TK? Does this overlap with existing IP rights (e.g. patent or plant variety) and if so, what then? Some guidance can be had from the recently enacted Swakopmund Protocol by Africa's ARIPO. http://www.aripo.org/images/Swakopmund_Protocol.pdf'.

[58] WIPO, The Protection of Traditional Knowledge: Draft Articles, Rev. 2 (April 26, 2013) contains draft provisions for the protection of TK and includes in its Policy Objectives that '*The protection of traditional knowledge should aim to: ... ensure that conventional intellectual property regimes operate in a manner supportive of the protection of traditional knowledge against misuse and misappropriation, and should effectively empower associated traditional knowledge [holders]/[owners] to exercise due rights and authority over their own knowledge*' (p.3) but should also '*... guarantee the fair and equitable sharing and distribution of monetary and non monetary benefits arising from the use of traditional knowledge*' (p.5). http://www.wipo.int/tk/en/igc/index.html.

[59] Gollin, above n 4, 99.

and oppression and restricts individual rights and freedoms.[60] Such people and organisations are likely to be more enthusiastic about disseminating knowledge than profiting from it. While they may not be very interested in the prospect of doing both, with some education about the benefits, they may come to embrace a balanced approach to protection and sharing. Indeed, the tension between competition and cooperation does require difficult choices about exploiting IP effectively and efficiently in a context where competition is, in some ways, frowned upon.[61]

The fact is that third sector enterprises often do operate in highly competitive environments that may also be characterised by increasing demand for services from the community, growing competition for contracts with the public and for-profit sector, declining volunteer support, and tight government funding. They can be expected to come under increasing pressure, and the effective management of IP will be correspondingly more important to their sustainability.[62]

Competence

Many third sector organisations do recognise the value of IP, as 'the increasingly competitive environment has forced traditional non-profit organisations to place great emphasis on innovation in all of their social value creating activities.'[63] However, even where a third sector organisation does have the motivation to manage IP, many organisations operating in the third sector may nonetheless be uncertain how best to exploit their IP, protect it, and achieve the balance between access and exclusivity. Deficiencies may also exist in their competence to do so.

Many of the same special characteristics of third sector organisations that can present philosophical challenges can also lead to difficulties in setting and maintaining consistent goals and monitoring organisational performance. In many third sector enterprises the challenges to effective

---

[60]Ibid 40–41. Gollin identifies 8 criticisms of IP laws: legal protection of IP keeps innovations out of the public domain, increases the cost of technology, creates monopolies, concentrates industry on what can be protected rather than what is most needed or best, that it pushes people from cooperation into competition, is expensive to obtain and maintain, requires elaborate national legal and regulatory institutions, and conflicts with moral views opposing property rights.
[61]Interview with Professor William van Caenegem (Bond University, August 2011).
[62]Kong, 97.
[63]Kong, above n 130, 160.

identification, valuation, and management of IP may be amplified significantly, due to the lack of infrastructure, management skills and funds typically experienced by these organisations. Practical impediments to effective IP management include a lack of awareness as well as the availability of resources and expertise. An organisation may lack an IP strategy out of ignorance, inertia, concern over costs, or a sense that the organisation is in a low risk or low yield situation.

The size of the organisation can be a determining factor in its level of competence and expertise. Typically, larger non-profit organisations will have a sound management infrastructure and an effective IP strategy.[64] In many cases a small to moderate size combined with multiple and often inconsistent objectives poses special challenges for separating strategic governance and day-to-day management, which can impact on expansion; financing; combating corruption; accountability; goal definition, alignment, measurement, and adjustment; and, of course, ensuring the integrity of IP.[65]

Whatever their attitudes, the workers, often volunteers, may lack the essential capabilities, knowledge and skillsets to maximise IP. Thus, an organisation's reliance on volunteers, not only as workers, but also as management and for board functions can involve, 'complacency about underperformance and lack of awareness about the board's inability to govern effectively.'[66] In some smaller third sector organisations, the same people may in fact be fulfilling more than one of these roles, and bringing the same deficiencies to each, thus compounding them. There may be problems 'recruiting or electing' people with the right skills and experience—there appears to be a limited supply of good people, and these are in demand, and on several boards. Boards often struggle to find appropriate people, which frequently contributes to a lack of strategic assessment/audit of the board expertise required. The areas of expertise that are commonly lacking, particularly in smaller organisations, include finance, business, and strategic skills.[67] The characteristics of third sector enterprise may also contribute to problems with accountability: '[t]here is sometimes insufficient clarity about board/staff roles, particularly in smaller organisations;

---

[64] Gollin, above n 4, 290.
[65] Billis, above n 121, 184.
[66] Spear, Cornforth and Aiken, above n 146, 59.
[67] Ibid.

and developing staff support for effective board functioning is often not achieved.'⁶⁸ Additionally, there may be conflicts between board and staff.⁶⁹

Constraints of IP Laws and Regulation

Third sector organisations are subject to the same IP laws as commercial enterprises. There is no general exception from infringement, with only limited exemptions for non-profit institutions conducting research.⁷⁰ A study on access by non-profits to other parties' technology concluded that most non-profits are ill-equipped to undertake the necessary measures to abide by others' IP.⁷¹ This is one consideration for third sector organisations in utilising technology, processes and other IP. On the other hand, they have to comply with laws and regulation in protecting their own IP. These regulatory considerations involve complex IP legislation and regulation issues and ensuring compliance on both fronts is an expensive exercise.

Furthermore, third sector organisations may be negatively impacted by global market regulation, which restricts the use of innovative patents that could benefit SEs committed to social causes, such as the promotion of health care in poor countries.⁷² There are also legal restrictions and compliance measures in respect of environmental technology which must be observed by third sector enterprise. Governments are increasingly passing laws requiring new beneficial technologies in 'technology-forcing regulations'⁷³ and a failure to comply could result in legal and environmental liabilities.⁷⁴

Tenenbaum suggests that third sector organisations should use copyright and trademark notices on all trademarks, service marks and

---

⁶⁸Ibid.

⁶⁹See Alter, above n 119; The Four Lenses Strategic Framework, above n 119. The UK-based Social Enterprise Coalition, http://www.socialenterprise.org.uk in which common characteristics of social enterprises have been identified as social aims, social ownership, and enterprise orientation.

⁷⁰Nottenburg, Pardey and Wright, 'Accessing Other People's Technology for Non-Profit Research' (2002) 46(3) *The Australian Journal of Agricultural and Resource Economics* 389, 390, 393.

⁷¹Ibid 391.

⁷²Gollin, above n 4, 330. Gollin notes, in relation to drug patent-holding companies, that patients in poor countries are at a disadvantage because of the small markets, low purchasing power, lack of incentive for development of drugs for public health problems such as malaria and tuberculosis, and the absence of intellectual property expertise.

⁷³Michael A. Gollin, 'Using Intellectual Property to Improve Environmental Protection' (1991) 4 *Harvard Journal of Law and Technology* 193.

⁷⁴Gollin, above n 4, 334.

certification marks owned and used by the association, and in addition register the organisation's name, logos and service marks with the Patent and Trademark Office.[75] Laws regulating patents are complex,[76] and international protection of patent rights is costly, both at registration stage and at enforcement level.[77] In addition, there is a dilemma concerning disclosure—the law of patents requires public disclosure in return for exclusive rights, and 'it is often impossible to disclose knowledge without potentially destroying its commercial value.'[78] There are costs associated with demonstrating that an innovation meets the necessary registration threshold, registration fees, periodic maintenance fees, and enforcement fees if the validity of the patent is challenged or to defend infringements.[79]

Registration and enforcement of trademarks are subject to the same limitations and cost implications as patent rights, although to a lesser extent, as patents incur the highest registration costs due to more stringent examination requirements.[80] The cost of trademark litigation is an important consideration in non-profit organisations. For example, in the US, for an average trademark infringement suit litigation costs can be as high as $775,000.[81] Copyright protection is the least affected by these considerations as it does not require registration to be enforceable,[82] however, international copyright regulation is complex and inconsistent, and enforcement can be expensive and problematic, especially in the digital context.[83]

Additionally, relevant legal regimes may be outdated, failing to keep pace with this important and dynamic sector. Alternatively they may have failed to mature to the stage of effective IP protection, particularly in

---

[75] Jeffrey S. Tenenbaum, 'Top Ten Copyright and Trademark Tips for Associations', *Venables News and Insights* (2001) <http://www.venable.com/top-ten-actually-eleven-copyright-and-trademark-tips-for-associations-01-01-2001/>.

[76] Gollin, above n 4, 335.

[77] Paul H. Jensen and Elizabeth Webster, 'Firm Size and the Use of Intellectual Property Rights' (2006) 82(256) *The Economic Record* 44, 47.

[78] Van Caenegem, above n 33, 7.

[79] Jensen and Webster, above n 185, 47.

[80] Ibid.

[81] Justin E. Pierce and Andrew D. Price, 'The "Bet the Company" Moment: Think Trademarks', *Venables News and Insights* (7 September 2011) <https://www.venable.com/the-bet-the-company-moment-think-trademarks-09-07-2011/>.

[82] William Van Caenegem, *Intellectual Property in Australia* (Wolters Kluwer 2010), 31. For example, the Australian *Copyright Act* 1968 (Cth) attaches no formal requirements to copyright protection.

[83] Francina Cantatore, *Negotiating a Changing Landscape: Authors, Copyright and the Digital Revolution*, (PhD thesis, Bond University, 2012), 11.

jurisdictions where strict IP regimes run counter to economic interests. A third sector organisation may be in a country without a strong system of IP laws so the risk of IP infringement and opportunities for licensing are minimal.[84] Of course, strong IP laws do not guarantee minimal infringement, countries with strong IP laws can still have major problems with enforcement.[85] Either way, implementing IP laws and regulations may pose a very real challenge for third sector entities. While it is acknowledged that these issues are not limited to such organisations, they can be a significant consideration, especially for financially constrained social enterprises. However, to omit a robust policy of IP management may prove a false economy of time and other resources.

Increased partnering and an explosion of hybrid organisations continue to blur the distinctions between various types of enterprise along the spectrum from non-profit to for-profit. It is understandable then that courts have shown little inclination to interpret the laws of IP protection more leniently for non-profit organisations than for their for-profit counterparts.

Third sector organisations must be just as vigilant in protecting IP, and they must do so in an environment in which conditions mitigate against the effective management of IP. Because the reasons that IP is not strategically managed are both operational and philosophical, they must not only be understood as discrete elements, but also as they interact with and potentially reinforce each other. Operational deficiencies may in some cases be due to philosophical impediments, such as their mission and purpose. Many of the factors underlying 'nonstrategy' commonly co-exist in the context of a third sector institution, synergistically reinforcing each other.

Moreover, there is a tension between the need to protect and manage IP rights, and the effective realisation of human and relational capital, which requires collaboration and cooperation. How effectively these conflicts are resolved will be determined by the ability of an organisation to recognise and capitalise on the intrinsic value of its IP while preserving its mission and purpose. Unless the conflicts are addressed, there can be little hope of translating human capital to the 'grail' of structural capital.

Third sector objectives and IP protection can be reconciled in practice only through balancing diverse interests and creating an effective

---

[84]Gollin, above n 4.

[85]'Certainly there's some deterrent effect, but South Korea is a good example of a country with strong IP laws but still a huge problem with enforcement.' Heather Forrest, correspondence, Third sector franchising and IP management, Sunday, 23 October 2011.

legal infrastructure within which to reap the benefits of the organisation's intellectual assets, human capital resources and strategic relationships. An appropriate solution will also align the organisation's internal identity, external image and its values and mission.[86] Many viable strategies can be employed—the range of creative approaches to meeting the challenges of third sector enterprise is growing exponentially, becoming more diverse, and extending far beyond the familiar classifications.[87] Because no single solution can be expected to suit every third sector enterprise context, it may be beneficial for third sector organisations to consider more flexible structures to accommodate their specific needs and alliances, taking cognisance of all aspects of their intellectual assets. Determining exactly what those structures should be and how they should be implemented is a topic which would benefit greatly from focused qualitative case studies and further empirical research.

Increased Challenges for Social Enterprises

While there is a growing recognition of the value of innovation,[88] SMSEs in particular may be resistant to IP protection or lack a coherent strategy, as evidenced by the research conducted in Australia. This may be because SMSEs are more focused on disseminating knowledge than profiting from it.[89] The research indicates that SMSEs often lack an effective strategy for identifying, valuing, and managing their IP.[90] SMSEs face a number of challenges in building and managing their organisations. As noted, because these organisations have a social benefit focus, the approach to the protection of IP appears to be different from that of commercial organisations, and additionally SMSEs face obstacles in managing their IP once they decide to take a proactive stance.

---

[86] Kylander and Stone, above n 82, 6. Kylander and Stone propose that 'A non-profit brand is most powerful when the organization's internal identity and external image are aligned with each other and with its values and missions.'
[87] Alter, above n 119; The Four Lenses Strategic Framework, above n 119.
[88] 'The increasingly competitive environment has forced traditional non-profit organisations to place great emphasis on innovation in all their social value creating activities': Kong, above n 130, 160.
[89] Gollin, above n 4, 345.
[90] Cantatore and Crawford-Spencer, above n 10, 225.

Lack of Motivation

There are a number of factors affecting the implementation of an effective IP management structure in SMSEs. These factors can constrain both motivation and capability.[91]

Firstly, SMSEs may lack the *motivation* to strategically manage IP for the following reasons:

- An SMSE's non-profit status can impose certain restrictions and requirements with respect to distribution of profit. For example, because profit cannot be distributed to members, there is less perceived reward and also less direct financial accountability for the protection of IP.
- Generally, SMSEs have a strong sense of mission and purpose and are driven by social objectives.[92] These objectives are as wide ranging as the human imagination; such as providing safe water supply, preventing domestic violence, or environmental protection. These objectives may detract from an organisation's motivation to protect IP, where the protection of IP is ordinarily perceived as a commercial objective. For example, there is an association of 'branding' with commercial pursuit of profit; SMSEs often overlook protection of brand for this reason, however, many SMSEs forget, or do not realise, that brand is also often critical to the success of non-profit enterprise (therefore profit correlates with success). It is not always clear whether lack of motivation is deeply principled and philosophical (e.g. with a social or humanitarian focus) at its core, or whether it is based on practical considerations and conditions (such as financial need). What is clear however is that the research suggests that philosophical and practical considerations do reinforce each other.
- SMSEs often specifically focus on sustaining industry relationships and cultivating partnerships. This focus can create tension between IP protection and collaboration in which the latter often takes precedence.
- The tendency to have informal agreements or a Memorandum of Understanding (MOU) in place with partner organisations, which do not have IP protection clauses, suggests a strong reliance on trust and a lower level of concern about the misuse of IP. Many organisations

---

[91]Ibid 220.
[92]Ibid 221.

surveyed had never considered the possibility of a third party misappropriating their IP for example to start a rival organisation with the same name, or to otherwise misuse their IP. However, in the research one of the survey participants did report that they had previously been deceived into revealing operational information to a group looking to start a rival enterprise.[93]

- In some instances, a combination of objectives causes tension between IP protection and collaboration.[94] Whilst some organisations may acknowledge a desire to protect their private property interests, this desire is often outweighed by the need to achieve social objectives, often in collaboration with other organisations. With respect to copyright, for example, values in favour of both sharing and innovation may prevail over self-interested ownership rights of copyrighted material. Litigation is often eschewed, as it could be perceived as highly non-collaborative; and similar views are often held regarding sequestration of, and monopoly over, rights.
- A lack of awareness is an important factor limiting the motivation for SMSE's to protect their IP. SMSE's often fail to appreciate the value of their IP and the direct link between IP rights (such as trademarks) and branding, which is an important aspect of an organisation's public image and value.[95] The fact is that the value of IP can be very hard to quantify accurately and precisely, which can facilitate a misperception that IP rights are not of sufficient value and importance to merit protection, particularly given limited funding.

Lack of Capabilities to Implement IP Protection

Additionally, there is often a perceived lack of capability to implement a useful IP protection strategy. Here, too, there are multiple contributing factors that can be listed as follows:

- There may be a lack of infrastructure for the necessary systems and human resources to apply such a strategy.

---

[93]Cantatore and Crawford-Spencer, above n 19, 336.
[94]Ibid 336–337.
[95]Ibid 334.

- Tested or sophisticated management skills (as many SMSEs grow organically from community need, without much if any, business know-how) are often absent although needed for the successful implementation of managerial structures to foster an IP protection program.
- The staff or volunteers of these organisations often have insufficient knowledge and skills to access or fully utilise outside expertise. Although there is significant scope for utilising pro bono legal advice to improve participants' IP management and protection, many SMSEs make no effort to obtain IP related advice, even when pro bono legal services are accessible for them. The research shows that, in some instances, where a SMSE obtained legal advice, the formal steps in protecting IP were seen as too onerous and/or expensive, and no further action was taken. This omission may indicate both a lack of concern or appreciation of the importance of IP rights as well as tendency to under utilise available legal assistance.[96]
- Typically SMSEs experience a shortage of resources (both financial and labour) to give effect to a viable IP protection program. Funding appears to be the primary constraint for organisations when considering their IP protection. There are significant funding problems if an enterprise has many sub-brands that need to be registered, as was the case for one of the organisations—examined in the research study—which was engaged in several projects simultaneously with different names. Registration of each name as a trademark was perceived to be either too difficult or too costly, or both. Often it is difficult for socially focused organisations to justify spending large amounts of money on an administrative task, such as registering IP interests, when those funds can be used to fulfil the group's social mandate. In addition, there are often concerns about the ongoing monitoring that would be required to ensure implementation.
- A 'lack of time' was often cited as a reason for not implementing an IP management scheme in conjunction with their failure to obtain legal advice, suggesting that many managers of SEs were too time poor to seek out the necessary advice. Some admitted that all their time was spent on pursuing their social purpose—much like in a small business, daily activities could be all-consuming, leaving little time for reflection and consideration of issues such as IP. It was apparent that most

---

[96]Ibid 336.

SMSEs would benefit from strategies to utilise their available human resources more effectively to strengthen their operations and to better access and utilise pro bono services.
- SMSEs are often reliant on funding sources that require ownership of the organisation's IP. Given that significant revenues now flow to organisations via government service contracts and grants, the clauses in such service and grant contracts often seek to reserve IP rights to the funder. This means not only that the SMSE loses control of its IP but that it shows the economic value of IP in SMSEs should not be underestimated and that, very often, their funding is reliant on the ability to offer IP rights as security.

Conclusion

This chapter reveals that there are important differences in the nature of social enterprise that should be taken into account with respect to management of IP and indeed many aspects of governance.

These factors include a lack of motivation to strategically manage their IP because of philosophical issues such as the tension between competition and cooperation; a perception that mission and purpose may conflict with commercial considerations; ownership issues related to 'social ownership' and constraints of IP laws and regulation.

The most common barriers to SMSEs' management of IP appear to be lack of knowledge about how to go about protecting IP, lack of time, lack of funding, lack of management and planning. Additionally the reliance on funding sources that require ownership of the organisation's IP could hamper effective IP management. The factors identified by SMSEs will be discussed in more depth in Chapter 4. Although the majority of SMSEs may blame their difficult position on a lack of funding, our research discussed in Chapter 4 suggests that the underlying reason may more accurately be described as a lack of understanding of the value of IP assets to the organisation.

CHAPTER FOUR

CASE STUDIES IN SME IP MANAGEMENT

Introduction

While third sector organisations must be just as vigilant in protecting IP as their for profit counterparts, they must do so in an environment in which conditions mitigate against the effective management of IP.[1] As explained in Chapter 3, SEs are subject to a variety of limitations and special considerations in developing, managing and protecting their IP. Third sector organisations can be prone to unique challenges because of their particular characteristics, such as their purposes and motivations; their ownership and stakeholder structures; non-distribution of profits to members; governance, management and workforce issues, including reliance on volunteers; the complexity of resource generation;[2] legal and regulatory considerations; and the increasing prevalence of hybrid forms. Many of these factors underlying 'non-strategy' commonly co-exist in the context of a third sector institution, synergistically reinforcing each other.[3]

The tension between the need to build and protect a recognisable brand in order to efficiently enable an organisation to procure funding, and the inherent non-commercial, collaborative, social focus of SE presents certain challenges to SMSEs in the SE arena. Such challenges often require a

---

[1]Cantatore and Crawford-Spencer, above n 10, 210–226.
[2]Lyons, above n 119, 5–7.
[3]Cantatore and Crawford-Spencer, above n 10, 226.

novel approach in dealing with their IP assets. Yet SMSEs often lack the knowledge, infrastructure and means to adequately manage their IP, which in turn may deter them from realising their full potential.

This chapter further examines the role and significance of IP management in SMSEs and presents findings from a qualitative interview-based study undertaken with 10 SMSEs over a three month period.[4] Following a discussion of available literature in this area, with an overview of some of the practical considerations faced by SMSEs, the research allowed us to draw on common themes from our findings in the context of the non-profit arena and make recommendations for effective IP management strategies and structures for SMSEs. We also suggest some practical solutions and present a proposed model for IP management in these organisations.

As we saw from previous chapters and case law the failure to adequately manage IP can have significant adverse consequences for third sector organisations.[5] In an earlier chapter we outlined the importance of effective management of IP for third sector and SE,[6] as IP is instrumental in the ongoing viability and innovative capacity of an organisation.[7] The ability of any enterprise to manage its IP effectively within the broader context of its intellectual capital is a significant factor in achieving its goals and in maximising the benefits of these assets. Third sector organisations do need to ensure best practice in their management practices, while, at the same time, it is incumbent upon courts and regulators to demonstrate sensitivity to the particularities of the sector. In our earlier chapter we also explored the potential differences in approach to the management of IP by third sector organisations from both philosophical and practical perspectives.[8] The approach to the management of IP in the third sector may be very different from that of organisations that are characterised principally by their profit-making orientation.

While there is a growing recognition of the value of intellectual innovation in these organisations,[9] at the same time third sector organisations may be resistant to IP management or lack a coherent strategy, as they 'are

---

[4]Cantatore and Crawford-Spencer, above n 19.
[5]Price, above n 100.
[6]Cantatore and Crawford-Spencer, above n 10, 210–226.
[7]Gollin, above n 4, 51–59.
[8]Cantatore and Crawford-Spencer, above n 10, 210–226.
[9]'The increasingly competitive environment has forced traditional non-profit organisations to place great emphasis on innovation in all their social value creating activities': Kong, above n 130, 160.

more focused on disseminating knowledge than profiting from it'.[10] Given that the efficient management of valuable IP assets is part of good governance, and given the evidence that third sector enterprise often fails to adequately manage its IP, this chapter explores how a group of Australian SMSEs deal with and manage their IP interests.

The Research Study

Methodology

The study was undertaken as a pilot study of a limited number of SMSEs from different geographical areas in Australia, in order to obtain some rich qualitative data in relation to their understanding and management of their IP rights. The study sought to explore the attitudes of management personnel of SMSEs on IP rights management, to ascertain what type of structures and practices the SMSEs currently had in place and the perceived limitations and difficulties in achieving effective IP management.

The sample was chosen as a purposive sample to represent the main aim of the research.[11] This is in line with Locke's observations that all qualitative research sampling is in effect purposeful, and aims to obtain the best possible data on the subject.[12] This method of purposive sampling (also described by Patton as 'purposeful sampling')[13] is explained by Stake as follows: 'For qualitative fieldwork, we draw a purposive sample, building in variety and acknowledging opportunities for intensive study'.[14] Such sampling is 'information rich and illuminative', offering insight about the phenomenon studied rather than empirical generalisation from a sample to a population.[15] Patton describes purposeful sampling as, '[q]ualitative enquiry typically focuses on a relatively small sample ... selected purposefully to permit enquiry into and understanding of a phenomenon *in depth*'.[16]

---

[10]Gollin, above n 4, 345.
[11]Jill Collis and Roger Hussey, *Business Research: APpractical Guide for Undergraduate and Postgraduate Students* (Palgrave Macmillan, 1997) 55.
[12]Karen Locke, *Grounded Theory in Management Research* (Sage, 2001), 17.
[13]Michael Q. Patton, *Qualitative Research and Evaluation Methods* (Sage, 3rd ed, 2002) 40.
[14]Robert E. Stake, 'Qualitative Case Studies' in Norman K. Denzin and Yvonna S. Lincoln (eds), *Handbook of Qualitative Research*, (Sage, 3rd ed, 2005) 443, 451.
[15]Patton, above n 217, 40.
[16]Ibid 46.

The participants were 10 SMSEs who were actively conducting SE activities, and who complied with the definition of SEs in the FASES report.[17] The definition prescribed by the ABS was used in determining whether the organisations fell within the scope of small and medium size organisations.[18]

Possible interviewees were identified through online research and sending out email invitations to participate in the research. All possible participants were asked screening questions and, for confidentiality purposes, all responses were de-identified, with no identifying features other than broad demographic information, such as the participant's State and where they conduct business.[19] The study did not favour any particular industry but sought to include a variety of SMSEs, as long as they met the FASES requirements.

The participants were approached as explained above, and were chosen based on:

- Meeting the FASES report definition through answering a set of questions by email;
- Their willingness to be interviewed and an interest in the research;
- Location and convenience of conducting an interview; and
- Availability of interviewees.

Of the 10 participants, three were from Victoria, two from New South Wales and five from Queensland. They represented a broad spectrum of industries, including a restaurant/cafe, printing services, employment, health services, creative media, food production, and motor mechanic services.

Additional interviews were conducted with two IP solicitors and a community financier, to further gain insight into the relevant issues discussed in this chapter. These interviews, regarded as 'elite interviews', provided valuable information on the research issues, as the interviewees possessed practical legal and financial knowledge of the benefits of effective IP management. Marshall and Rossman note some of the advantages of elite interviews as their possible familiarity with legal and organisational

---

[17]Barraket, Collyer, O'Connor and Anderson, above n 138.
[18]See above n 20 and accompanying text.
[19]Elizabeth A. Buchanan, *Readings in Virtual Research Ethics: Issues and Controversies* (Idea Group Publishing, 2004) 146.

structures.[20] It was envisaged that the findings of the research would be strengthened by the inclusion of a purposive sample of such high-profile or 'elite' participants with a high level of knowledge on the subject matter, as proposed by Patton.[21]

In-depth face-to-face interviews with the managers or key staff members of the organisations formed the nucleus of the research and provided rich qualitative data.[22] The interviews were semi-structured and open-ended in nature, based on an interview guide. The use of an interview guide leaves the interviewer 'free to explore, probe and ask questions that will elucidate and illuminate the particular subject,' and according to Patton 'it provides for better use of the limited time available for an interview; interviewing is more systemic and comprehensive and the issues to be explored are delineated in advance'.[23]

Based on the purposeful sampling strategy with the inherent purpose of 'in-depth understanding' as identified by Patton,[24] the results of the interviews provided sufficient qualitative data for meaningful analysis and discussion within the framework of this research. The interviews were recorded and transcribed, which was regarded as more effective than note taking alone and also less intrusive.[25] An in-depth content analysis followed, whereby the data was categorised into primary issues, for the purpose of identifying patterns or themes, described by Cavana, Delahaye and Sekaran as 'the process of identifying, coding and categorising primary patterns in the data'.[26] The questions in the interview guide assisted in categorising the qualitative data, allowing themes to emerge from the raw data and developing theories that were 'adequately grounded in the data'.[27]

---

[20]Catherine Marshall and Gretchen B. Rossman, *Designing Qualitative Research* (Sage, 5th ed, 2010) 155–156.

[21]Patton, above n 217, 46.

[22]Norman K. Denzin and Yvonna S. Lincoln (eds), *Handbook of Qualitative Research* (Sage, 3rd ed, 2005) p 12.

[23]Patton, above n 217, 343.

[24]Ibid 230.

[25]Robin Legard, Jill Keegan and Kit Ward, 'In-depth interviews' in Jane Ritchie and Jill Lewis (eds), *Qualitative Research Practice: A Guide for Social Science Students and Researchers* (Sage, 2003) 139.

[26]Robert Y. Cavana, Brian Delahaye, and Uma Sekaran, *Applied Business Research: Qualitative and Quantitative Methods* (John Wiley & Sons, 2001) 171.

[27]Mark Saunders, Philip Lewis and Adrian Thornhill, *Research Methods for Business Students* (Prentice Hall, 2007) 479.

Data Analysis and Findings

The findings are presented below with a discussion of the emerging themes and the dominant issues arising from these interviews.

Legal Structures

Although the organisations made use of a variety of legal structures, of those surveyed four operated as a company limited by guarantee ('Ltd'), two were structured as companies with limited liability ('Pty Ltd'), and only one operated as a cooperative.

Interestingly, some participants were unaware of their organisational structure, perhaps suggesting that they had no formal structure. The incidence of the different organisational structures and types of enterprises are set out in Table 1 below:

Table 1 Legal Structures.

Structure	Participants	Type of industry
Company Limited by Guarantee	40%	Creative enterprises, motor mechanic service, health services.
Company (Proprietary Limited)	20%	Employment, food production.
Cooperative	10%	Café and community service sponsor.
Unknown	20%	Restaurant, food production
No specific structure	10%	Business venture of a charity, e.g. printing

Importance of Branding

Participants generally acknowledged that branding was a very important part of their operations. Most organisations are locally based, some with a view to expanding nationally. As the organisations surveyed were locally based, the brand of the organisation is even more important as it seeks to grow and expand its customer base. Though many are keen to expand they have not considered long-term IP strategies.

Significantly, although participants recognised the importance of branding, there was a disconnect between this realization and taking positive steps to ensure protection of their brand. This appeared to be related to a lack of knowledge of trademark protection and not understanding the value of IP assets. For example, most have not considered the IP in respect of their websites, yet they rely on their websites for marketing—closely associated with branding. Another example involves goodwill in the name of the enterprise, which was considered to be very important, as customers and philanthropists associated it with the social mission of the enterprise. All participants acknowledged that it would be very damaging if, for example, someone used the name for a different purpose and undermined their social purpose. Yet most of them had taken little or no action to protect their brand. It was evident that, prior to the interview, many had not seen the connection between brand management and IP protection. Very often an organisation is instantly recognizable by its trademark or trade name, which reflects its brand. It follows then that a lack of IP management in relation to trademarks may translate into a loss of confidence in the enterprise, both internally and externally.

Registered Trademarks

Participants mostly agree that their trademarks were important. Four participants had registered a trademark in their names and/or logos. These organisations had all obtained pro bono assistance from lawyers and all of them had an online presence or website.

However, six of the 10 participants had not registered any trademarks. This seemed to be due, predominantly, to a lack of knowledge. In particular half of the organisations surveyed seemed to be under the misconception that registration of a business name was sufficient to protect their organisations' names. These participants did not appear to understand the difference between registering a business name and having a trademark. There was also a perception that it was costly and complex to register a trademark. This preconceived notion that registration of trademarks would be a very expensive process was a barrier that had prevented participants from seeking more information about IP. Furthermore, most were not familiar with the IP Australia website and did not know that it was possible to register a trademark yourself without the assistance of a lawyer.

Registered Patents

Only one of the participants had registered a patent in respect of the equipment and machinery used in the production of its products. However, with the exception of one other enterprise, most of the participants did not utilise innovative technology that was worth patenting in the first instance. The owner of that innovative enterprise was of the view that the cost of patenting the product was not worth it, particularly as enforcement costs in the event of an infringement would be too large.

Copyright Protection

Most of the participants utilised materials in which they could claim copyright yet there was a lack of knowledge on the issue of copyright protection and the steps that could be taken to protect their copyright in these materials. Examples of materials identified that could be subject to copyright were: education and teaching resources; training manuals; books and instructional materials available to the public, e.g. cookbooks and guides; software code; website content; and PowerPoint slides.

About half the participants claimed to have some knowledge of copyright and 30% of interviewees were aware of Creative Commons licences. Most organisations, however, had no conception of the Creative Commons licence and the way that it could be utilised to share content while providing some protection from commercial exploitation.[28]

Only one participant had made use of a Creative Commons licence in a book publication; however, it was uncertain if there was sufficient notice of the conditions of the licence when the book was being downloaded. Despite the extensive range of materials that could benefit from copyright protection measures, none of the other participants had taken any steps to prevent infringement of their copyright in publications or online content.

On a related note, one of the participants who had taken no steps to protect any of its IP rights, only considered possible infringements once an ex-employee who had been appointed as the administrator of the organisation's Facebook page, took control of the page and refused to give it back to the organisation. This incident illustrated the importance of being in control of an organisation's digital content, and the ramifications of allowing another party control over these assets.

---

[28] A Creative Commons licence provides a way to share content while protecting it from commercial exploitation with 'baseline permissions and core conditions'; however, it provides voluntary licensing options and would be difficult to enforce if breached. See: http://creativecommons.org.au/.

Regulation of IP Ownership by Agreement

Participants were questioned about the level of protection afforded to their IP in the context of agreements with others. These agreements included both intra-organisational and inter-organisational measures. In this regard two issues were relevant: first, whether there were agreements in place with volunteers, partners, contractors and customers which specifically protected their IP and confidential information; and second, whether they were able to claim the IP in work/inventions/meta data created by others at their request, such as website developers, employees, contractors and volunteers.

Whether they had contracts in place differed from organisation to organisation, usually depending on the level of legal advice they had obtained. There were conflicting views in the perceptions of organisations on IP protection, and a tension between the desire for SMSEs to share information and work in a collaborative environment while still protecting the organisation's interests. For example, two organisations were happy for recipes or ideas created by employees/volunteers to be used for the employees/volunteers own benefit. Another organisation had registered a patent and had ownership of their IP but indicated that if someone copied their processes, they would not take enforcement actions against them as long as a social purpose was being fulfilled.

Fewer than half of the participants had formal agreements with volunteers, and of those, fewer than half (i.e. less than 25% of all participants) addressed protection of the organisation's IP assets in their agreements. Two creative organisations admitted that they did not have measures in place to manage shared IP ownership with volunteers and users of their services who created stories and images. Only one participant had a formal agreement in place with the software developers who created the online system used to operate their business model, making provision for ownership of the website and software by the participant organisation. Another participant had a formal agreement with its logo designer in respect of ownership of the IP in the logo designs on its website. In total, only three participants made use of service agreements with service providers.

The most common agreement SMSEs had with other organisations was a MOU. This may or may not be legally binding depending on the terms of each agreement. In general, the MOUs set out the relationship between the parties and gave some guidelines about their responsibilities, rather than regulating issues such as IP. Most organisations had either informal agreements or a MOU in place with partner organisations—there was a definite lack of any formal agreements in joint enterprises, and no IP protection in place. As there were no perceived dangers to their IP rights in relation to partnerships, they did not regard it as necessary to protect it.

Pro Bono Legal Advice

Participants obtained varying levels of legal advice in respect of IP and agreements with other organisations. Significantly, most of them (80%) had access to some form of pro bono legal advice, either through committee/board members or contacts in the legal profession, or through Government funded bodies; yet very few (only 20%) sought advice on protection of their IP rights. This omission may indicate a lack of concern or appreciation of the importance of IP rights, or a tendency to under utilise available legal assistance.

Problems with Implementing an IP Management Structure

The general view amongst participants was that it was difficult for socially focused organisations to justify spending large amounts of money on an administrative task such as registering IP interests, when those funds could be used to fulfil the group's social mandate. In addition, there were concerns about the ongoing monitoring that would be required to ensure implementation. Several main considerations were identified as impeding their interest or ability to prioritise IP management.

The most common problems cited by participants are set out in Table 2 below:

Table 2 Perceived Problems in Managing IP.

Impediment	Participants
Lack of knowledge	50%
Lack of time	40%
Lack of funding	70%
Lack of management and planning	40%
Satisfactory management	10%

As is evident, most participants claimed a lack of funding as an important reason for the absence of an effective IP management structure.

The funding sources of organisations varied—some were funded by a combination of government funding, donations and business activities, some by government funding and business activities and others by government funding and/or business activities. Only one organisation relied purely on donations for their provision of meals. All of them were involved in the provision of goods or services.

Half of them admitted to a lack of knowledge and 40% cited a lack of time, and a lack of management and planning as reasons for not having an IP management structure in place. Although the majority blamed their position on a lack of funding, it could be argued that the underlying reason may more accurately be described as a lack of understanding of the value of IP assets to their organisation; had it been important enough, IP protection would have been a greater priority to the participants.

Furthermore, as stated above, many had access to pro bono legal advice but had not utilised the opportunity to gain advice on IP management. Even where they obtained legal advice, with the exception of one participant, the formal steps in protecting IP was seen as too onerous and/or expensive. There were significant funding problems if an enterprise had many sub-brands that needed to be registered, as was the case for one organisation that was engaged in several projects simultaneously with different names. Registration of each name as a trademark was perceived to be either too difficult or too costly, or both. Two participants stated that, even if they had considered establishing an IP management regime, it would be too costly to enforce, and therefore pointless.

IP management was generally not seen as very important when compared with Health and Safety policies for example—most participants stated that they had never considered that someone could steal their IP and start a rival organisation with the same name, or misuse their IP. One of the participants admitted, however, that they had previously been deceived into revealing operational information to a group looking to start a rival enterprise.

Emerging Themes

Attitudes Towards IP Management

A critical consideration of the problems identified by participants reveals that there are a number of issues affecting an organisation's desire and ability to implement an effective IP management structure. First, funding appeared to be the primary constraint for participants when considering their IP protection. However, on closer examination it becomes evident that the perception of most participants is that IP rights are not of sufficient importance to merit the use of their limited funding. There is also a distinct lack of understanding associated with this perception—participants by and large did not appreciate the value of their IP and the direct link between IP rights (such as trademarks) and branding, which is an important aspect of an organisation's public image and value.

Furthermore, in some instances a diversity of objectives caused tension between IP protection and collaboration—whilst some organisations acknowledged a desire to protect their private property interests, their main focus was on social objectives, which were often achieved through collaboration with other organisations. The tendency to have either informal agreements or a MOU in place with partner organisations—with no provision for IP protection—suggests a strong reliance on trust-based relationships and a lack of concern about misuse of their IP.

SMSEs Can Make Better Use of Pro Bono Resources

As the findings indicate, there is significant scope for utilising pro bono legal advice to improve participants' IP management and protection. Many participants currently make no effort to obtain IP related advice, even when it is accessible to them. Interestingly, once they were questioned on the issue, most participants agreed that they should make more/better use of the resources at their disposal. Significantly, 'a lack of time' was often cited as a reason for not implementing an IP management scheme in conjunction with their failure to obtain legal advice, suggesting that many managers of SMSEs were too time poor to seek out the necessary advice. Some admitted that all their time was spent on pursuing their social purpose—'much like in a small business, daily activities could be all-consuming, leaving little time for reflection and consideration of issues such as IP'. It was apparent that most participants would benefit from strategies to utilise their available human resources more effectively to strengthen their operations.

Agreements Used to Protect IP and Confidential Information to Varying Degrees

As discussed above, there was heavy reliance on 'trust' arrangements between parties and MOUs with collaborators or partner organisations. These types of agreements are by and large not legally enforceable, yet most participants were content to rely on the goodwill and honesty of other organisations. This may be attributed to the social focus of SMSEs, and an expectation that others shared similar, selfless objectives. None of the participants had addressed IP rights in their MOUs.

Furthermore, less than 25% of all participants addressed protection of the organisation's IP assets in their volunteer agreements, and only 20% had agreements in place with service providers in relation to their IP. This signified a marked absence of suitable legal agreements addressing IP related issues, potentially leaving participants' trademarks and copyright material at risk.

Most Have IP Assets that Require Trademark and Copyright Protection

Of the surveyed participants, all had IP interests in their trade and business names, logos and web presence, most of them had copyright interests in written and visual materials, and only one had an interest in a patent. Considering the reliance that SEs place on their brands to gain credibility and communicate their mission, there was a surprisingly low implementation of trademark registrations (40%), and a distinct lack of awareness or interest in protecting their copyright.

Disconnect Between Branding and IP Management

It follows that there is a significant disconnect between the importance participants placed on branding and the lack of protective steps taken in respect of their IP. This disparity indicates a lack of a deeper understanding of the significance of brand protection, which may rely heavily on trademarks and logos, as well as a general failure to recognise the intrinsic value of their tangible and intangible IP assets.

Reasons for IP Management Failure

Overall the data suggests that the barriers to effective IP management are due more to attitudes than conditions. Whilst participants identified a number of issues that contributed to the absence of an effective IP management structure, few recognised how relatively simple intra-organisational measures, if approached proactively, could contribute to an effective IP strategy.

An effective IP management model takes into account the interactive relationship between an organisation's employees/volunteers, collaborative relationships and its IP rights. If implemented efficiently, these components should support one another and contribute to strengthening the SMSE's IP management structure. For example, collaborative relationships should include sharing of IP management strategies and ideas, and utilising resources such as licencing and confidentiality agreements to facilitate protection of organisations' IP rights.

Conclusions and Recommendations: A Suggested Model

Chapter 1 outlined some of the factors that can create challenges for the third sector in managing IP; this includes motivation, mission and purpose, non-distribution of profit, issues of ownership, competence and constraints of IP law and regulation.[29] The research conducted here indicates that many SMSEs do not have adequately formalised IP management structures in place. When specifically asked, participants mostly agreed that they needed a better IP management structure, yet they were constrained by the issues outlined above, or an apparent apathy towards the benefits of having an effective IP structure. The findings from our interviews suggest two fundamental barriers to the effective management of IP. The first barrier can be described as *attitudes* to IP and its management, whilst the other barrier is *conditions* for effective management of IP. These two barriers are of course interrelated; they can, and often do, reinforce each other.

First, with respect to attitudes, this was arguably the most important problem identified. There was a significant lack of knowledge and implementation of IP management strategies on the part of SMSEs for which

---

[29]Cantatore and Crawford-Spencer, above n 10, 210–226.

various reasons were cited, such as a lack of knowledge, funding and/or time. Significantly, participants generally prioritised other issues, such as raising money, over IP concerns and some felt that they did not need IP management structures.

The question then arose—what was the real reason behind their failure to implement an effective IP management structure? Could it be a lack of awareness of the value of their IP assets and branding? Could it be apathy, or that they really do not understand how to do it or that it is 'too hard'? It appears that these reasons may be the true impediments to their lack of proactive measures with respect to their IP rights.

Second, with respect to conditions, it was evident from the qualitative data that IP management issues had not been a priority for any of the participants at the time of the interviews. The participants cited their financial conditions or lack of knowledge and/or time as reasons for their failure to prioritise this part of their operation. However, linked with their sometimes difficult operational conditions, their underlying attitudes towards the importance of IP management determined their lack of appropriate action. They were generally more concerned with their SE focus, earnings and meeting their social objectives, whilst IP was often regarded as a less important issue to be dealt with if and when time allowed. Mostly it was not considered or dealt with adequately at all, with important resources such as time and money applied in favour of other objectives.

There were also misconceptions about trademark and copyright protection, and a lack of useful knowledge in these areas. The issue of patents was only relevant in one organisation but trademark and copyright issues affected all participants. Branding was generally regarded as a significant part of the organisation, yet few participants made a connection between branding and trademark protection, and most failed to take protective steps in this regard.

Significantly, on a deeper level, the issue of IP management often presented SMSEs with a challenge due to the dichotomy of private interest perceptions (protecting their assets) and a public/social benefit focus which has at its base a culture of sharing. There was a tension between their desire to share information and protect their IP. Some participants indicated a desire to share but to retain some control over how their IP was used. This diversity of objectives could be observed in their reluctance to spend money on IP management and, on the other hand, recognition of the importance of protecting their brand.

Therefore it was recommended that SMEs take the following steps in improving their IP management structures:[30]

1. *Devise an IP Management Model*: At its foundation, effective IP management requires a structure and the motivation to implement the necessary changes in the organisation to give effect to the IP management plan. In this context the *IP Management Model* suggested below in Figure 2 provides a workable structure for SMEs to apply in their day-to-day operations. Such a model should be supported by an *IP Management Plan* which deals with the different aspects addressed by the model.

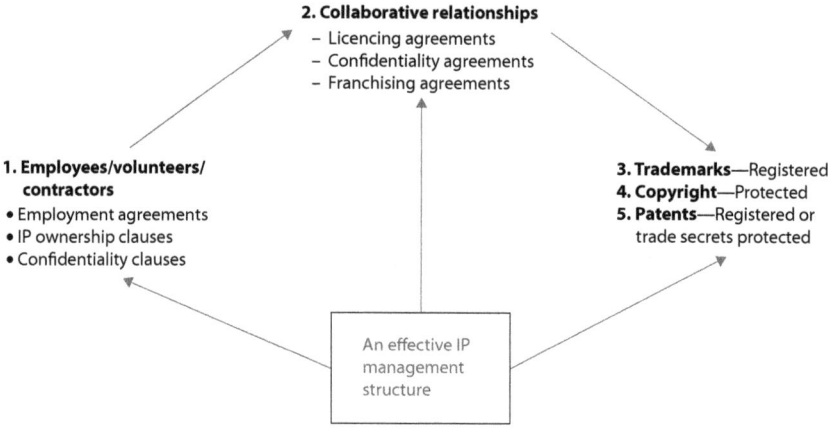

Figure 2 IP Management Model for SMEs.

The proposed model depicts the interaction between human resources (staff, volunteers and contractors), collaborators and IP assets. A strong and effective IP management strategy takes cognisance of all three of these aspects within the organisation (intra- and inter-organisational relationships as well as important IP assets), and ensures that each is addressed and protected.

Intra-organisational relationships can be effectively managed by means of appropriate legal agreements: whether employment, volunteer or service agreements. These agreements should include provisions

---

[30] Cantatore and Crawford-Spencer, above n 19.

dealing with the protection of IP assets belonging to the SME, confidentiality clauses, as well as provisions dealing with ownership of IP creation for and within the organisation. *Inter-organisational relationships* may be facilitated by way of licencing agreements, franchising arrangements or agreements including confidentiality and IP protection clauses to ensure protection of the SMEs IP assets. Pro bono legal advice can be utilised to achieve these objectives, and once agreements have been drafted, they become part of the organisation's IP assets for future use. Examples of a 'Contractor's Service Agreement with Confidentiality Clause' and a 'Confidentiality Agreement' have been included in this book as Appendices C and D respectively.

Lastly, there needs to be a strategy in place to deal with *registration of trademarks and patents, and the licensing of copyright*—each category should be carefully considered and where possible, a SMSE should obtain legal advice and assistance on the best way to secure these assets. For trademarks and patents, the option of registration should be considered, as well as the costs involved. In relation to copyright, it may be important to—in addition to licensing where appropriate—consider digital protection mechanisms on the internet, e.g. where materials are available and downloadable online.

2. *Address conflicting objectives*: An effective IP management strategy should support the social/community focus and collaborative relationships of a SMSE, while protecting its IP assets and branding. This can be achieved through appropriate licensing of IP rights (e.g. trademarks) and confidentiality agreements.

3. *Need for education and assistance*: Overall the data suggests that the barriers to effective IP management are due more to attitudes than conditions. Therefore we suggest that education and initiatives to increase awareness could have a very beneficial effect in raising the standard of IP management in SMSEs. We note that there was often a marked change in the interviewees' viewpoints once they became aware that there may be merit in a closer examination and management of their IP rights. In this regard a government funded initiative or website would be a useful tool in providing education and assistance for SMSEs. SMSEs would also benefit from further practical guidance on issues such as, for example, registering their own trademarks, or implementing basic copyright protection measures.

4. *More beneficial use of pro bono resources*: Often board members or volunteers can assist SMSEs with IP related issues; alternatively a SMSE may have access to free legal assistance. Our research shows that these resources are typically under-utilised in relation to IP management and branding, and that they can be more effectively used in relation to issues such as copyright and trademark advice. It is however acknowledged that patent registration, being a highly specialised area of law, may be more difficult to implement through pro bono resources.
5. *More effective use of agreements to protect and secure IP*: It has been shown above that SMSEs can make better use of agreements to regulate relationships between themselves and their volunteers, employees, partners and collaborators, as in many instances, such legal measures are entirely absent.

IP creation should be addressed in volunteer and employee agreements in two areas. First, the creation of IP by volunteers and employees in the course and scope of their activities or work with the organisation. Second, the protection of IP owned by the organisation. In both instances clauses should be utilised to protect the interests and ownership rights of the organisation. It would also be useful to include clauses dealing with trade secrets and confidential information of the organisation. Similarly, relationships with service providers such as web designers and software providers should also be regulated by agreements in respect of these issues, with the object of securing and protecting an organisation's IP assets.

Last, in relation to partners, collaborators, and customers, consideration should be also given to the impact of these relationships on the SMSE's IP rights. For example, it would be beneficial to enter into licensing or franchising agreements with organisations using a SMSE's trademarks or other IP, to ensure protection of its brand and its IP generally. Relevantly, in respect of patents it may be more useful for SMSEs to have confidentiality agreements in place to protect their trade secrets rather than registering a patent, not only due to the high cost of registration and enforcement, but also because of the consideration that once a patent is filed, it becomes public knowledge, and could conceivably be adapted by competitors to be non-infringing.

In the context of a competitive marketplace and the reduction of government funding in the non-profit sphere, more emphasis is being placed on self-help and the encouragement of entrepreneurial and innovative initiatives by third sector organisations. It is proposed here that, by implementing an IP management structure and executing the basic steps suggested in this chapter, SMSEs can control their IP assets in a more effective way. However, a proactive and focused approach is needed to achieve the desired results, and more detailed guidelines may be needed for industry-specific organisations.

CHAPTER FIVE

IP MANAGEMENT IN A GLOBAL MARKETPLACE

Introduction: A Tailored Approach to IP Rights Protection

Time, money, and management skills are all limited, and SMSEs may fail to see the value in expending limited resources on IP management. Consequently, SMSEs' approach to the management of IP in the third sector may be very different from that of an organisation that is characterised principally by a profit-making goal. In the absence of a profit motive, the competitive considerations that govern the behaviour of a company wishing to assert and enforce IP rights do not apply to an SMSE. Where motivation is lacking, and where time, funding and management skills are being employed elsewhere, the best ideas and approaches to IP management and protection can be elusive. While there are no simple solutions, there are some strategies and approaches to help ensure better protection of IP among SMSEs.

In considering protective measures, it is useful to summarise which kinds of IP a SMSE may have and what the importance and relevance of each type of IP is to that organisation. The type of IP in an organisation will usually depend on the nature and focus of the enterprise. Some types of IP are more common than others in smaller non-profit organisations and social enterprises; for example, not all SMSEs will have patentable materials or trade secrets. Trademarks tend to constitute the most important types of IP rights relating to SMSEs—most rely on some form of branding to distinguish their organisation and/or describe their activities.[1] Of the survey participants referred to in Chapter 4, all had IP interests in their trade and business names, logos, and a web presence. Many of them had copyright interests in written and visual materials, and there was a lack of awareness or interest in protecting copyright. Considering the reliance that SMSEs place on their brands to gain credibility and communicate their mission, there was a surprisingly low implementation of trademark registrations (40%) and only one of the participants had an interest in a patent.[2]

In deciding whether and how to protect its IP, an SMSE should consider the nature of the IP rights used in the enterprise, any existing claims to the ownership of the IP, and the value of the IP. In addition SMSEs must also consider the burdens of protecting the IP (such as the cost and procedures of identification), statutory protections (such as registration), and monitoring and enforcement of IP. The different types of IP rights most commonly affecting SMSEs—namely trademarks, copyright and patents—are discussed in turn below.

Managing and Protecting Different Types of IP

In Chapter 4 we proposed an IP Management Model that took account of the different rights and interests of stakeholders. In this chapter we discuss in more depth how different types of IP may be dealt with by SMSEs.

Trademarks

Described simply, a trademark is a word, phrase, symbol, and/or design that identifies and distinguishes the source of the goods of one party from those of others, and as noted, some examples include brand names, slogans, and logos. Unlike patents and copyrights, trademarks do not expire after a set term of years.[3] Trademark rights come from actual "use" (see below).

---

[1] Kylander and Stone, above n 82.
[2] Cantatore and Crawford-Spencer, above n 19, 335.
[3] See United States Patent and Trademark Office, *Trademark, Patent or Copyright?* <https://www.uspto.gov/trademarks-getting-started/trademark-basics/trademark-patent-or-copyright>.

Therefore, a trademark can last forever provided the owner continues to use the mark in commerce to indicate the source of goods and services.

In the US trademark registration is not mandatory. It is possible to establish common law rights in a mark based solely on use of the mark in commerce, without a registration. However, federal registration of a trademark with the United States Patent and Trademark Office (USPTO) has several advantages, including a notice to the public of the registrant's claim of ownership of the mark, a legal presumption of ownership nationwide, and the exclusive right to use the mark on or in connection with the goods or services set forth in the registration.[4]

The Australian *Trademarks Act* (the TMA) describes a trademark as a 'sign used, or intended to be used, to distinguish goods or services dealt with or provided in the course of trade by a person from goods or services so dealt with or provided by any other person'.[5] A trademark may be an unregistered common law mark or a mark registered under s 19 of the TMA.[6] Article 18 of *The Agreement on Trade-Related Aspects of Intellectual Property Rights* (TRIPS) allows World Trade Organisation (WTO) members to protect a trademark for a minimum term of seven years, which is indefinitely renewable. Registration of a trademark establishes ownership and with it the right to use the registered word, phrase or letters etc. in relation to the classes of goods and services for which it is registered. As an asset, a trademark has value reflected in its owner's balance sheet and can be sold and licensed to other users.

In practice, anyone can register a trademark—in Australia this occurs through IP Australia by registration on the Trademark Register under the TMA. In a case such as the *Freecycle* case referred to in Chapter 2, for example,[7] it would be necessary to register two separate trademarks— one in respect of the name of the organisation (i.e. the word 'freecycle') and one in respect of the logo (as it appears). A slogan or 'tagline' would need a separate registration. Trademarks may also need to be registered in more than one class. For example, a non-profit vegetarian restaurant might want to register its trademark in several classes, such as 'restaurant', 'café'

---

[4] Ibid.
[5] *Trade Marks Act 1995* (Cth) s 17.
[6] Registration gives the owner of the mark the exclusive rights listed in s 20 of the TMA. Registered trade marks are the personal property of the registered owner under s 21 of the TMA.
[7] *Freecycle Sunnyvale v Freecycle Network*, 626 F 3d 509 (9th Cir 2010). In this case the United States Court of Appeal found that a non-profit organisation, Freecycle Network, had abandoned its trade marks by allowing another party to use them without sufficient quality control.

and 'vegetarian food'. There is a fee for each separate registration, and in cases where multiple registrations are necessary or it is unclear which class applies, a SMSE should obtain legal advice on the best course of action. The registration process may take a few months and involves a procedure whereby the proposed trademark is assessed for originality and advertised, and affected parties may make objections. Where available, pro bono legal advice should be sought; this could effectively limit a SMSEs cost to the necessary registration fees involved.[8]

An owner of a registered trademark can pursue an infringer without having to prove its business reputation, or to prove there has been misrepresentation or deception. In contrast to the improper use of an unregistered trademark, the unauthorised use of a registered trademark is a criminal offence and an owner of a registered trademark can, for example, obtain Australian Customs' assistance to stop foreign shipments of goods that bear fraudulent or deceptive trademarks. Though unregistered trademarks cannot be 'owned', and lack many of the associated benefits of registered trademarks, unregistered trademarks can be useful if a brand is not registrable. Consumer and IP protection is offered under the common and statutory law of passing off and misleading or deceptive conduct, and more explicitly under the TMA. Nevertheless, it is registration which provides organisations with maximum protection.

In the research study, participants mostly agreed that their trademarks were important, but this did not translate to registration of trademarks. There appeared to be a misconception that registration of a business name was sufficient to protect the organisations' names and marks. Many SMSEs may be unaware that mere registration of a business name does not protect their rights in that name. There also appeared to be some confusion about the nature of registering a business name and the nature of protecting trademarks. At the same time there was a perception that it was costly and complex to register a trademark. The perception of expense appeared to pose a barrier that prevented participants from seeking more information about IP.[9] Enforceable property interest in names, logos and other identifying marks or wording requires that they be identified and registered under the relevant legislation. Pro bono advice from non-profit

---

[8]This is on the assumption that there are no objections by other affected stakeholders with similar trade marks.

[9]Cantatore and Crawford-Spencer, above n 19, 335.

board members or outside legal practitioners can prove invaluable in this process. Tenenbaum,[10] suggests the use of copyright and trademark notices on all materials and trademarks owned and used by an organisation and registration of the organisation's name, logos and service marks.[11]

Trademarks and Branding

A trademark is often integral to an organisation's identity. The more successful the enterprise, the more important a trademark becomes as a reflection of the brand. As previously mentioned, 'brand' can be defined as a 'name, term, design, symbol, or any other feature that identifies one seller's goods or service as distinct from those of other sellers'.[12]

Apart from being an important IP asset, a trademark can be a valuable marketing tool. Often, an organisation is instantly recognisable by its trademark or trade name, which reflects its brand. It follows then that a lack of IP protection may translate into a loss of confidence, internally and publicly. This occurred in the case of *WWP Inc v Wounded Warriors*,[13] where the organisation's brand had been affected by wrongful use of its IP by other organisations. The Court in that case specifically recognised that the reputation and goodwill of charitable institutions are as important to SMSEs as they are to their commercial counterparts. This holding underscores the importance of protecting the name and image of the organisation.[14]

As discussed in Chapter 2, the public image of a SMSE may also influence its ability to attract funding and investment, as an organisation's social objectives and reputation are often closely associated with its branding. It would thus be beneficial for a SMSE to take steps to protect its brand as effectively as possible, to guard against infringements of its IP assets.

---

[10]Tenenbaum, above n 31.
[11]In the United States the relevant authority is the Patent and Trade Mark Office. In Australia it is IP Australia and in New Zealand it is the IP Office of New Zealand.
[12]Keller, above n 84, 10.
[13]*WWP Inc v Wounded Warriors Inc*, 566 F Supp 2d 970 (D Neb, 2008)
[14]In *WWP Inc v Wounded Warriors Inc*, 566 F Supp 2d 970 (D Neb, 2008) a jury awarded $1.7 million to the Wounded Warrior Project (WWP) of Jacksonville and entered a permanent injunction against Wounded Warrior Family Support. The $1.7 million included $1.295 million for deceptive trade practices and $400,000 for unjust enrichment as a result of confusion.

It has been acknowledged that large non-profit organisations usually have detailed policies to manage the use of their names and logos,[15] and that many non-profits use brand management as a tool for fundraising. Kylander and Stone's suggestions of two necessary types of brand management activities for social enterprise are useful: those that focus on growing brand equity through alignment and mission implementation in partnership and cooperation with other organisations; and those aimed toward protecting brand equity (put at risk in part by the very partnerships and cooperation that grow the brand).[16] Within this dichotomy, IP rights play a central role. This was an important aspect of the *Freecycle* dispute and one that many SMSEs may fail to recognise and appropriately address.[17]

It was evident that, while the study participants generally acknowledged that 'branding' was an important part of their operations, they often failed to appreciate the relationship between branding and IP rights.[18] As the organisations surveyed were generally operating within their local geography, the brand of the organisation would become more important as it sought to grow and expand its customer base. Though many of the organisations were keen to expand, they had not considered long-term IP strategies. Thus, despite recognition of the importance of branding, there was a disconnect between the desire to expand and taking positive steps to ensure protection of their brand.

We noted that this 'disconnect' appeared to arise principally from lack of knowledge of trademark protection and failure to recognise the value of IP assets. For example, most participants had not considered the IP in respect of their websites, though they relied on their websites for marketing—closely associated with branding. Another example involves goodwill in the name of the enterprise, which was considered by survey participants to be very important, as customers and philanthropists associated it with the social mission of the enterprise. All participants acknowledged that it would be very damaging if, for example, someone used the name for a different purpose and undermined their social purpose; yet most of them had taken little or no action to protect their brand. It was evident that, prior to the interview, many had not appreciated the connection between brand management and IP protection. This disparity indicates a lack of a

---

[15] Kylander and Stone, above n 82, 37.
[16] Ibid 4.
[17] Cantatore and Crawford-Spencer, above n 10, 221.
[18] Cantatore and Crawford-Spencer, above n 19, 334.

deeper understanding of the significance of brand protection, which may rely heavily on trademarks and logos, as well as a general failure to recognise the intrinsic value of their tangible and intangible IP assets. Inadequate attention to IP management in relation to trademarks therefore can translate into, not only a financial burden, but a loss of confidence in the enterprise, both internally and externally.

Some recent court cases such as the *Freecycle* case,[19] demonstrate a lack of interest in protecting IP among third sector organisations. While the consequences for these organisations are significant, and the lesson is clear that such organisations must comply with trademark laws in the same way as commercial enterprises in the US, it is worth questioning whether or not Australian courts should follow a similar approach. In that case the organisation was found to have abandoned its trademarks, by allowing 'naked licensing', a phenomenon that occurs when a licensor fails to retain or exercise adequate quality control over a licensee's use of its licensed trademark, resulting in the trademark no longer representing the quality of the licensor's product or service.[20]

The Court's judgment in the *Freecycle* case recognised that the organisation had an interest in sharing the name and logo, which underpinned its failure to exercise control over the trademark. Nevertheless, the fact that Freecycle brought suit indicates that they may have intended to protect their IP rights, rather than promote a culture of sharing. These inconsistencies highlight the SMSE community's confusion and unease with respect to IP protection in the context of trademark and branding.

In the Australasian context, the New Zealand case of *Te Runanga O Toa Rangatira Incorporated v Prokiwi International Limited*,[21] also illustrates some of the problems that can confront SMSEs in registering trademarks that are integral to their organisation. In that case the Intellectual Property Office of New Zealand found in favour of Prokiwi International Limited (Prokiwi), a New Zealand themed souvenir company, and refused to register applications by Te Runanga o Toa Rangatira Incorporated, a SMSE (the Runanga) for 'KA MATE', 'UPANE KAUPANE', 'WHITI TE RA', and 'KA ORA'. The words of the trademarks applied for form part

---

[19] *Freecycle Sunnyvale v Freecycle Network*, 626 F 3d 509 (9th Cir 2010).
[20] Price, above n 100.
[21] *Te Runanga O Toa Rangatira Incorporated v Prokiwi International Limited* [2012] NZIPOTM 14 (1 June 2012).

of the Haka Ka Mate, a traditional Maori dance.[22] The decision amounted to a failure to grant protection for unregistered Maori trademarks, and the question has subsequently arisen whether the New Zealand IP framework is adequate to protect Maori IP rights held by SMSEs.[23]

It has been recognised that in Australia, despite the assisted filing services for trademark applications offered by IP Australia at www.ipaustralia.gov.au, 'the average filer still considers that business names are all that are required when setting up a business.'[24] Thus, there is a perception amongst trademark application filers that if they are guided by IP Australia in the course of their filing, their application is 'bullet-proof' and that they have received endorsement from a third party. This is despite the fact that the support provided is only administrative in nature, not legal. Slater points out that there is evidence of both ignorance and misunderstanding of the nature and purpose of business name registration. Findings suggest that there is not only a degree of uncertainty but also a range of widely and mistakenly held beliefs,[25] and that business names are thought of by many businesses as a form of entitlement, 'an active title that is owned more or less exclusively by a business'.[26] Furthermore, Slater notes that the average person does not know what IP is, how to obtain a strong portfolio, or how to commercialise it for real profit.[27] He also expresses the view that in the Australian arts and sciences the average citizen does not know what IP exists in what they create; '[i]f they do, they don't know how to collect it, or if they collect it, they don't know how to exploit it on a global scale.'[28] As evidence he cites an example of a doctor who introduced IVF to Australia and achieved the world's first clinical IVF pregnancy. When he was asked why IVF was not patented he said that at the time they did not think about it—they did not know that they had the option.[29] Slater also

---

[22]Usually performed at the beginning of certain New Zealand sporting events, such as rugby matches.

[23]See Lynell Tuffery Huria, 'New Zealand intellectual property framework inadequate to protect Maori IP', *AJ Park* (online), 4 September 2012 <http://www.ajpark.com/ip-central/news-articles/2012/09/new-zealand-intellectual-property-framework-inadequate-to-protect-maori-ip/>.

[24]A Slater, 'The Case for a New Federal Arts and Sciences Policy and Practice' (2006) 19(5 & 6) *Australian Intellectual Property Law Bulletin* 75.

[25]Survey conducted by Eureka Strategic Research on behalf of Advisory Council on Intellectual Property Issues, Australia in 2005.

[26]Slater, above n 258, 75.

[27]Ibid.

[28]Ibid 78.

[29]Ibid.

argues that the aim for creative products should be to protect the work in such a way that it allows for effective licensing, as 'licensing is where the real money can be made,'[30] and that public education should be improved. He acknowledges that the US has a far better track record of public education around IP,[31] which Australia should seek to emulate.

Another judicially considered issue is whether a name or logo amounts to a Geographical Indicator (GI) or a trademark.[32] In the case of *Deckers Outdoor Corporation v Australian Leather Pty Ltd*,[33] US company Deckers Outdoor Corporation sued Australian Leather Pty Ltd, a small Australian business, for use of the word UGG in relation to their goods. Decker had trademarked the word UGG in most places in the world. In Australia it did not have exclusive ownership of the word as Australian courts recognised that the word is descriptive.[34] Some politicians had called on the Australian government to make UGG a protected word—similar to 'feta' in Greece (designating it to be a GI and not a trademark). Barcelon examines the tension between whether Decker is acting as a bully that is taking advantage of the trademark system or if it should be entitled to profit from its marketing efforts to make the UGG boot popular.[35] He considers whether UGG could also be a GI in Australia 'provided that local manufacturers can agree on the rules and the required standards of quality to be able to use the sign'. He acknowledges that this is problematic overseas as Decker already owns UGG trademark in most jurisdictions and conflict with a prior mark would be an obstacle to registration.[36] Finally he suggests SMEs should use savvy online marketing to distinguish products without using the word UGG, highlighting that Decker boots are made in China, not Australia. This case illustrates potential issues that SMEs can face dealing with a product that on face value would seem to have been properly trademarked.

---

[30]Ibid 76.
[31]Ibid 77.
[32]*Deckers Outdoor Corporation v Australian Leather Pty Ltd*—(ND Ill, 1:2016cv03676, 28 March 2016).
[33]*Deckers Outdoor Corporation v Australian Leather Pty Ltd*—(ND Ill, 1:2016cv03676, 28 March 2016).
[34]*Deckers Outdoor Corporation v B&B McDougall* (2006) 68 IPR 322; *Deckers Outdoor Corporation v Luda Productions Pty Ltd* (2006) 70 IPR 402.
[35]Raya Barcelon, 'David and Goliath battle gets UGG-ly' (2016) 29(8) *Australian Intellectual Property Law Bulletin* 197.
[36]Ibid.

Actual Use and Control

An issue that was considered in the case of *Lodestar Anstalt v Campari America LLC*[37] was the practical and contractual control that trademark owners have over licensees. In that case it was found that a sufficient connection between the owners and the product was needed. Lodestar applied to have the 'Wild Geese' trademarks owned by Campari removed for non-use. Campari itself did not use the marks but one of its licensees did. In order to rely on this, the licensee's use needed to be authorised to do so by Campari. Prior to this litigation, Campari had contested the licensee's use of the mark. A settlement had been reached between them whereby the licensee transferred its ownership of the marks in Australia to Campari and retained a perpetual licence to use the marks. Significantly, the licence included control provisions but in the relevant period Campari did not exercise any of its rights of control.

The Court considered 'control as a matter of substance' so as to 'indicate a connection in the course of trade with the registered owner'. The Court took guidance from jurisprudence under previous Australian and UK law, particularly in relation to the importance of maintaining the connection between the goods and the registered owner. However, the Court noted that since the introduction of the Trademarks Act 1994 (UK) and the TMA, the UK law has taken a different path, and the legislative differences rendered foreign jurisprudence irrelevant. In conclusion the Court held that the licensee's use of the mark was not enough to defeat a non-use application as Campari did not exercise *actual* control over the licensee's use, and that theoretical control was not enough. The implications of this case were that practical and contractual control that trademarks owners have over licensees should be carefully considered, and that a sufficient connection between the owners and the product was required.[38]

Trademarking a Name

Often there may be a need to trademark a personal name. Dillon considers the situation where a person wants to use their personal name or

---

[37] *Lodestar Anstalt v Campari America LLC* [2016] FCAFC 92.

[38] Ibid. L Davis, 'Trade mark cases update: wild geese and smoking cigars' (2016) *Australian Intellectual Property Law Bulletin* 206.

surname as a branding or marketing tool.[39] Such a step requires consideration of a few issues, namely: whether other family members may also be involved in the same industry, in which case it might be better to not use the name; considering using an acronym or nickname instead to protect the brand and avoid disputes with other family members; and considering what would happen if the person were no longer involved with the business that is tied to their name. In general there exists a prohibition against trademarking common surnames—however, there are many exceptions in Australia, e.g. Allens, Myer, Paul's, David Jones. In these cases the 'ordinary signification' of words will be considered. Are they common to a particular trade or to indicate a common heritage? If so, then they are not capable of distinguishing goods and services and as a result are not able to be registered.

In the case of Garrett Electronics Inc,[40] it was held that the surname Garrett was capable of distinguishing metal detectors because it was highly unlikely that a person manufacturing metal detectors in Australia would have the surname Garrett—that is, the name Garrett was not common to, or descriptive of, that particular trade—and so the 'ordinary signification' of the name Garrett in this context would be a specific supplier of those goods.

Dillon considers examples where individuals have lost the right to use their own names,[41] for example Bob Jane T-Mart and Alannah Hill—both left their companies in acrimonious circumstances and have lost the right to trade under their own names. Bob Jane Corporation brought proceedings against Bob Jane's newly formed companies for trademark infringement, misleading and deceptive conduct, and passing off. The Federal Court of Australia found for Bob Jane Corporation on all grounds.[42] In particular, the Court found that Bob Jane's behaviour was antagonistic and displayed a lack of regard for the consequences of his conduct. Not only was he found to have breached Bob Jane Corporation's trademark rights, Bob Jane's behaviour meant that he was unable to rely on any 'good faith' defence he might have sought under the TMA. While Bob Jane's behaviour was perhaps not ideal, it is easy to appreciate the immense frustration

---

[39] K Dillon, 'Trade marks in business—you've gotta fight (for your naming rights)' (2015) *Australian Intellectual Property Law Bulletin* 265.
[40] *Re Garret Electronics Inc* (2015) 114 IPR 155.
[41] Dillon, above n 273.
[42] *Bob Jane Corp Pty Ltd v ACN 149 801 141 Pty Ltd* (2013) 97 ACSR 127.

Bob Jane must have felt, having built a business in his name, in his field of expertise, to then be in a position where he was unable to use that name or the goodwill he had built in it.

It seems clear that individuals who retain the rights to use their names are much better-placed moving forward where a parting of the ways or a dispute occurs—but what if it is already too late and you find yourself in a position where someone else owns your naming rights? Can you use your name at all? In a case[43] where the registered trademark was SWEETHEART, a company called Sweetheart Plastics Inc was unable to use that mark in reliance on s 122(1)(a)(i) TMA as it was not characterised as a use of the company's name (which would have to have been Sweetheart Plastics or Sweet-heart Plastics Inc).

If a person no longer owned their name, they could still use it under the good faith defence (s 122(1)(a)(i) TMA). This does not apply, however, if the mark is only part of a company or person's name. It also does not apply if the mark is being used to wrongly divert business.[44]

Descriptive Words

Some caution also needs to be exercised against using trademarks that contain highly descriptive words. Webb and Landerer suggest that, where a brand name is largely descriptive, an organisation should include the top level domain component as part of the trademark, for example include '.com', '.net' and '.org'.[45] A case where this issue arose was *REA Group Ltd v Real Estate 1 Ltd*,[46] where the defendant infringed a trademark by operating the websites realestate1.com.au and realcommercial1.com.au. The plaintiff in this case owned realestate.com.au and realcommercial.com.au. The Court advised considering other vendors' trademarks when developing a Google search optimisation strategy, as it may amount to infringement if one—even inadvertently—used another's mark as a trademark. It has been held that there is no infringement if the word is used in a

---

[43] Dillon, above n 273, 269. *Smith & Nephew Plastics (Australia) Pty Ltd v Sweetheart Holding Corporation* (1987) 8 IPR 285.
[44] Dillon, above n 273, 267.
[45] T Webb and N Landerer, 'Descriptive words, trademarks and use on the internet—how far can protection extend?' (2014) 27(10) *Australian Intellectual Property Law Bulletin* 307.
[46] [2013] FCA 559 (7 June 2013).

descriptive sense,[47] and it appears to be the settled position in offline cases that the law is reluctant to grant a monopoly in descriptive words.[48] But words can also become descriptive, for example 'granola'. In concluding that this was infringing use, Bromberg J suggested that the distinguishing feature of REA's mark was the domain name in its entirety because 'real estate' alone would not be distinctive enough to establish brand identity. There was a real danger of confusion between REA's mark and realestate1.com.au because, in the context of the scanning process that internet users undertake when looking at a search results page, the "1" is not very distinctive and was likely to be missed. His Honour similarly found trademark infringement in relation to the "realcommercial1.com.au" domain name.

The decision emphasises the importance of registration for brands that comprise a domain name, even if the second level domain on its own would be highly descriptive. It should be noted that Bromberg J expressed some discontent with conferring this kind of monopoly on a trader:[49]

> ... it is troubling that terms that are highly descriptive of a particular area of commerce and which provide significant commercial advantage should not be readily available for use by all who seek to participate in that commerce.

In the case of *Mantra Group Pty Ltd v Tailly Pty Ltd (No 2)*,[50] Tailly admitted that it had used words that were substantially identical with or deceptively similar to the Mantra Group's marks. However, Tailly contended that it had used the words in a descriptive sense to refer to the name and location of the Circle on Cavill apartment complex and not as a trademark. Reeves J rejected Tailly's argument and found that it had infringed the Mantra Group's trademark by using the words in domain names, as a banner-style heading and in stand-alone format on the webpages, and sometimes without any descriptive content. In light of these factors, his Honour found that a consumer viewing the domain names and various websites to which they linked would conclude that the words were being used as a badge of origin to denote Tailly's accommodation

---

[47] *Lift Shop Pty Ltd v Easy Living Home Elevators Pty Ltd* [2014] FCAFC 75.
[48] *Hornsby Building and Information Centre Pty Ltd v Sydney Building Information Centre* (1978) 140 CLR 216.
[49] Webb and Landerer, above n 279, 309.
[50] *Mantra Group Pty Ltd v Tailly Pty Ltd (No 2)* [2010] FCA 291.

services. This decision demonstrates that the use of a trademark in domain names and on the webpages can constitute use 'as a trademark'. Whether it does so will depend on the manner of use in the domain name and on the website. In rejecting the 'good faith' defence, Reeves J held that the phrase 'geographic origin ... of ... services' refers to the name of a country, region, city, or town from which a person's goods or services have been derived and not to a privately owned building. Further, his Honour suggested that the good faith element of the defence was negated on the basis that Tailly had used the words excessively as meta tags and on the website for search engine optimisation purposes. This decision demonstrates that an alleged infringer who uses a competitor's trademark consistently as meta tags in source code for their own website will have difficulty in establishing a defence under the TMA that involves an element of good faith.[51]

The related case of *Google Inc v Australian Competition and Consumer Commission (ACCC)*[52] concerned the publication of 11 advertisements using Google's AdWords platform in which advertisers reproduced competitors' names and trademarks as keywords. For example, a search for Harvey Norman Travel generated an advertisement for STA Travel with a clickable link 'Harvey World Travel' that redirected consumers to the STA website. The ACCC also sought injunctive relief against the advertisers. However, the ACCC's claims against the advertisers were settled. In finding that Google had not engaged in misleading and deceptive conduct, the High Court distinguished Google from other intermediary or agents who engage in misleading or deceptive conduct by publishing, communicating or passing on someone else's misleading representation. The High Court held that Google is not responsible in an authorial sense for the sponsored links published in response to a user's search request. The result is determined by the keywords and other content of the sponsored link that the advertiser has chosen. While the advertisers were liable, the Court was not convinced that the facilitation of the misleading and deceptive conduct by Google meant that it breached the *Trade Practices Act 1974* (Cth).[53]

---

[51] Webb and Landerer, above n 279, 309.
[52] *Google Inc v Australian Competition and Consumer Commission* (ACCC) [2013] HCA 1.
[53] Webb and Landerer, above n 279, 310.

A Question of Balance

Despite the purported benefits of registering a trademark, in the context of SMSE IP management, it is necessary to consider the fundamental underlying policies of trademark protection. In the US there have been some concerns raised about trademark law. For example, Carter expressed the view that:

> [T]he Federal law of trademarks ... rests on unstated assumptions about how marks are selected and marketed, and, because of its assumptions, it might be granting too much in return for too little. In theory, legal protection of trademarks provides incentives for firms to make investments aimed at gaining consumer confidence in their marks. Successful marks are like packets of information. They lower consumer search costs, thus promoting the efficient functioning of the market. Too few ask the question, however, whether Federal trademark law is consistent with this theory.[54]

Similarly in Australia and New Zealand, trademark law may not always serve the needs of SMSEs, and the difficulties and inconsistencies imply further questions, such as whether trademark protection really protects all the value and goodwill of a SE, which, by nature of its social welfare focus, has a much broader value base.

Again, it is essentially a question of balance—how do the benefits of trademark protection (e.g. certainty, asset protection and brand protection) weigh up against potential negatives such as higher costs and impact on collaborations? Sharing and collaboration are important values in the SMSE context, and these principles need to be accommodated in a trademark strategy. On the other hand, without trademark protection, a SMSE is in danger of losing or severely compromising its valuable IP assets and branding, which could potentially lead to a loss of funding and lack of credibility in the market place. The SMSE also needs to be realistic about enforcement policies, and whether the cost of enforcement justifies the end result. Most importantly, its trademark strategy needs to reflect the organisation's social purpose and ideals and be compatible with its collaborative partnerships. Registration of a trademark does not exclude

---

[54] Stephen L Carter, 'The Trouble with Trade Mark' (1990) 99 *Yale Law Journal* 759.

collaborative arrangements, but would enable the SMSE to effect responsible licensing of its trademark and protect its brand at the same time. This can be achieved through registration of the central trademark used by the SMSE and suitable licensing agreements with collaborators and partner organisations.

Copyright

The Internet and the availability of digital information have changed perceptions of what users may do with information they see on the screen. Where content is the online manifestation of a formally published work such as a book or a journal, most people may understand that copyright applies to it. However, often there is insufficient understanding that if a website does not carry a copyright notice it does not mean that it is free to download and use regardless of the rights of the content owner.[55]

Copyright is a statutory right regulated in the US by the *Copyright Act 1976* and in Australia by the *Copyright Act 1968* (Cth) (the CA) and provides the owner of copyright exclusive privilege for a limited period of time over original literary, musical, dramatic, or artistic works fixed in a tangible medium.[56] Pursuant to the *Berne Convention for the Protection of Literary and Artistic Works*[57] there are no formalities for the protection of copyright. Significantly, *The Agreement on Trade-Related Aspects of Intellectual Property Rights* (TRIPS),[58] an international agreement administered by the WTO in relation to IP rights, states that members shall comply with Articles 1 through 21 of the Berne Convention and the Appendix thereto.[59] Copyright protection applies only in the territory of the granting state, for 70 years after author's death in Australia,[60] as is the case in the US.

No registration of an interest is possible in Australia (as there is no copyright register), although it is regarded as prudent to include a © mark on anything under copyright, followed by the name of the copyright owner,

---

[55] J Cox, 'As I See It-Copyright in the Digital Age: Has the Balance of Interest Between Owners and Users Really Changed?' (2010) 22(6) *Against the Grain* 80.
[56] *Copyright Act 1968* (Cth) s 31.
[57] Opened for signature 9 September 1886, 828 UNTS 221 (entered into force 5 December 1887).
[58] Opened for signature 15 April 1994, 1869 UNTS 299 (entered into force 1 January 1996).
[59] *The Agreement on Trade-Related Aspects of Intellectual Property Rights* s 1(1).
[60] Copyright Act 1968 (Cth) s 33.

the place and the year of creation, to dissuade others from copying the material without consent. In the US registration on the copyright register is voluntary, and copyright exists from the moment the work is created. In order to bring a lawsuit for infringement of work in the US however, registration is required.[61] As noted before, copyright can be held in written materials, but also in software programs, photos, videos, etc.

However, for databases to be protected there has to be some creative effort involved—for example, in *IceTV Pty Ltd v Nine Network Australia Pty Ltd*,[62] lists of names or television program schedules have been held not to be protected. In that case Nine News failed to show that they had copyright in their weekly television program schedules. The Court held that a literary work will only be 'original' if it has been created by some 'independent intellectual effort' which requires some evidence of creative effort in order to claim copyright in something.[63] Additionally, it should be noted that, where an employee makes, in the course of his or her employment, a literary, dramatic, musical, or artistic work, that person's employer is the first owner of any copyright in the work.[64]

Copyright protection is beneficial for the creation of new literary, musical, dramatic and artistic works, as it provides an incentive for creators. It has been recognised that the general objective of the system of IP law in Australia is utilitarian and economic in character,[65] rather than aimed at protecting the personal rights of copyright holders. Thus the value of incentivising creativity and transformation of creative ideas is foundational to copyright protection.

In the commercial sphere, as well as SEs, copyright often exists in online materials and other materials used in the organisation. Whether or not the copyright should be asserted and protected depends on the prerogatives of the organisation and its social purpose. In many instances—as opposed to commercial enterprises—its social focus and collaborative objectives may outweigh or obviate the need for copyright protection. The cost factor in enforcing copyright may also be a relevant consideration.

---

[61] See https://www.copyright.gov/help/faq/faq-general.html#register.
[62] *IceTV Pty Ltd v Nine Network Australia Pty Ltd* (2009) 239 CLR 458.
[63] Ibid [33] and [48].
[64] *Copyright Act 1968* (Cth), s 35.
[65] Intellectual Property and Competition Review Committee, Intellectual Property Legislation, *Review of intellectual property legislation under the Competition Principles Agreement (2000)*, Australia, 33.

What could amount to copyright infringement? This issue is discussed by Givoni[66] in a broader context, by explaining that copying the 'look and feel' of an artwork and putting it on a T-shirt can be copyright infringement even if it is not an identical copy.[67] Furthermore, it is not necessary for the infringer to know that the act was an infringement of copyright.[68] These issues may be overlooked by SMEs who use artwork without proper authority. Permission should always be requested before using copyrighted work. In the context of SMEs or SMSEs, where copyright may be a consideration when dealing with IP rights in relation to certain materials, such as sound recordings, films and videos, which are commonly used on websites or in social media where organisations promote their initiatives. These creative works may constitute IP created for the organisation and as such would automatically be protected by copyright. Although no registration is required, technical measures such as digital rights management (DRM) are often used to prevent illegal downloading of the materials.

A SMSE may take steps to assert copyright in its materials, programs and written work by noting the copyright sign or taking formal protection measures such as DRM. On the Internet, DRM is generally employed by organisations desiring copyright protection;[69] however, this requires technical knowledge or assistance and there are costs involved with their implementation. As noted, SMSEs generally have a social benefit focus and may thus be more inclined to share their copyright materials with partner organisations and beneficiaries. However, the advantage of implementing protection measures is that it may avoid unauthorised commercial exploitation of their materials by external users and commercial enterprises.

When examining the use of copyright in the research study, it was apparent that most of the participants used materials in which they could claim copyright, yet few implemented protective measures. Relevant materials included education and teaching resources; training manuals;

---

[66] S Givoni, 'Dotting your IPs and crossing your Ts (shirts)' (2016) X *Australian Intellectual Property Law Bulletin* 107.

[67] *Elwood Clothing Pty Ltd v Cotton On Clothing Pty Ltd* [2008] FCAFC 197.

[68] *Fenty v Arcadia Group Brands Ltd (t/a Topshop)* [2013] EWHC 2310 (Ch) (England, High Court, 31 July 2013).

[69] 'DRM refers to a collection of systems used to protect the copyrights of electronic media. Digital Rights Management is important to publishers of electronic media since it helps ensure they will receive the appropriate revenue for their products. By controlling the trading, protection, monitoring, and tracking of digital media, DRM helps publishers limit the illegal propagation of copyrighted works': <http://techterms.com/definition/drm>.

books and instructional materials available to the public, e.g. cookbooks and guides; software code; and website content. Nevertheless there was a lack of knowledge on the issue of copyright protection and the steps that could be taken to protect their copyright in these materials. Although participants had some knowledge of copyright and were aware of the concept of Creative Commons licences, there was little understanding as to how the Creative Commons licence worked and the way that it could be utilised to share content while providing some protection from commercial exploitation.[70] Despite the extensive range of materials that could benefit from copyright protection measures, few participants had taken any steps to prevent infringement of their copyright in publications or online content.

This was the case even where they had contracted for work to be done by external contractors. While copyright in work undertaken by employees within the scope of their employment will generally be owned by the organisation,[71] written copyright assignments should be obtained for work done by external contractors, including work such as written copy, graphics or videos.[72] Failure to do so can result in a lack of control over materials commissioned by the SMSE. Computer programs—also subject to copyright—commissioned by a SMSE are similarly not protected unless covered by a written assignment.

Where DRM may not be a desirable option for a SMSE or proves too costly to implement online, there are other options, for example, the Creative Commons is a free online licensing system that provides creators with licensing options for various uses of their materials, which can be appended to copyright materials.[73] The advantage of the Creative Commons is that it enables the copyright holder to determine ways in which its copyright materials may be used by the public. The disadvantage of the system is that it relies upon an 'honesty box' system to operate,[74] and there are no legal remedies (other than the usual rights under copyright legislation) available

---

[70] A Creative Commons licence provides a way to share content while protecting it from commercial exploitation with 'baseline permissions and core conditions'; however, it provides voluntary licensing options and would be difficult to enforce if breached. See <http://creativecommons.org.au/>.
[71] Tenenbaum, above n 31.
[72] Gollin and Taylor, above n 36, 8.
[73] See Creative Commons in general, http://creativecommons.org; in Australia, http://creativecommons.org.au; in New Zealand, http://creativecommons.org.nz.
[74] Francina Cantatore 'From Vault to Honesty Box: Australian Authors and the Changing Face of Copyright' (2013) 25(1) *Bond Law Review* 98.

for breach of the licensing provisions. It does, however, have a global reach and is internationally recognised, and if used correctly, will provide the copyright owner with copyright protection in respect of the licence issued. There have been a number of cases where Creative Commons licences have been upheld.[75]

A case brought against Virgin Mobile Australia provides an example of the use of a licence as a way of managing IP rights, and sets out the limits of the Creative Commons licence.[76] In that case it was established that a photographic image on Flickr used by Virgin and protected by a Creative Commons 'by attribution' licence, only covered the rights of the photographer and did not allow him to give away the privacy rights of his subject.[77] Thus, in using photos covered by a Creative Common licence, it would be necessary to ensure that the privacy rights of persons appearing in the photograph were not infringed.

Overall, our research suggested that copyright is often important to SMSEs, especially for certain projects and applications, e.g. the recipe book of one participant,[78] and a training manual devised by another participant.[79] However, as noted, SMSEs often value sharing and collaboration over protection in this area, which supports the notion that copyright protection need not be approached in the same way by SMSEs as in commercial enterprises.

'Soft' regulation options such as the Creative Commons, which promote controlled sharing and attribution, may be more suited to SMSEs, due to their social purpose objectives and the fact that there are no costs associated with this approach. This is in contrast with the relatively high cost of implementing DRM or other technical measures, as well as legal costs of enforcement in the case of breach. Furthermore, agreements with external contractors and collaborators could regulate assignment and licensing of copyright materials. Unlike trademarks, there is no registration necessary of copyright, and it could be argued that it is unlikely that infringement

---

[75]See, e.g.: 09-1684-A (Lichôdmapwa v. L'asbl Festival de Theatre de Spa); Jacobsen v. Katzer; Gerlach vs. DVU; and Curry v. Audax, available at https://wiki.creativecommons.org/wiki/Category:Case_Law.

[76]*Chang v. Virgin Mobile USA, LLC* (ND Tex, 2009 WL 111570, 16 January 2009).

[77]Noam Cohen, 'Use My Photo? Not Without Permission', The New York Times (online), 1 October 2007 <http://www.nytimes.com/2007/10/01/technology/01link.html>.

[78]Research participant: *Lentil as Anything*, a not for profit restaurant chain in Sydney and Melbourne.

[79]Research participant: a not-for-profit restaurant in Brisbane.

of copyright would impact as severely on the SMSE as infringement of its trademark (which is central to its branding).

Transformative Use and 'Fair Use'

Technology and the use of derivative material in transformative works has also been a consideration in copyright debates. The issue of 'fair use' has been an issue hotly debated in Australia. Despite Productivity Commission recommendations[80] that Australia should follow the US's lead in applying a doctrine of fair use, instead of the 'fair dealing' system provided for by the CA, many have opposed the recommendation. In the US 'real and fair abridgment' emerged as a defence to copyright infringement in 1740 to allow works that made a marked progression on the original copyrighted work were protected.[81] This was the foundation for the doctrine of fair use in the US.[82]

Collins and Young[83] state that there is a tension between modern copyright which includes the right to create derivatives and the doctrine of fair use, and that 'fair use is a necessary ingredient in ensuring that copyright remains limited and does not "stifle the very creativity which that law is designed to foster"'.[84] Fair use is described as a mechanism to balance private and public interests; however it must be acknowledged that there is often uneven bargaining power between the creative permission seeker and creator of transformative works, and the corporate copyright owner, which raises that question whether fair use is 'a right or a defence'. In their article Collins and Young point out that copyright was created to incentivise creativity, including transformative activities like mashups and remixes and argue that content hosts like YouTube and SoundCloud need a more balanced implementation of fair use in their content management policies as these digital platforms rely on users to generate content and often this

---

[80]In 2013 the Australian Law Reform Commission (ALRC) released a report that proposed reforms for simplifying aspects of the Copyright Act. As part of this, the ALRC proposed the replacement of the fair dealing defence with a flexible fair use defence in order to address technological advancement. https://www.alrc.gov.au/publications/copyright-report-122.
[81]*Gyles v Wilcox* (1740) 2 Atk 142, 143.
[82]In the US fair use is codified in s 107 of *Copyright Act 1976* (US).
[83]S Collins and S Young, 'Fair enough? How technology and the law shape creative mashups' (2017) 30(3) *Australian Intellectual Property Law Bulletin* 46.
[84]Ibid citing SCOTUS in *Campbell v Acuff-Rose*.

content will draw on copyrighted works.[85] They caution that the unpredictability of fair use means relying on it can be a huge risk financially and the integrity of the work can be threatened if copyrighted portions have to be removed.[86] From a practical perspective copyright enforcement is now automated on some websites by using a content identification system that identifies matches to copyrighted content. However, use of an automated system does not create the ability to distinguish between infringement and fair use as the technology has not yet advanced to that extent. They criticise the fact that digital platforms in general have taken a very conservative approach to fair use but this has a chilling effect on creativity.[87]

This approach is in line with Leval's viewpoint that fair use 'should not be considered a bizarre, occasionally tolerated departure from the grand conception of the copyright design but something that is integral to the constitution of copyright law an essential in ensuring that copyright's goals can be fulfilled.'[88]

What is meant by a transformative work? In the US the courts consider whether the defendant used the copyright work for a different expressive purpose from that with which the work was created. Such use should 'employ the quoted matter in a different manner or for a different purpose from the original'.[89] For example, the finding that the use of copyright material by Google Books fell within the fair use exception in the US was in part based on the transformative nature of the use. The digitisation by Google of complete books so that they could be searched was found to be transformative, as it transformed expressive text into a comprehensive word index to assist readers, scholars, researchers and others in finding books.[90]

Wilkenson also considers the proposed changes to a 'fair use' system instead of fair dealing and proposes a different viewpoint.[91] He explains that the flexible fair use would set out 'Fairness Principles' and the existing exceptions under the CA would be illustrations of fair use purposes. In this regard, a key consideration in relation to the principle of 'purpose

---

[85] Ibid.
[86] Ibid 47.
[87] Ibid.
[88] Pierre Leval, 'Toward a Fair Use Standard' (1990) 103 *Harvard Law Review* 1105.
[89] Ibid 1111.
[90] *Authors Guild v Google (Google Books)* (SD NY, CIV 8136, 14 November 2013). N Weinstock Netanel, 'Making Sense of Fair Use' (2011) 15 *Lewis and Clark Law Review* 715, 768.
[91] G Wilkinson, "Simple and flexible? Considering the proposed changes to fair dealing" (2014) 27(2) *Australian Intellectual Property Law Bulletin* 92.

and character of use' will be if the work is transformative. Technology has made it easier to 'sample' copyrighted work and many copyright owners are against the introduction of a flexible fair use defence because they believe it would make it even easier than it already is for their copyright to be accessed and infringed.[92] An alternative to the flexible fair use defence proposed by Australian Law Reform Commission (ALRC) is a New Fair Dealing Exception that clearly defines the purposes for which the dealing might be considered fair. In that case the Fairness Principles would be applied to each of the defined purposes. However, Wilkenson sees this proposal as more flexible than the existing fair dealing defence but still not capable of easy adaptation to new technology, and as akin to amendments that were being made in the UK.[93] In view of these challenges an application of Fairness Principles to range of exceptions to infringement currently in the Act, was desirable.

Fairburn and Milicevic also discuss the 'polarisation' caused by the fair use proposal—noting that flexibility and certainty are mutually exclusive and that flexibility enables adaptation.[94] They state that

> Certainty and flexibility are often mutually exclusive outcomes. The Act is replete with flexible and, to some extent, uncertain concepts—such as "originality", "substantiality" and "authorisation"—and this makes it adaptable to new situations. In principle, it is difficult to see why a similar approach should not be available to exceptions.[95]

Furthermore, depending on how the provisions are drafted, Australian courts could have recourse to overseas decisions interpreting fair use, as well as Australian precedents that have considered whether certain uses amount to a 'fair' dealing under the current fair dealing exceptions.

Cox states that the nature of the fair use tests invites litigation, and points out that it is surprising how few reported case law on breach of copyright exists, given their vagueness. While the user may regard the use as fair, the rights holder may disagree. If the rights holder is a large corporation in publishing, movies, or software, it will undoubtedly have the

---

[92] Ibid.
[93] Ibid.
[94] J Fairburn and Z Milicevic, 'Digital revolution for copyright—the ALRC releases its discussion paper for copyright reform' (2013) X *Australian Intellectual Property Law Bulletin* 58.
[95] Ibid 60.

resources to initiate legal action and take the matter before a court. Most breach of copyright cases involving legal cost of half a million dollars or more. That automatically disadvantages the individual and the SME—the very users that are needed to drive economic growth.[96]

As at the date of publication of this book, the ALRC and Productivity Commission[97] have called on Australia to adopt the US style system of fair use. It has been proposed that adoption of fair use could provide a potentially proportionate measure that allows transformation where it is reasonable, as opposed to the current fair dealing regulation which creates a closed class with new exceptions having to be added via legislation.[98] The government's approach following the recommendations of the ALRC will greatly impact how copyright in transformative work is treated in the future.

Patents

A patent is a statutory right which gives the inventor the exclusive right to use or sell a patented product, method or process, for a limited time,[99] and is regulated by the *U.S. Patent Act* in the US and the *Patents Act 1990* (Cth) in Australia. A patent may be a standard patent, innovation patent, petty patent, or a foreign patent granted upon substantially similar principles. Patent rights are personal property, and may be assigned, willed, sold, licensed, or otherwise dealt with by the patentee. The patented product usually enters the public domain after a maximum of 20 years, but an innovation patent enters the public domain after eight years. Under article 33 of TRIPS, there is a minimum protection of 20 years for WTO members. Usually a patent is valid only in the granting state, but the international *Patent Cooperation Treaty*[100] allows for a simplified procedure of registration in member countries. Patent law is highly specialised and usually requires specialist legal assistance to effect registrations under the relevant Patents Act in a specific jurisdiction, especially when patents are sought internationally. Furthermore, the cost of registration may amount

---

[96]Cox, above n 289.
[97]See ALRC Report at https://www.alrc.gov.au/publications/copyright-report-122.
[98]Ibid.
[99]WIPO, Fields of Intellectual Property Protection, p17 at http://www.wipo.int/export/sites/www/about-ip/en/iprm/pdf/ch2.pdf
[100]Opened for signature 19 June 1970, 1160 UNTS 231 (entered into force 24 January 1978).

to a considerable sum, and for smaller SMSEs it may prove difficult and costly to enforce a registered patent overseas. Because patents are publicly searchable, others can potentially examine an organisation's patent, make certain modifications to it and create a competitive product.

Exclusive right to use or sell a patented product, method or process, for a limited time may be useful to certain types of SEs, which use or trade in a patentable product. It is likely, however, that an SMSE may want to disseminate a patentable invention. This raises the question of whether patent protection undermines or alternatively can be used to support that process.

The advantage of registering an effective patent is that the SMSE will hold and be able to claim ownership of an IP asset that could be licensed to other parties. Relevantly, where an employee (or volunteer) invents a product or process which may be subject to IP rights, under Australian law,[101] inventions will be owned by the employer organisation only if they were invented in the course and scope of an employee's duties.[102] Using an employer's resources will not automatically entitle the organisation to the assignment of an invention, thus a written contract should be concluded to protect both parties' interests.[103]

There are two schools of thought on the advisability and utility of registration of patents. While registration does provide the patent holder with a certain degree of protection, it is an expensive process, especially if registration in more than one country is required. Some SMSEs may have patentable goods or services that are material to the success of their organisations or central to their social activities. Despite its social benefit focus an SMSE may have an interest in protecting patents from potential infringement by commercial or competing organisations. In the research study, our research indicated that there was a perception of a high cost of patenting as well as of enforcement, which discouraged patent registration. Significantly, however, most of the participants did not utilise innovative technology that was deemed to be worth patenting.

Another option is to rely on confidentiality agreements, rather than registration, to protect a SMSEs patentable and confidential material. Confidentiality agreements can be useful in dealings with partnership organisations, customers, employees and volunteers, and pro bono legal

---

[101] *Patents Act 1990* (Cth).
[102] Van Caenegem, above n 33, 97.
[103] Ibid.

assistance could be sought to prepare appropriate documents. They are discussed further below. The downside of non-registration is that if there is no patent registered, the invention will not generally be amenable to licencing.[104]

Registering IP can also have commercial advantages for SMEs, as pointed out by Konya.[105] SMEs raising equity capital in Australia can be subject to onerous disclosure requirements under the *Corporations Act 2001* (Cth) but innovative SMEs can take advantage of disclosure exemptions to attract a unique pool of sophisticated and professional investors without the need for formal disclosure. Konya proposes that registering IP early is a good way that SMEs can then access these investors. From an IP perspective, business owners need to demonstrate to investors that they have conducted a thorough audit of all potential IP in the business. An IP audit is an essential exercise that should be undertaken prior to the capital raising exercise, and should identify any IP that is or is not capable of being registered in Australia and around the world, and also identify any IP that might be a potential infringement of a third party's IP. In this way, SME owners can feel more confident in convincing good quality investors that they are developing a viable enterprise worth investing in.

Innovation Patents

Specific mention needs to be made of innovation patents, which are subject to a lower patentability threshold, is quicker and cheaper, but also has a reduced patent term with more restrictions on patent subject matter. Hind discussed the review done of the innovation patent by the Advisory Council on Intellectual Property Law in 2014, and explained the process:[106] On filing an application for an innovation patent, the only check is one of formalities and then the patent will be granted. In these applications no assessment of patentability is undertaken. However, he points out that 'although the patent has been granted, it cannot be enforced until it has successfully undergone substantive examination for patentability which

---

[104]See, e.g., in Australia, as regulated by the *Patents Act 1990* (Cth) s 13(1).

[105]Victoria Konya, 'Raising Capital for IP SMEs—understanding the disclosure requirements' (2016) X *Australian Intellectual Property Law Bulletin* 99.

[106]Ray Hind, 'Innovation patents—useful but unloved by some' (2014) X *Australian Intellectual Property Law Bulletin* 219.

can be requested by the patent owner or a third party at any stage throughout the term of the innovation patent'.[107]

Only after that stage does it becomes a certified patent. While intended for the use of SMEs, there is evidence that innovative patents are also being used by large corporations in both Australia and the US. It is also being used as a strategic tool to target specific infringements—often an innovative patent is filed as a divisional application for a pending standard patent. The novelty threshold for these patents is low—the applicant needs to show novelty and 'an innovative step' (as opposed to an inventive step).[108] An innovative step is considered to exist when the differences over the prior art make a substantial contribution to the working of the invention, and this has to be considered in the light of the common general knowledge.[109] The case of *Dura-Post (Aust) Pty Ltd v Delnorth Pty Ltd*,[110] which concerned a roadside post of spring steel, dealt with a number of innovation patents by Delnorth. Dura-Post argued that reference to a contribution to the working of the invention in the innovative step test required a consideration of the advance in the art represented by the invention. That argument was rejected both at first instance and by the Full Court on appeal. The Delnorth decisions clarify that the test requires an assessment as to whether the differences between the invention as claimed and the applicable prior art contribute to the working of the invention. At first instance and as accepted on appeal, it was held that 'substantial' contribution in the context of the innovative step test meant 'real' or 'of substance'.

In general the requirements for the specification of an innovation patent application are broadly the same as those applicable for a standard patent in terms of disclosure sufficient for others to perform the invention, and disclosure of the best method for performing the invention. The processing regime and patentability threshold are, however, significantly different and it is those differences which give rise to the advantages and related criticisms of the innovation patent system. Other differences are a reduced patent term of eight years, in comparison with 20 years for a standard patent.[111] An objective of the innovation patent system as introduced in 2001 was, as the Advisory Council on Intellectual Property (ACIP)

---

[107]Ibid.
[108]See the test in *Dura-Post (Aust) Pty Ltd v Delnorth Pty Ltd* [2009] FCAFC 81.
[109]Hind, above n 339, 220.
[110]*Dura-Post (Aust) Pty Ltd v Delnorth Pty Ltd* [2009] FCAFC 81.
[111]Hind, above n 339, 219.

Review notes, to stimulate innovation in Australian SMEs by providing Australian businesses with IP rights for their lower level inventions. An intention was also to provide easier, cheaper and quicker rights.[112]

Not surprisingly, this type of patent application has seen an increase in usage since its inception. In its first year in Australia, only 163 innovation patent applications were filed. This figure later increased to 1050 in the next year.[113] However, over the next nine years, that number increased by only 31% to 1376 applications. While the innovation patent, with its shorter term and lower inventive threshold, was aimed at SMEs, the statistics published by IP Australia do not include data about who is most actively filing innovation patents.[114]

The 2014 ACIP Review[115] was unable to discern whether the introduction of innovation patents did or did not stimulate innovation in Australian SMEs.[116] The ACIP review recommended an increase in the level of innovation needed to amount to an innovative step, and said that the test should be that in *Minnesota Mining & Manufacturing Co & 3M Australia Pty Ltd v Beiersdorf (Aust) Ltd*;[117] and the invention should be non-obvious to a non-inventive skilled worker when compared to general knowledge anywhere else in the world. IP Australia proposed raising the standard to a non-obvious inventive step (requiring the same test as standard patents); however the distinction between an innovation patent and standard patent persists, providing SMEs with an easier and cheaper option of patent registration.[118]

Contractual Arrangements

In contemplating protective strategies for SMSEs, it is important to recognise that IP protection measures include not only the registration of IP rights but also inter- and intra-organisational agreements, including

---

[112]Ibid 220.
[113]S Givoni, 'IP Australia data' (2011) X *Australian Intellectual Property Law Bulletin* 62.
[114]Ibid.
[115]Advisory Council on Intellectual Property Review of the Innovation Patent System: Final Report, May 2014, <www.acip.gov.au>.
[116]Hind, above n 339, 219.
[117](1980) 144 CLR 253.
[118]See IP Australia, 'Types of Patents' <https://www.ipaustralia.gov.au/patents/understanding-patents/types-patents>.

licensing arrangements. While copyright, trademarks and patents are protected under statutory law, not all protection of IP is accomplished by means of legislated regimes. Some IP, such as confidential information, trade secrets and know-how, does not lend itself to protection according to these processes. For these types of IP, suitable agreements, such as confidentiality clauses that prohibit others from revealing knowledge, are often better suited to protect and manage IP such as recipes, formulas, processes and know-how. Contractual arrangements that include confidentiality clauses are supported by the law of contract, property and tort. An example of an IP licencing agreement is included as Appendix A.

Such provisions may be used in agreements entered into with board members, managers, employees, volunteers, business partners, business associates, research collaborators, contractors and other organisations regarding the use and disclosure of confidential information. They may be used in the context of management, employment, contracting, volunteer arrangements and cooperative ventures. For example, an employment agreement may provide that an employee must maintain the confidentiality of trade secrets even after leaving that employment. In environmental law, persons who gain knowledge of trade secrets in the course of considering applications for permits to emit pollution, or otherwise in the course of administering the legislation, may commit an offence if details are improperly disclosed.

Private agreements can eliminate the need to go through formal and costly processes of government agencies. Such agreements can be used to protect trade secrets with respect to some technologies and proprietary knowledge (know-how) or indeed any formula, pattern, device, or compilation of information used in an enterprise and that gives that person an opportunity to derive an advantage over other persons who do not know or use it. With respect to patent protection, confidentiality measures may be preferable to registration when it is difficult to copy a product, or where the cost of registration may be prohibitive for an SMSE. However, proving a breach of confidentiality or trade secrets can be complex and can be costlier than defending a registered right.

The use of a contract to protect confidential information may, however, reduce avenues of enforcement, for example, by and through independent government authorities or agencies. Also, although these agreements are widely used to protect against competition, they must be carefully drafted to avoid infringing the prohibition against contracts in restraint of trade.

Participants in the research study were questioned about the level of protection afforded to their IP in the context of agreements with others. These agreements included both intra-organisational and inter-organisational measures. In this regard two issues were relevant: first, whether there were agreements in place with volunteers, partners, contractors and customers which specifically protected their IP and confidential information; and second, whether they were able to claim the IP in work/inventions/metadata created by others at their request, such as website developers, employees, contractors and volunteers. Whether they had contracts in place differed from organisation to organisation, usually depending on the level of legal advice they had obtained.

As we saw there were conflicting views in the perceptions of organisations on IP protection, and a tension between the desire for social enterprises to share information and work in a collaborative environment while still protecting the organisation's interests. For example, two organisations were happy for recipes or ideas created by employees/volunteers to be used for the employees/volunteers own benefit. Another organisation had registered a patent and had ownership of their IP but indicated that if someone copied their processes, they would not take enforcement actions against them as long as a social purpose was being fulfilled. Fewer than half of the participants had formal agreements with volunteers, and of those, fewer than half (i.e. less than 25% of all participants) addressed protection of the organisation's IP assets in their agreements. Two creative organisations admitted that they did not have measures in place to manage shared IP ownership with volunteers and users of their services who created stories and images. Only one participant had a formal agreement in place with the software developers who created the online system used to operate their business model, making provision for ownership of the website and software by the participant organisation. Another participant had a formal agreement with its logo designer in respect of ownership of the IP in the logo designs on its website. In total, only three participants made use of service agreements with service providers.

The SMSEs surveyed placed heavy reliance on 'trust' arrangements between parties and MOUs with collaborators or partner organisations. Though such trust arrangements may not be legally enforceable, most participants were content to rely on the goodwill and honesty of other organisations. None of the participants had addressed IP rights in their MOUs; less than 25% of all participants addressed protection of the organisation's

IP assets in their volunteer agreements, and only 20% had agreements in place with service providers in relation to their IP. This signified a marked absence of suitable legal agreements addressing IP related issues, potentially leaving participants' trademarks and copyright material at risk.

Important issues to consider here would be the relationships an organisation has with its web developers, external contractors and people creating IP for the organisation. A SMSE needs to have agreements in place to ensure that they own the contents of their website and other IP, and that any work done for the organisation by volunteers, employees or contractors becomes the property of the organisation.

While it may be possible for SMSEs to make better use of agreements to regulate relationships between themselves and their volunteers, employees, partners and collaborators, in many instances, such legal measures are entirely absent. IP creation should be addressed in volunteers' and employees' agreements to address both the creation of IP by volunteers and employees in the course and scope of their activities or work with the organisation and the protection of existing IP owned by the organisation. In both instances contractual clauses should be utilised to protect the interests and ownership rights of the organisation. It would also be useful to include clauses dealing with trade secrets and confidential information of the organisation. Similarly, relationships with service providers such as web designers and software providers should also be regulated by agreements in respect of these issues, with the object of securing and protecting an organisation's IP assets.

Last, in relation to partners, collaborators and customers, consideration should be also given to the impact of these relationships on the SME's IP rights. For example, it could be beneficial to enter into licensing or franchising agreements with organisations using a SMSE's trademarks or other IP, to ensure protection of its brand and its IP generally. Relevantly, in respect of patents it may be more useful for SMEs to have confidentiality agreements in place to protect their trade secrets rather than registering a patent, not only due to the high cost of registration and enforcement, but also because of the consideration that once a patent is filed, it becomes public knowledge, and could conceivably be adapted by competitors to be non-infringing.

In Australia the courts have recognised employment agreements in order to protect the IP of an organisation. For example, in *IceTV v Duncan Ross* [2007] NSWSC 635 the court enforced a restraint of trade contract which had the effect of protection confidential information. IceTV had been established as a shelf company that purchased the IP rights of a failed start up. IceTV had employed the founder and former CEO of the start-up as employees. Following product launch, and poor sales, IceTV terminated the contracts of both former start up employees whose technology was being sold. The former employees began to work as consultants at a company which would have been one of IceTV's customers. IceTV brought the litigation to enforce a 12 month restraint contained in the employment contract of the former employees, and succeeded in their action. The judge held that this was the most convenient means of upholding IceTV's 'legitimate' interest in 'confidential information'.[119] Riley criticises the Court's decision that a potential employee, who IceTV had been unable to engage, was a 'legitimate interest'.[120] He argues that

> The hole in the contract lawyers' argument, however, is that traditionally the common law has refused to enforce such contracts, on the basis that that they are illegal restraints of trade. This ancient doctrine depends on a similar rationale to the 'incentive' rationale of intellectual property protection. The public interest is served by maintaining the freedom of individuals to exploit their creative, innovative and just plain productive talents in a freely competitive market.[121]

He also expressed the view that 'customer connection' was a legitimate interest, as the goodwill of the customer was developed at the expense of the employing firm. However, the inherent talent of the employees 'including their ability to generate ideas and come up with product innovations and marketing strategies' should not be regarded as a 'resource' produced by the employing firm. Although it may have been a resource that the firm once employed, as soon as they terminated the contracts of the staff members, they forfeited any entitlement to control the future exploitation of their talents.[122] However, despite this criticism, the decision illustrates the readiness of the courts to recognise agreements protecting confidential

---

[119] *IceTV v Duncan Ross* [2007] NSWSC 635.

[120] J Riley, 'Innovation put on ice? Jealous IP protection may discourage creativity' (2008) 20(7) *Australian Intellectual Property Law Bulletin* 102.

[121] Ibid 103–104 citing *Maggbury Pty Ltd v Hafele Australia Pty Ltd* (2001) 210 CLR 181.

[122] Ibid.

information and IP held by companies at the expense of ex-employees. It could be argued that in extending the protective mantel in such a broad manner, this approach by the Court indicates a willingness to extend the interests of organisations to include human capital rather than merely IC, which could discourage creativity and undermine the incentive to create.

IP Issues Among SME's in the UK: The Hargreaves Report

In his 2011 report Ian Hargreaves recognised the issues facing SMEs in the UK in dealing with their IP rights online.[123] He noted that the extent of information available on IP could act as a significant barrier for SMEs as 'one quarter (27 per cent) of surveyed SMEs agreed that there are too many services available—it's difficult to choose the right one.'[124]

He also referred to a number of anecdotal accounts involving SMEs who had initially received poor advice and subsequently faced even higher costs in damage limitation.[125] Furthermore, it was shown that SMEs wanted an integrated source of advice that combined technical and commercial insight to allow them to commercialise and simultaneously protect their IP.[126] In support of this statement he cited that

> 'two thirds (66 per cent) of surveyed SMEs indicated that they would be interested in having access to an intermediary who can provide basic advice on IP rights (applications, maintenance, licensing, disputes or enforcement) in place of a legal advisor or attorney—with interest even higher amongst the smallest firms who had started trading recently'.[127]

He mentioned an example of the detrimental effects of the UK's failure to keep up with developments in consumer technology. The Brennan J7 music player, the brainchild of Martin Brennan, a young British entrepreneur, enabled consumers to store music from CDs which they had

---

[123]Ian Hargreaves, 'Digital Opportunity: A Review of Intellectual Property and Growth' (May 2011).
[124]Ibid para 9.6.
[125]Ibid para 9.7.
[126]Ibid para 9.8.
[127]Ibid.

purchased on its hard disk, making them easily accessible for playing from one point. He stated that it was difficult to see that product as an undesirable innovation, or to see it as requiring actions any different than those already done by millions of consumers with other digital music players. However the Advertising Standards Authority had ruled (given where the law stood on the issue) that advertisements for the Brennan should include a warning that using it involved copyright infringement. Hargreaves pointed out that the UK could not afford to place unnecessary obstacles in the way of innovation in consumer products.[128]

The lack of integration was particularly significant when considering that research commissioned by the Review into the financial constraints experienced by small businesses revealed that only around one quarter of intangibles-intensive SMEs wrote down an IP strategy and a similarly small proportion explicitly aligned their IP strategy with their business plan. These findings were important because interviews with investors as part of the same research indicated that SMEs' ability to present a strong business plan (incorporating intangibles and IP) was a key factor in their decisions on whether to offer financial assistance. The Review also saw evidence that some creative firms, especially in the music industry, experience considerable difficulty in accessing finance.[129]

The Review therefore asked firms to estimate their true costs of obtaining registered IPRs. The average cost to an SME of applying for, maintaining and protecting a patent, was reported to be £20,700; the equivalent figure for a trademark or design is £4,800. The mean fee paid for external advice on applying for, maintaining and protecting a patent was estimated to be £13,800; the comparable figure for a trademark or design was £6,300. Among surveyed SMEs who had withdrawn, or considered but not launched, an application for registered rights, cost was given as the reason by three in 10 (28%). That the cost of obtaining or maintaining IP protection is a significant issue is also acknowledged by practitioners. In its submission to the Call for Evidence, the Chartered Institute of Patent Attorneys noted that

> many practitioners have experience of … businesses not being able to continue with [patent] protection because of shortage of

---

[128]Ibid para 5.29.
[129]Ibid para 9.10.

funding ... This has been reported as a particular issue for smaller biotechnology/pharma type companies, where revenues from products many be substantially later than in other technology fields and the costs can be very high.[130]

Hargreaves further noted that it was evident that SMEs felt that the cost of IP management was prohibitively high, and made the following suggestions for improvement: implementing business mentorship and outreach by connecting firms with a well-established IP portfolio with a new or smaller firm; government provision of cheap IP advice; and more online engagement.[131]

As a result of the report, the changes that were suggested by Hargreaves were considered for introduction in the *Intellectual Property Act 2014* (UK).[132] One of the aims of the reforms was to make the UK IP system clearer and more accessible to SMEs. Chamberlain summarises the benefits of reform, which would includes measures that would: make it easier for businesses to understand what is protected by design law, with a view to aiding innovation and making investment in the design sector safer and clearer; make the issue of design ownership clearer, with a view to encouraging trade in intangible assets and reducing the costs for businesses; strengthen design protection with the introduction of criminal penalties (in relation to the copying of UK registered designs) with a view to helping designers enforce their rights; introduce a design rights opinion service with a view to more IP disputes being settled without the need to resort to what is often time-consuming and expensive litigation; provide a power to implement the Unified Patent Court based in London, with a view to introducing a single patent system in almost all EU countries so British businesses can protect inventions internationally in a single patent; and allow the UK to share information on unpublished patent applications with a view to clearing existing application backlogs and speeding up clearance times at other patent offices.

These changes substantially improved access of SMEs to IP information. The same observations and issues apply to SMEs as well as SMSEs

---

[130] Ibid para 9.12–9.13.
[131] Ibid para 9.8.
[132] P Chamberlain, 'Intellectual Property Act 2014—helping SMEs drive innovation and growth' (2014) 19(3) *Communications Law* 96.

globally, with lack of education and advice playing a major role, which need to be addressed.

Conclusion

The necessity for SMSEs to create partnerships and attract funders means that a collaborative framework is essential to promote the sharing of ideas and enhancement of social impact. As noted above, the IP of an organisation may be a consideration in government service contracts and grants, and, if adequately protected, may provide the organisation with an asset capable of significant leverage. All these objectives need to be balanced with a strategy that encourages creativity and protects its intellectual assets. The interaction of IP rights protection and branding is central to the decision making process. Questions such as: 'Do the brand protecting activities limit a non-profit's ability to take risk and stretch the organisation?' and 'What are the other potential downsides or detrimental aspects of traditional brand management activities?' need to be asked and answered by each organisation. Additionally, the financial cost and benefits of IP protection measures should be carefully weighed by the SMSE.

A considered approach should meet an organisation's mission and purpose and also protect the assets of the organisation. No single solution can be expected to suit every SMSE, and it may be beneficial to consider more flexible structures such as private agreements to accommodate specific needs and alliances. A proactive and informed approach can help a SMSE to resolve apparent conflicts and overcome the challenges inherent in the non-profit sphere.[133]

Contractual clauses and other forms of private agreements can serve the particular needs and interests of an SMSE. As with trademarks SMSEs do need to ensure the value and integrity of the organisation, its information and practices, and its brand. Analysis of our findings suggests that trademarks and agreements are the areas that SMSEs often do and rightly should emphasise in an IP management strategy. Copyright should be assessed in terms of the aims of the organisation, and whether the property is related to the internal workings, identity and success of the organisation

---

[133]Francina Cantatore and Elizabeth Crawford-Spencer, 'Strategies for Intellectual Property Protection in the Third Sector' (2015) 21(2) *Third Sector Review* 149, 166.

or whether it is material that the organisation seeks to disseminate for public benefit. A similar analysis can be undertaken for potentially patentable property.

More research is needed to assess individual SMSEs as case studies of different approaches to managing and protecting IP. We hope to gauge over time and compare the effectiveness of different approaches in SMSEs. It would also be useful to explore particular sectors and types of organisations to better understand variations in attitudes and capabilities. This further research may provide more detailed guidelines to SMSEs and to industry-specific organisations. It can also contribute to better practice in the commercial arena and inform policy and the ongoing development of legal frameworks around IP.

Overall the data from the research study suggested that the barriers to effective IP management are due more to attitudes than conditions. Whilst participants identified a number of issues that contributed to the absence of an effective IP management structure, few recognised how relatively simple intra-organisational measures, if approached proactively, could contribute to an effective IP strategy. An effective IP management model takes into account the interactive relationship between an organisation's employees/volunteers, collaborative relationships and its IP rights. If implemented efficiently, these components should support one another and contribute to strengthening the SMSE's IP management structure. For example, collaborative relationships should include sharing of IP management strategies and ideas, and utilising resources such as licencing and confidentiality agreements to facilitate protection of organisations' IP rights.

It is incumbent upon SMSEs to evaluate the importance of IP rights protection within the context of their collaborative relationships and implement a cohesive IP rights management structure. We have previously suggested a suitable IP management model for SMSEs which takes cognisance of employees, volunteers, contractors and other collaborative relationships. Central to our recommendations was the valuable role played by licencing and confidentiality agreements as part of the IP management strategy, as well as the advantages of registering trademarks to protect an organisation's goodwill and branding.[134] However, whether or not SMSEs

---

[134] See Cantatore and Crawford-Spencer, above n 19, 340.

choose to implement these strategies will depend on their attitudes and motivation in view of their social objectives.

Protection of IP rights is integral to good governance practice, but it cannot be assumed that management of IP should be the same for SMSEs as for their commercial for profit counterparts. The research that has been conducted to date provides useful information about what some SMSEs are doing with respect to their IP management. This book recognises the very different needs and attitudes in these organisations and so implies that different approaches are suitable for SMSEs arising both out of their philosophical orientation and mission as well as out of their practical structures and capabilities. The research study discussed in this book contributes to an understanding of what is desired by SMSEs in respect of their IP rights, and the aims that SMSEs wish to achieve. The study, our resulting findings, and this book as a whole support the design of a more comprehensive legal support framework that genuinely reflects the interests and needs of civil society, consistent with their philosophies and modes of function, as well as with the practicalities of such practices in a local and global context.

Following on this framework the next two chapters deal with special topics related to IP and SMSE management. Chapter 6 explains with the nature of IP as collateral in security transactions, the significance of the *Personal Property Securities Act 2009* (Cth) (PPSA), approaches to maximising IP protection and challenges for organisations manner in their management of intellectual property under the PPSA, while Chapter 7 looks at structuring SEs according to models of franchising and examines the nature of IP protection and management as it varies under emerging models of social franchising.

CHAPTER SIX

IP AS COLLATERAL IN SECURITY TRANSACTIONS

Introduction: IP as Collateral

The significance of IP as intellectual assets of an organisation becomes apparent when it is valued in economic terms. This holds true not only for large organisations but also for SMEs and SMSEs viewing their IP rights as personal property assets which may be used as security in financial transactions, or licensing agreements. In respect of security arrangements caught by the provisions of security legislation, organisations—including SMEs and SMSEs—need to be vigilant in protecting their IP rights.

IP rights have become a sought after form of security for financing in recent years,[1] which raises various issues in relation to how IP is treated when viewed as a security interest. In the case of social enterprises and non-profits, security legislation also becomes relevant in licensing arrangements with partners or franchisees, e.g. where an enterprise (such as in the *Freecycle* example described in Chapter 2) enters into a licencing arrangement of its trademarks or other branding materials (including patented software and copyright materials) with other organisations. In these instances, organisations may need to register a security interest over their own IP assets in order to protect their interests.

---

[1] Brian Jacobs, 'Using Intellectual Property to Secure Financing after the Worst Financial Crisis Since the Great Depression' (2011) 15 *Intellectual Property Law Review* 450.

Thus, the importance of IP being used as collateral in a commercial transaction applies not only to commercial enterprises, but also to social enterprises. It may well be the means by which they are able to secure funding or attract investors or partners, and as such, becomes a valuable commodity. In order for organisations to have a better understanding of the regulation of IP as security interests in Australia, it is necessary to provide a brief overview of the applicable legislation.

In Australia the entry into force of the PPSA in 2012 made significant inroads into traditional norms of dealing with IP ownership and rights. Modelled on the Canadian and New Zealand personal property securities legislation,[2] the PPSA requires that security interests in personal property be registered on a national register (the Personal Property Securities Register, or PPSR), instead of the previous state-based Office of Fair Trading registers,[3] the ASIC companies' register[4] and the various IP registers.[5] In addition, certain transactions that previously provided security for an owner, such as retention of title arrangements, with no need for registration, now require registration on the PPSR to afford the seller the same level of protection. These requirements have caused the PPSA to impact significantly on a range of commercial transactions dealing with personal property, including the interests of lessors and lessees, consignors and consignees, sellers and buyers, licensors and licensees, and lenders and borrowers. It has also had a marked effect on the treatment of IP interests such as licences, which commonly occur in copyright and other licensing agreements.[6]

Under the PPSA a transaction that 'in substance secures payment or performance of an obligation' in respect of personal property, including IP rights such as copyright, patents, trademarks and designs, may give rise to a 'security interest',[7] which has been a rather novel concept in Australian

---

[2]More specifically the Saskatchewan *Personal Property Security Act, RSS 1993, c P-6.2* and New Zealand *Personal Property Securities Act* 1999, (NZ).
[3]Established under the various state-based *Fair Trading Acts*.
[4]Established under the *Australian Securities and Investment Commission Act* 2001 (Cth).
[5]Such as the *Register of Patents, Register of Designs, Register of Trade Marks* and *Register of Plant Breeder's Rights*.
[6]Cantatore, above n 11, 141–154.
[7]*Personal Property Securities Act 2009* (Cth) s 12(1).

law.[8] The 'in substance' test means that the form of transaction is immaterial, as is the identity of the owner of the property.[9] In the context of IP the definition thus includes transactions whereby, for example, trademarked products are used as security in commercial transactions or copyright licences are partially assigned or used as security.[10] Once a transaction gives rise to an interest which meets the PPSA definition of 'security interest',[11] the transaction is regulated by the PPSA and registration on the PPSR is generally required[12] to preserve a party's priority interest in the property as against third parties, such as competing creditors or receivers.

These issues have become particularly relevant as the value of IP rights is increasingly recognised in commercial dealings. Businesses are more frequently using intangible property as collateral, and creditors are more readily accepting such assets as security in financial transactions.[13] In this way organisations have been increasing their ability to obtain financing by offering intangible property, e.g. copyright in a film or in musical works,[14] as collateral. The way the importance of tangible property such as real estate, machinery and inventory has diminished, and intangible property has gained greater significance,[15] has been described as a paradigm shift.[16] Moreover, the inclusion of IP rights is often incidental under transactions

---

[8] At the time of writing this article, only a small number of substantive cases have been dealt with under the Australian PPSA. See *Carson, in the matter of Hastie Group Limited* (No 3) [2012] FCA 719; *Maiden Civil (P&E) Pty Ltd (in Receivership) v Queensland Excavation Services Pty Ltd* [2013] NSWSC 852; *NCO Finance Australia Pty Ltd v Australian Pacific Airports (Melbourne) Pty Ltd* [2013] FCCA 2274; *Albarran v Queensland Excavation Services Pty Ltd* [2013] NSWSC 852; *Auto Moto Corporation Pty Ltd v SMP Solutions Pty Ltd* [2013] NSWSC 1403; *Cirillo v Registrar Of Personal Property Securities* [2013] AATA 733; *Central Cleaning Supplies (Aust) Pty Ltd v Elkerton* [2014] VSC 61; *Pozzebon (Trustee) v Australian Gaming and Entertainment Ltd, in the matter of Australian Gaming and Entertainment Ltd (in liq)* [2014] FCA 1034. This has resulted in reliance on New Zealand and Canadian case law to interpret this generic concept that has been introduced into Australian law.

[9] *Personal Property Securities Act 2009* (Cth) s 12(1).

[10] *Personal Property Securities Act 2009* (Cth) s 12(1) and s 12(2)(j). Note: The assignment of a copyright licence will only create a security interest if, in substance, the assignment secures payment or performance of an obligation.

[11] *Personal Property Securities Act 2009* (Cth) s 12(1).

[12] *Personal Property Securities Act 2009* (Cth) s 21(2)(a). Perfection can also occur if the secured party has possession of the collateral [*Personal Property Securities Act 2009* (Cth) s 21(2)(b)], but this is unusual in the case of most commercial transactions, other than pledges, where possession will provide perfection. Certain interests are excluded from the PPSA under section 8 of the PPSA, such as common law liens, which need not be registered, and under s 12(5).

[13] Tosato, above n 12, 93.

[14] Lam, above n 13.

[15] Tosato, above n 12, 93.

[16] Smith and Parr, above n 15, 1.

where security is taken over all the assets of a company,[17] in what was previously a 'floating charge'. How these IP rights are dealt with under security transactions in Australia has been affected substantially by the introduction of the PPSA, and some of the challenges need to be recognised and addressed in the context of this book.

Below this section briefly considers how IP is treated under the PPSA, and how owners (e.g. businesses and social enterprises) and disseminators of IP may deal with some of the challenges presented by the inclusion of IP rights under the law, and contains recommendations for protective measures in dealing with problematic issues.

IP and the PPSA

The PPSA regulates security transactions involving all property, other than land and certain statutory exclusions.[18] Thus dealings in intangible property, including IP, may also be regulated by the PPSA.[19] IP under the PPSA includes registered rights under the *Designs Act 2003* (Cth), *Patents Act 1990* (Cth), TMA and unregistered rights under the *Plant Breeder's Rights Act 1994* (Cth), *Circuit Layouts Act 1989* (Cth) and the CA.[20] Trade secrets, internet domain names and unregistered trademarks are not included under this definition, but may still be 'intangible property' under the PPSA.[21] In commercial transactions the PPSA inclusion will affect owners of, or interested parties in registered rights in designs, patents and trademarks, interest holders in copyright in literary, dramatic, musical or artistic works,[22] and persons with the right to do an act under the *Circuit Layouts Act*[23] during

---

[17] Tosato, above n 12.

[18] *Personal Property Securities Act 2009* (Cth) s 10 definition of 'personal property'. The definition is a negative one; it refers to 'personal property' as 'Property (including a licence) other than (a) land; or (b) a right, entitlement or authority' that is granted by statute and declared 'not to be personal property for the purposes of the Act'.

[19] *Personal Property Securities Act 2009* (Cth) s 10 definition of 'intangible property'.

[20] *Personal Property Securities Act 2009* (Cth) s 10(a)—(g) definition of 'intellectual property'.

[21] Anthony Duggan and David Brown, *Australian Personal Property Securities Law* (Butterworths, 1st ed, 2012) 33.

[22] As defined in the *Copyright Act* 1968 s 189.

[23] *Circuit Layouts Act* 1989, s 17.

the protection period of the layout, or under the *Plant Breeder's Rights Act*[24] in relation to 'propagating material of a plant variety.'[25]

More specifically, under the PPSA '*intellectual property*' is defined as:[26]

> ... any of the following rights (including the right to be a party to proceedings in relation to such a right):
>
> (a) the right to do any of the things mentioned in paragraphs 10(1)(a) to (f) of the Designs Act 2003 in relation to a design that is registered under that Act;
> (b) the right to exploit or work an invention, or to authorise another person to exploit or work an invention, for which a patent is in effect under the Patents Act 1990;
> (c) the rights held by a person who is the registered owner of a trademark that is registered under the Trademarks Act 1995;
> (d) the right to do, or to license another person to do, an act referred to in section 11 of the *Plant Breeder's Rights Act* 1994 in relation to propagating material of a plant variety;
> (e) the right to do an act referred to in section 17 of the *Circuit Layouts Act* 1989 in relation to an eligible layout during the protection period of the layout;
> (f) the right under the Copyright Act 1968 to do an act comprised in the copyright in a literary, dramatic, musical or artistic work or a published edition of such a work, or in a sound recording, cinematograph film, television broadcast or sound broadcast;
> (g) a right under or for the purposes of a law of a foreign country that corresponds to a right mentioned in any of paragraphs (a) to (f).

Thus, given that IP is personal property under the PPSA,[27] the PPSA deals with security interests in these IP rights in the same way as with any other security interest in tangible property,[28] as enunciated in *Viacom*

---

[24] *Plant Breeder's Rights Act* 1994, s 11.
[25] As per the definition under the *Personal Property Securities Act* 2009 (Cth), s 10(d) definition of IP.
[26] *Personal Property Securities Act* 2009 (Cth), s 10.
[27] *Personal Property Securities Act 2009* (Cth) s 10 definition of 'personal property'.
[28] This is subject to specific provisions relating to intangible property in some instances, e.g. pursuant to the s 62 priority requirements. There are also specific registration requirements for IP rights described by serial number pursuant to s 153(1) read with *Personal Property Securities Regulations* sch 1, pt 2, cl 2.2.

Global v Scene One Entertainment (in Receivership),[29] and more fully discussed below.

IP Licences

Significantly, a transferable licence to exercise rights comprising IP is specifically included under the definition of *'licence'* under the PPSA,[30] even if its transferability is limited[31] or the licence is non-exclusive. An issue may sometimes arise as to the nature of the transaction and whether or not it can be described as a licence, or more accurately as an assignment. As we will see below this characterisation could materially impact on the status of the transaction under the PPSA, and the legal interests of the contracting parties. For businesses and social enterprises this could mean the difference between retaining or losing control of their IP.

An issue which may be potentially perplexing for interest holders and practitioners is the exclusion of a licence as a 'security interest' under the Act, which states: 'A ***security interest*** does not include: (a) a licence'.[32] In the context of IP interests, the exclusion of a licence from this definition means that an IP licence itself is not per se a security interest under the PPSA—rather, the transferrable IP licence is personal property (as explained above), which may be an asset or collateral[33] used for the purpose of creating a security interest.[34] Thus, a security interest can be registered over such licences on the PPSR, a practice which is becoming increasingly important, especially in the various technology and creative industries where licensing agreements are operative and typically used by licensees as collateral to secure finance.[35]

With respect to licensing agreements, the nature and terms of the agreement will usually determine whether a proprietary right is being conferred

---

[29] *Viacom Global v Scene One Entertainment (in Receivership)* CA 600/09 [2009] NZCA 457.

[30] '(Whether or not the right, entitlement, authority or licence is exclusive, and whether or not a transfer is restricted or requires consent),': *Personal Property Securities Act 2009* (Cth) s 10 definition of 'licence'.

[31] Jason Harris and Nicholas Mirzai, *Annotated Personal Property Securities Act 2009* (Cth) (Wolters, 1st ed, 2012) 61.

[32] *Personal Property Securities Act 2009* (Cth) s 12(5)(a).

[33] Personal property to which a security interest is attached or which is described in a registration on the PPSR. See definition of 'collateral': *Personal Property Securities Act 2009* (Cth) s 10.

[34] Harris and Mirzai, above n 397, 61.

[35] Tosato, above n 12, 94; Australian Copyright Council, *Personal Properties Securities Act (PPS Act) and copyright*, <http://www.copyright.org.au/find-an-answer/>.

or merely a contractual one (which will then fall outside the scope of the PPSA).[36] The difficulties sometimes associated with determining the status of such transactions in relation to assignment of copyright in particular, as well as accurate description of the collateral, will be discussed below.

IP Specific Provisions

In addition to the application of the general provisions of the PPSA, IP is specifically dealt with in Part 3.5.[37] This part of the Act deals with situations:

- where 'the exercise of rights by a secured party in relation to goods necessarily involves the exercise of intellectual property rights covered by the security interest';[38] or
- where there is 'a transfer of intellectual property that is the subject of a licence (or sub-licence).'[39]

In the case of scenario (a), the PPSA provides that it will apply to the IP rights in the same way as it applies to the relevant goods,[40] e.g. patented machinery, patented pharmaceuticals, computer hardware with embedded software or branded clothing. Thus in a case where a patent is necessary to operate a piece of machinery the secured party's interest will include the patent rights required to make the machinery operational.[41] Similarly, if a computer is subject to a security interest it will include the patent, trademark and other embedded IP that is essential to its operation. The application of this provision can be problematic where different parties

---

[36] See Duggan and Brown, above n 387, 33; Anthony Duggan, 'In the wake of the Bingo Queen: Are licences property?' (2009) 47 *Canadian Business Law Journal* 225.
[37] *Personal Property Securities Act* 2009 (Cth) ss 104–106.
[38] *Personal Property Securities Act* 2009 (Cth) ss 104–105.
[39] *Personal Property Securities Act* 2009 (Cth) s 104, s 106.
[40] *Personal Property Securities Act* 2009 (Cth) ss 104–105.
[41] The *Explanatory Memorandum* to the *Personal Property Securities Act* 2009 (Cth), provides the following example: 'Grantor A owns a factory that produces car parts using robots whose only function is to manufacture those particular car parts. The process used to manufacture the car parts was patented by Grantor A. Grantor A obtains a loan from Bank A and receives value for a security interest. The security agreement refers to "the robots". Bank A registers the security interest. Grantor A defaults under the security agreement. Bank A enforces the security agreement. The security agreement only refers to a security interest over the robots, but the court determines that the security interest extends to the patent to the extent required to permit the robots to operate. The exercise of Bank A's rights to the robots under the security agreement necessarily involves the use of the patent rights exploited in the robots. Bank A's security interest will therefore be enforceable against both the robots and the patent.'

have security interests in the goods and the IP rights respectively, an issue that will be further discussed later in this section.

In scenario (b), the Act provides that a security agreement will bind successors in title to the licensor or sub-licensor to the same extent that they were bound.[42] This means that, if the original licensor had consented or was a party to a security agreement entered into by the licensee, the transferee would be bound to this agreement in the same way as the original licensor (transferor).[43] For example, if A acquires a licence to use a patent from B (the licensor), and later gives Bank C a security interest over all its present-and-after-acquired property with B's consent, and B (licensor and owner of the patent) assigns the patent to a transferee D, but the licence stays with the original licensee (A), then the Bank C's security agreement will bind all successors in title (or transferees) to the original owner of the IP (licensor), to the extent that the security agreement bound the original owner. Accordingly, this will only be the case if the owner consented to the Bank's security interest or was a party to the security agreement.[44] This provision accords with the relevant provision of the *Copyright Act* in relation to transfer of copyright interests by the owner.[45]

However, while the *Copyright Act* provision means that a transferee (recipient) of a copyright interest needs to be vigilant about possible liabilities of the transferor under existing licensing agreements with licensees, the PPSA takes the transferee's prospective liability one step further, by binding them under the licensee's obligations to a secured party, if the original copyright owner consented or was a party to that transaction. A diagrammatic depiction of this scenario would look as set out in Figures 3 and 4 below, illustrating the difference in the transferee's liability where the PPSA applies.

For example, if there is an existing software licensing agreement with the licensee, it means that the transferee could be bound by the original licensor's agreement with the licensee, in respect of issues such as updating and maintaining the licensed software. However, the PPSA amplifies the transferee's deferral of interest to the registrant of a personal property security signifi-

---

[42] *Personal Property Securities Act* 2009 (Cth) s 104, s 106.
[43] *Personal Property Securities Act* 2009 (Cth) s 106(1); Duggan and Brown, above n 387, 39.
[44] Duggan and Brown, above n 387, 39.
[45] *Copyright Act 1968* (Cth) s 196(4): A licence granted in respect of a copyright by the owner of the copyright binds every successor in title to the interest in the copyright of the grantor of the licence to the same extent as the licence was binding on the grantor.

cantly where the licensee has entered into secured transactions with other parties with the consent of the transferor as illustrated in Figure 4 below.

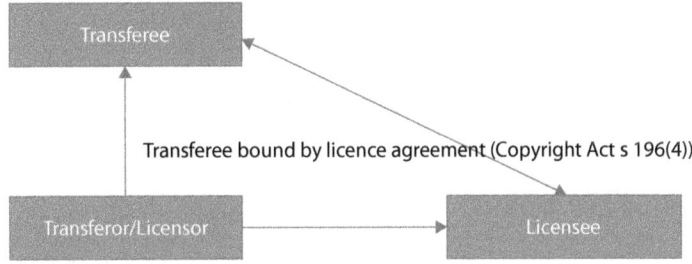

Figure 3 Transferee Liability Under the *Copyright Act*.

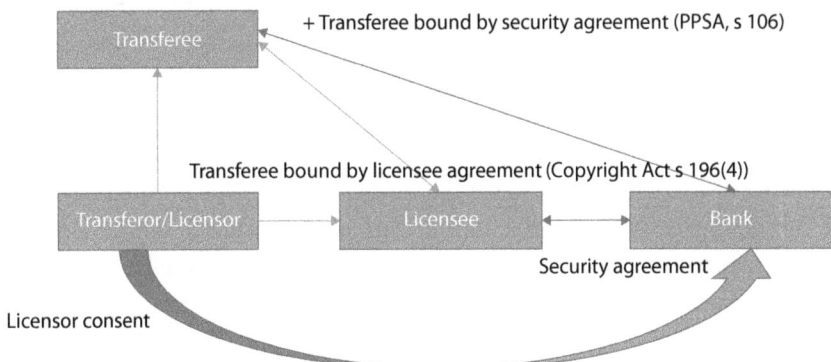

Figure 4 Transferee Liability Under the PPSA.

In this example, if the licensee has obtained a loan from the bank under a security agreement[46] which encumbers all its assets, with the consent (express or implied) of the licensor, the transferee will be bound to the same extent as the original licensor. This is a potentially dangerous situation for a transferee and would require them to firstly, ascertain the identity of all licensees of the copyright material; secondly, to conduct searches on the PPSR to ascertain the existence of any security interests over the licensee's assets (including its rights under the licensing agreement); and thirdly, to ascertain whether the original licensor would be bound under

---

[46]Usually this would have been in the form of a charge, which gives rise to a security interest under the PPSA (s 12(2)(a) & (b). The charge will be a security agreement under the PPSA (s 20(2)).

that agreement, should the bank exercise any rights they hold over the licence. Thus, if the licensee defaults on its bank loan—unless specific provision is made in the licence for its termination in the event of the licensee defaulting on any future loans secured by the licence (which would be unlikely)—the bank could potentially sell or transfer the licensing rights without the express consent of the transferor, and retain the proceeds, as explained below.

Maximising IP Protection

Priorities

How do IP owners then ensure that their IP rights do not become subject to security interests without their express consent in light of the PPSA requirements, and why is it important to do so? Priority disputes may arise between owners of IP, secured parties, competing creditors, receivers of insolvent estates and so on, and in such instances, the issue of perfection under the PPSA may be a determining factor.[47] We have noted that the PPSA definition of a security interest includes transactions whereby, for example, patented materials are used as security in commercial transactions or copyright licences are partially assigned or used as security.[48] Where an IP licence is involved, the situation is complicated by the fact that a licence is excluded as a 'security interest', which may create uncertainty for a party unfamiliar with the workings of the PPSA who wishes to use an IP licence as collateral in a loan transaction. In practice, this means that the parties may need to enter into a security agreement in respect of the licence, in addition to the licensing agreement, as the licence itself is not registrable on the PPSR as a security agreement.[49]

The PPSA prescribes a 'perfecting process' whereby a secured party can achieve the maximum amount of protection in collateral,[50] which requires that the security interest must firstly 'attach' to the collateral[51] in order to have an enforceable right against the grantor. Attachment occurs[52] when

---

[47] *Personal Property Securities Act 2009* (Cth), s 55.
[48] *Personal Property Securities Act 2009* (Cth) s 12(1).
[49] *Personal Property Securities Act 2009* (Cth) s 12(5).
[50] Note ss 19–21 as well as the possibility of achieving 'super-priority' under s 14, in the case of a purchase money security interest (PMSI).
[51] *Personal Property Securities Act 2009* (Cth) s 19(1).
[52] Unless the parties agree otherwise—*Personal Property Securities Act 2009* (Cth) s 19(3).

the grantor has rights in collateral[53] or power to transfer rights in collateral, and either: value is given for the security interest,[54] or the grantor does an act by which a security interest arises.[55] In the case of granting a security interest in IP rights, this requirement will usually be achieved when the grantor (the IP owner) enters into the security agreement.[56]

For the security interest to be enforceable against third parties, a written security agreement which describes the collateral,[57] signed or accepted by the grantor,[58] is a specific requirement under the PPSA, unless the secured party is in possession of the collateral.[59] Because of the intangible nature of IP (and the scope for dispute about actual and constructive possession of the IP), a written security agreement is essential to ensure protection of an interest in IP. However, as will be discussed below, the accurate description of IP rights as collateral can be problematic and give rise to uncertainty where no serial number exists, as is the case with a copyright interest. It may also be difficult to accurately describe the 'work' or 'subject matter other than work' subject to copyright in sufficient detail on the PPSR.

Significantly, a security interest in the *proceeds* derived from the collateral is enforceable against third parties even if 'proceeds' are not specifically included in the security agreement.[60] This means that, for example, periodic payments made in respect of an IP licence to a licensor, which has been used as collateral, will also be covered and may be recoverable by a secured party under the security agreement. However, *priority* in proceeds will be subject to perfection and proper description of the IP collateral in the PPSR registration, as will be seen below.[61]

---

[53] Any proprietary interest is sufficient, even voidable title—see *iTrade Finance Inc v Bank of Montreal* [2011] 2SCR 360.

[54] 'This is in effect consideration—a promise of finance is sufficient and it can be provided at a later date—see *Agricultural Credit Corp of Saskatchewan v Pettyjohn* (1991) 1 PPSAC (2d) 273.

[55] E.g. obtaining rights to the property (collateral), signing the security agreement or taking possession of the property; *Personal Property Securities Act 2009* (Cth) s 19(2).

[56] See Harris and Mirzai, above n 397, 103.

[57] See *Re Apollo Fitness Academy Inc* (1984) 3 PPSAC 280. Detail of description is a question of commercial reality—see ibid 112; E.g. 'shelving' was sufficient in *GE Capital Canada Acquisitions Inc v Dix Performance* [1995] 2 WWR 738.

[58] *Personal Property Securities Act 2009* (Cth) s 20(1)(b)(iii).

[59] *Personal Property Securities Act 2009* (Cth) s 20(1)(b)(i).

[60] *Personal Property Securities Act 2009* (Cth) s 20(6), subject to the provisions of s 32.

[61] *Personal Property Securities Act 2009* (Cth) s 153 provides for requirements of the 'financing statement' which is lodged on registration of the security interest.

It has been firmly established that, in a dispute with other parties, 'perfection' is the most important step of the process to determine priority[62] and the date of perfection will usually determine the priority of the secured party vis-à-vis other claimants,[63] rather than the date of attachment. In the case of IP rights, perfection is achieved, either by force of the PPSA through 'temporary perfection';[64] or if the security interest is (a) attached to the collateral; (b) enforceable against third parties;[65] and (c) an effective registration is in place.[66] Temporary perfection may occur upon the transfer of collateral to another secured party, where a 'grace period' applies to the new secured party to enable perfection in the ordinary way.[67] Notably, perfection can occur prior to attachment,[68] i.e. a secured party can register before attachment has been completed.[69] Indeed, it could be argued that it would be courting disaster to provide funds to a prospective borrower unless an effective registration is in place.[70]

Registration Requirements

Registration of a security interest is effected on the PPSR by way of a Financing Statement,[71] which must include the information required

---

[62] *Bank of Montreal v Innovation Credit Union* [2010] 3 SCR 3; *Graham v Portacom NZ Ltd* [2004] 2 NZLR 528; see also the landmark case of *Waller v NZ Bloodstock Ltd* [2006] 3 NZLR 629. These decisions were followed in the Australian case of *Maiden Civil (P&E) Pty Ltd (in Receivership) v Queensland Excavation Services Pty Ltd* [2013] NSWSC 852 and *NCO Finance Australia Pty Ltd v Australian Pacific Airports (Melbourne) Pty Ltd* [2013] FCCA 2274.
[63] *Graham v Portacom NZ Ltd* [2004] 2 NZLR 528.
[64] *Personal Property Securities Act 2009* (Cth) s 21(1)(a).
[65] Through possession or entering into a written security agreement as provided for in s 20(1)(b)(iii) of the *Personal Property Securities Act 2009* (Cth).
[66] *Personal Property Securities Act 2009* (Cth) s 21(2)(a); or if the secured party has possession of the collateral (s 21(2)(b), which is unlikely in the case of IP).
[67] Harris and Mirzai, above n 397, 132.
[68] *Personal Property Securities Act 2009* (Cth) s 21(3).
[69] See also *674921 BC Ltd v Advanced WingTechnologies Corp* (2006) 9 PPSAC 43. However, in some cases registration may be required prior to attachment (see s 62), where 'super priority' in an IP security interest is being asserted.
[70] Under *Personal Property Securities Act* 2009 (Cth), s 62. Especially if "super priority" is being claimed in respect of a "purchase money security interest". The issue of super priority in "purchase money security interests" (PMSI) falls outside the scope of this article; however, it is possible to create a PMSI in an IP asset where the secured party is the seller/lessor of the IP or is financing the purchase or lease of the IP asset—see *Personal Property Securities Act 2009* (Cth) s 14(1).
[71] *Personal Property Securities Act 2009* (Cth) s 150.

by s 153, such as the parties' particulars,[72] a description of the collateral, the registration end time and whether a purchase money security interest (PMSI) is being claimed.[73] The description requirements here[74] are different from and more stringent than the description required in the security agreement,[75] as it provides for description as either consumer or commercial property;[76] the class of collateral;[77] and a provision that 'collateral may or must be described by serial number, if allowed or required by the regulations.'[78]

These provisions require strict adherence, as a mistake on the financing statement may render the registration ineffective, if it is regarded as a seriously misleading defect.[79] Examples of ineffective registrations would be where the grantor is misdescribed[80] or where a required serial number is omitted.[81] In relation to describing IP collateral there are specific requirements set out in the *Personal Property Securities Regulations* (PPS Regs).[82] For example, the regulations distinguish between consumer and commercial property, which have different registration requirements.

In the context of this discussion, it is more likely that the subject collateral will be commercial property,[83] rather than consumer property, as the IP will usually be held by an organisation rather than an individual; or if held by an individual, be used in the course or furtherance of carrying on a business or enterprise. The PPS Regs provide that 'commercial property'— which is intangible property and one of the following: a design, patent, plant breeder's right, trademark; or a licence in respect of any of these types of property—may be described by serial number.[84] Thus it is the secured

---

[72]Except in the case of consumer property which must be described by serial number, where the grantor's particulars are omitted.
[73]*Personal Property Securities Act 2009* (Cth) s 153.
[74]*Personal Property Securities Act 2009* (Cth) s 153 (Item 4).
[75]*Personal Property Securities Act 2009* (Cth) s 20(1)(b)(iii).
[76]*Personal Property Securities Act 2009* (Cth) s 153 (Item 4(a)).
[77]*Personal Property Securities Act 2009* (Cth) s 153 (Item 4(c)).
[78]*Personal Property Securities Act 2009* (Cth) s 153 (Item 4(b)).
[79]*Personal Property Securities Act 2009* (Cth) s 164(1)(a); or if it is a defect mention in s 165.
[80]E.g. recording the grantor's name as 'Grandstrand' instead of 'Granstrand' (*KJM Leasing Ltd v Granstrand Brothers Inc* (1994) 7 PPSAC (2nd) 44; 158 AR 78).
[81]Pursuant to *Personal Property Securities Act 2009* (Cth) s 165(a); failing to include a serial number where required to do so (*Kelln (Trustee of) v Strasbourg Credit Union Ltd* (1992) 3 PPSAC (2d) 44; 89 DLR (4th) 427).
[82]*Personal Property Securities Regulations* 2009 sch 1, pt 2, cl 2.2.
[83]*Personal Property Securities Act 2009* (Cth) s 10: "**Commercial property** means personal property other than consumer property".
[84]*Personal Property Securities Regulations 2009* (Cth) sch 1, pt 2, cl 2.2(1)(c).

party's choice whether or not to include a serial number in the registration. The voluntary nature of this provision means that a potential credit provider may have to conduct a number of searches on the PPSR to ascertain whether the IP rights on offer are, in fact, encumbered.

Significantly, copyright is omitted from these serial number provisions, as copyright is not registrable in Australia[85] and, consequently, does not have a serial number to be registered. This means that a full description of the copyright interest (or the copyright licence) that is being provided as collateral needs to be made for identification purposes. It also complicates any searches by a prospective credit provider, who will have to carry out careful (and perhaps numerous) searches on the PPSR.[86] This anomaly illustrates why organisations using IP as collateral in their dealings need at least a working knowledge of the PPSA, or alternatively, need to obtain legal advice in these matters.

Australian court decisions under the PPSA have emphasised the need for effective description of the collateral on the PPSR.[87] For example, in the *Hastie* case administrators appointed to a number of companies that comprised the Hastie Group applied to the Court for permission to dispose of plant and equipment—with an estimated value of $6.4 million—held by various companies in the group. One of the main problems was that the administrators had difficulty identifying property that was subject to the security interests of third parties, due to incomplete or general descriptions on the PPSR. Yates J granted the order allowing for the sale of the property, illustrating the importance of providing an accurate description for each item of secured property and as much particularity as possible.[88] Although this case dealt with tangible property, it also serves to caution parties with security interests in intangible personal property to ensure that their registration is effective, not only from a compliance perspective, but also on a practical level should they need to identify the secured property. This point is discussed in more depth below.

---

[85] William Van Caenegem, *Intellectual Property in Australia* (Wolters, 1st ed, 2010) 31–32.
[86] Tim Golder, Tom Reid and Thomas Middleton, 'The Personal Property Securities Act and IP: A simpler way?' (2012) 7 *Journal of Intellectual Property Law & Practice* 536.
[87] *Carson, in the matter of Hastie Group Limited (No 3)* [2012] FCA 719 (5 July 2012).
[88] *Carson, in the matter of Hastie Group Limited (No 3)* [2012] FCA 719 (5 July 2012) at 727.

Challenges for Organisations in Dealing with IP Under the PPSA

SMEs and SMSEs

It is worth noting that SMEs—and SMSEs especially—will face the same challenges discussed in Chapters 3 and 4 in relation to protection of their IP rights under securities legislation. The PPSA makes no distinction between commercial and social enterprises, or between small business and large corporations. There is no 'sliding scale' and all organisations and individuals, irrespective of size, need to observe the provisions of securities legislation in their dealings with personal property. This means that the issues discussed in earlier chapters are once again relevant here: SMEs and SMSEs are likely to have fewer financial resources, less knowledge or access to knowledge about the PPSA, lower levels of training in these aspects of the law, and—especially in the case of social enterprises—less motivation to devote resources to these issues. These factors could affect their ability and inclination to take protective measures in respect of the IP rights.

Multiple IP Registers

The first challenge lies in the fractured treatment of IP under Australian law, which is reflected in both the legislation and registration requirements. Pre-PPSA security over IP rights was dealt with in a number of different Acts, namely: the *Circuit Layouts Act* 1989, *Plant Breeder's Rights Act* 1994, *Patents Act* 1990, *Designs Act* 2003, the CA and the TMA. The Register of Patents, Register of Designs, Register of Trademarks and Register of Plant Breeder's Rights (known collectively as the IP Registers), continue to be administered by IP Australia. The various IP Acts have been amended to avoid overlap with the PPSA, and although IP ownership is still recorded on these registers (e.g. the relevant details of a registered trademark are recorded on the Register of Trademarks),[89] registration of security interests in IP rights are now regulated by the PPSA and require registration on the PPSR to protect the holder's interests.[90] Significantly, these registrations were voluntary before the application of the PPSA and in many instances a

---

[89] *Trade Marks Act* 1995 (Cth), s 69; *Trade Marks Regulations* 1995 (Cth), reg 7.2.
[90] See general discussion of *Personal Property Securities Act* 2009 (Cth) in Parts I and II above.

security interest over a trademark would remain unregistered.[91] Whilst the PPSA provides greater certainty for persons searching for security interests, it also means that persons searching IP rights need to conduct separate searches on both the relevant IP register (to ascertain the particulars of the IP right) and the PPSR (to establish whether the IP right is subject to any security interests).

Unlike prior registered interests which appeared on the ASIC register, for example, registered IP security interests were not migrated to the PPSR. The rationale was the fact that registrations of security interests were not compulsory on the IP registers.[92] Thus, the onus was placed on all prior secured parties with a registered interest in IP rights to re-register their interests during the transitional period.[93] Any parties who failed to do so are now in the position of an unsecured party and would need to register in order to secure their interests.[94]

The effect of the concurrent application of the PPSA and IP legislation is that security interest disputes will be regulated by the PPSA, but other disputes (e.g. competing ownership claims or licence-holder/transferee disputes) continue to be regulated by the various IP Acts. Thus, for parties undertaking due diligence on IP, a search of both the PPSR and the relevant IP register would be appropriate.

Copyright

As noted above, copyright is not registrable in Australia[95] and as such, no registered copyright interests exist. It has been noted that, for registration purposes on the PPSR, copyright is treated in a different manner to other IP rights as it does not have a serial number to be recorded, unlike for example a patent, which 'may or must' be described by the

---

[91] Robert Burrell and Michael Handler, 'The PPSA and registered trademarks: when bureaucratic systems collide' (2011) 34 *UNSW Law Journal* 603.
[92] Duggan and Brown, above n 387, 339.
[93] This period ended on 31 January 2014, as noted above.
[94] However, any registrations effected after the end of the transitional period will only be effective from registration date, parties will lose the benefit of transitional provisions under s 320 of the Act, and other creditors whose registration preceded theirs may have priority over their interests.
[95] *Berne Convention for the Protection of Literary and Artistic Works*, art 5(2); Van Caenegem, above n 451, 31–32.

patent number mentioned in the Patents Register.[96] This may mean credit providers, funders, or potential partners could be carrying out numerous searches on the PPSR to establish whether a copyright interest is free from encumbrance, as—unlike other commercial IP interests—it is not readily searchable by serial number.[97] It also means the secured party will have to ensure that the copyright is fully described in the security agreement, and as accurately as possible on the financing statement, to adequately protect their interests.

Knopf points out other considerations when taking security over copyright:[98]

> Even a copyright, which is ironically (given its artistic association) normally the most readily transferable and "liquid" of intellectual properties can lose its value if, for example, the original author does not wish to participate in adaptations, derivative works, or sequels. Moreover, the original author will normally have moral rights which simply cannot be assigned and can only be waived. Moral rights can, and indeed should, be scary stuff to a banker unless the author has irrevocably and completely waived her entitlement. In a film or a computer program, there can be many dozens or hundreds or more of "authors." There may also be reversion rights in the case of Canada or termination of transfer rights in the case of the U.S.A. that may severely compromise the value of an older copyright.

He further says:[99]

> Copyright registration in the U.S.A. is backed up by deposit of a work, but in the case of computer software it is unlikely to contain any useful quantity of actual source code. In Canada, the work cannot be deposited at all. None of the systems in Canada is reliable in terms of conclusively showing current ownership. There is no on-line copyright system in Canada in any event.

---

[96] *Personal Property Securities Regulations 2009* (Cth) sch 1, pt 2, cl 2.2(2).
[97] Golder, Reid and Middleton, above n 452.
[98] Howard Knopf, (2002), 'Security interests in intellectual property: An international comparative approach' (2002) 7 *International Intellectual Property Law & Policy* 90–91.
[99] Ibid.

Similar considerations apply to Australian copyright, as Van Caenegem points out:[100]

> 'No formal requirements are attached to copyright protection under the Copyright Act ... No copyright symbol needs to be displayed on a work or subject matter as a condition of protection, and no official registration of copyright works is either possible or required.'

Thus, Australian parties have to contend with similar limitations as Canadians in their ability to secure copyright interests in copyright works. They need to follow a diligent approach by being aware of the pitfalls and providing detailed copyright descriptions.[101]

Licensing Copyright: Licence or Assignment?

In the case of licencing agreements, it can sometimes be difficult to determine whether a proprietary right is being conferred or merely a contractual one (which will then fall outside the scope of the PPSA).[102] Examples of an 'Licencing agreement: Licence of IP' and an 'Assignment of IP Agreement' have been included in this book as Appendices A and B respectively, which illustrate the difference in terms and conditions included in these types of agreements. Distinguishing between licencing and assignment of IP interests is a consideration for SMEs and SMSEs entering into licencing arrangements with other parties. It may be especially relevant where, for example a bank (the secured party) agrees to take security over a copyright licence held by a licensee in return for a bank loan. Duggan points out that that a fishing licence, for example, has been held to be property (and thus subject to the PPSA) by the Canadian Supreme Court in *Saulnier v Royal Bank of Canada*.[103] It is clear from the earlier discussion that a licence is indeed personal property under the PPSA, and a transferable

---

[100] Van Caenegem, above n 451, 31–32.
[101] As illustrated by the *Hastie* case: *Carson, in the matter of Hastie Group Limited (No 3)* [2012] FCA 719 (5 July 2012).
[102] See Duggan and Brown, above n 387, 33; and Duggan, above n 402.
[103] *Saulnier v. Royal Bank of Canada*' (2008), 298 D.L.R. (4th) 193 (S.C.C.).

licence to exercise rights comprising IP is specifically included under the definition of *licence* under the PPSA.[104]

Whether or not a proprietary right in a copyright licence has been transferred will depend on the terms of the contract between the IP rights owner and the transferee/licensee, and especially whether or not reversionary rights are included in the contract. As registration on the PPSR does not require the filing of supporting documentation, the secured party will have to ensure that it obtains a copy of the contract to ascertain the true nature of the licence. It may also not be clear to the secured party whether any registered interests exist over the copyright licence being offered as security, because of the difficulties of searching for an accurate description of such a licence on the PPSR, as no registration number exists in the case of copyright. Clearly the value of a copyright licence which has been assigned to the licensee will be significantly more valuable than a licence granted with restrictions or reversion rights; and this status can only be determined by carefully studying the agreement between licensor and licensee. An absolute assignment will indicate the transfer of property rights; whereas a 'licence' may only signify a contractual right, which makes it difficult to secure licensing rights with any certainty. Where a copyright licensing agreement (or an assignment for that matter), is subject to reversionary rights of the licensor, there may be a registered interest in favour of the licensor on the PPSR which protects his or her rights, which could be difficult for a credit provider to find for the reasons explained above.[105] If the credit provider fails to find this registered interest during a search of the PPSR, and takes the copyright licence as security, it may suffer a significant loss in the event of a dispute vis-à-vis the licensor. Where this concerns large projects such as film productions which rely on copyright material, or valuable copyright interests in the music industry,[106] it may have dire repercussions for the investor. Whilst this specific scenario may

---

[104] "(Whether or not the right, entitlement, authority or licence is exclusive, and whether or not a transfer is restricted or requires consent)," *Personal Property Securities Act 2009* (Cth) s 10 definition of 'licence'.

[105] As the holder of the reversionary right, the licensor should register an interest over the licence on the PPSR pursuant to s 12.

[106] The value of copyright in songs can be considerable, for example, in 1984 Michael Jackson paid $47.5 million to purchase ATV Music Publishing, which owned the copyright of more than 200 songs written by John Lennon and Paul McCartney, viewed at <http://www.celebritynetworth.com/articles/entertainment-articles/how-michael-jackson-bought-the-beatles-catalogue-then-turned-it-into-a-billion-music-empire>.

not directly affect SMEs or SMSEs who are licensors, it could have a chilling effect on their ability to raise funds based on their IP assets, due to uncertainties in this area of the law.

Clearly if there has been an outright assignment to the assignee, property has been transferred and the secured party will be safe in dealing with the transferee; but as Harris and Mirzai point out the true nature of the transaction must always be considered:[107]

> An assignment is absolute in essence, that is, there remains behind no interest held by the assignor. Where ... an interest remains, the instrument is rarely an assignment at all, rather a revocable mandate or creation of a trust ... Where parties attempt to mask a security interest behind the veil of assignment, this will not prevent the PPSA from applying pursuant to the "in substance" test (see s12(1)).

Thus, when dealing with rights held under a copyright licence being offered as security, three issues bear consideration. First, is it a transferable licence? Second, has there been an absolute assignment, or a licensing agreement or assignment with residual rights held by the licensor. Third, if the latter applies, are there any security interests registered against the licence or the underlying copyright which would have priority over any subsequent interest holders? As illustrated above, this can be difficult to determine with certainty.

From a different perspective, the transferee of an IP asset (e.g. where the licensor sells its business to another party and includes the copyright in a sound recording as part of the assets)[108] should heed the provisions of s 106 mentioned above, which deals with the 'transfer of intellectual property that is the subject of a licence (or sub-licence).'[109] As we saw, if the transferor has granted a licence to a licensee who has encumbered the licence (e.g. a licence to reproduce the sound recording commercially), the Act provides that a security agreement will bind successors in title to the licensor (or sub-licensor) to the same extent that they were bound.[110] This requires considerable caution on the part of a transferee to avoid its property interest being deferred to a secured party of a licensee of the

---

[107] Harris and Mirzai, above n 397, 54.
[108] As illustrated by *Figure 2* above.
[109] *Personal Property Securities Act 2009* (Cth) s 104, s 106.
[110] *Personal Property Securities Act 2009* (Cth) s 104, s 106.

transferor (licensor), a difficult task, as it needs to ensure the licensor was not bound by any security agreement over the licence. It may be possible to deal with this dilemma by requesting a warranty from the transferor (licensor) that the transferor has not previously consented to security interests in the licence.[111]

IP Intrinsically Associated with Collateral

Another peculiarity of IP under the PPSA is how it deals with IP that is intrinsically part of the property involved,[112] e.g. patented machinery, patented pharmaceuticals, computer hardware with embedded software or branded clothing. This could affect the interests of both the owner of the IP as well as the secured party. Thus, we have noted that, in a case where a patent is necessary to operate a piece of machinery, the secured party's interest will include the patent rights required to make the machinery operational.[113] The application of this provision can be problematic where different parties have security interests in the goods and the IP rights respectively, in other words, in respect of the tangible property and intangible property involved.

In this respect, Mirzai and Harris express the view that: 'The Australian Courts have generally been reluctant to imply a licence to deal with the IP associated with tangible property, enforcing the view that such rights are separate and distinctive.'[114]

The PPSA deals with this situation by providing that, where the security agreement necessarily involves an exercise of the IP rights, the underlying

---

[111] Australian Copyright Council, *Personal Properties Securities Act (PPS Act) and Copyright*, 7 <http://www.copyright.org.au%2Fadmin%2Fcmsacc1%2F_images%2F51175436952f9a69b99b19.pdf&ei=OpqeU4XSBsvIkQXKuYGIAQ&usg=AFQjCNFtfD2vpQOaGMdmfU5KJjonKMOrfg&sig2=hyAewE-TPAb wOKB0nHx6iQ>.

[112] *Personal Property Securities Act 2009* (Cth) s 104, s 105.

[113] The *Explanatory Memorandum* to the *Personal Property Securities Act* 2009 (Cth), provides the following example: 'Grantor A owns a factory that produces car parts using robots whose only function is to manufacture those particular car parts. The process used to manufacture the car parts was patented by Grantor A. Grantor A obtains a loan from Bank A and receives value for a security interest. The security agreement refers to "the robots". Bank A registers the security interest. Grantor A defaults under the security agreement. Bank A enforces the security agreement. The security agreement only refers to a security interest over the robots, but the court determines that the security interest extends to the patent to the extent required to permit the robots to operate. The exercise of Bank A's rights to the robots under the security agreement necessarily involves the use of the patent rights exploited in the robots. Bank A's security interest will therefore be enforceable against both the robots and the patent.'

[114] Harris and Mirzai, above n 397, 322. See *R and A Bailey and Co v Boccaccio Pty Ltd*.

rights will attach to that collateral, unless the security agreement provides otherwise.[115] This reverses the common law position, under which the secured party need not include a specific reference to any IP rights in the security agreement. Accordingly, in these circumstances, the grantor now has the onus of expressly excluding IP from the agreement.[116] Thus, in order to avoid the implied inclusion of IP, from a grantor's perspective, security agreements should clearly state the extent to which the IP or IP licences form part of the collateral.

Conclusion

It has become evident that, when considering dealings with IP in commercial transaction—whether entered into by commercial or non-profit organisations—the PPSA plays a central role. Additionally, any licence granted in respect of that IP should be carefully scrutinised to ensure that it has not been encumbered under the PPSA. A prospective secured party will have to conduct detailed searches in respect of any IP collateral on offer, under its serial number as well as other possible descriptions, to ascertain whether any prior registered security interests exist against the collateral. When viewed from this perspective, it can be argued that dealing with IP rights (including licences) as collateral can be a perilous affair under the PPSA.

IP licences, in particular, raise a number of issues which a prospective secured party of a licensee (e.g. a credit provider of a licensee) should consider. First, is the licence transferable? If so, it will be regulated by the PPSA[117] and can be used as collateral in a transaction.[118] Second, have any security interests been registered over the licence by the licensor or any other secured parties, and have they described the IP (which is the subject of the licence) by a serial number?[119] If uncertainty exists as to the unencumbered nature of the licence, it would be advisable for a secured party to require a subordination agreement from the licensor or assignor, who may

---

[115] *Personal Property Securities Act 2009* (Cth) s 105.
[116] Harris and Mirzai, above n 397, 322.
[117] *Personal Property Securities Act 2009* (Cth) s 10 definition of "licence".
[118] This requires an understanding of the s 12(5) PPSA provision that the licence itself is not a security interest, but can be used as security in commercial dealings.
[119] As per *Personal Property Securities Regulations 2009* (Cth) sch 1, pt 2, cl 2.2(1)(c).

hold ownership or reversionary rights in the licence and whose security interest may be difficult to establish with certainty via a PPSR search. A similar approach should be followed in respect of any other parties holding security over the assets of the licensee, and especially secured parties with a registered security interest over all 'present and after-acquired assets' of the licensee, as this will include any IP rights.

For the acquirer or transferee of IP rights—perhaps as part of the acquisition of a business—it is vital to be aware of existing licensing agreements of the IP with other parties, and any potential liabilities that may arise in that regard. It has been noted above that there may be ongoing service liabilities such as the maintenance of licensed software under licensing agreements;[120] but under the PPSA further diligence is required.[121] If the original owner (licensor) would have been bound under an agreement with a secured party, for example a creditor of the licensee, that secured party could potentially exercise any rights they hold over the licence if the licensee defaults on its security agreement, rendering the transferee (new owner) of the IP subordinate to the rights of the licensee's secured credit provider under an existing agreement. This situation may be averted by—in addition to conducting diligent searches under IP serial numbers as well as against all known licensees—obtaining a warranty and indemnity from the IP owner/transferor to address the onerous s 106 provision,[122] and ensuring that the transferee does not take on more than he or she bargained for.

While it cannot be disputed that the PPSA has, in general, achieved its intended goal of facilitating 'the creation of personal property security interests to ensure efficient transactions and increased certainty in financing,'[123] the effect of the discretionary description requirements of commercial IP under the PPS Regs[124] is to cast some doubt over the 'certainty' of the PPSR. For this reason, and because of the other compelling considerations highlighted in this section, dealings by businesses and social enterprises in IP interests should be approached with caution under the PPSA. And where IP rights are transferred, the main danger for transferees of IP rights and prospective secured parties, is that the effect of the

---

[120] As explained by *Figure 1* above.
[121] As explained by *Figure 2* above.
[122] *Personal Property Securities Act 2009* (Cth) s 106. Pursuant to s 106, the Act provides that a security agreement will bind successors in title to the licensor or sub-licensor to the same extent that they were bound.
[123] Golder, Reid and Middleton, above n 452.
[124] *Personal Property Securities Regulations 2009* (Cth) sch 1, pt 2, cl 2.2(1)(c).

PPSA provisions on such dealings may not be readily apparent, and could well have dire consequences if overlooked. It is evident that organisations who deal with IP rights in commercial transactions without due regard for the impact of the PPSA, and without obtaining professional advise, do so at their own peril.

As noted, security legislation has implications for the IP rights of SMEs and SMSEs, especially in relation to licencing arrangements with franchisees, which require them to be vigilant about protecting their IP assets. As explained, in instances where they fail to register a security interest over their licences or other IP, they may lose in a priority contest against parties with registered interests against the grantor's (or licencee's) assets. SMEs and SMSEs are generally more vulnerable to financial uncertainty than their large counterparts, which renders it even more essential to obtain legal advice with regard to security interests, where their own (or their partner organisations') IP or licencing rights may be affected.

CHAPTER SEVEN

APPROACHES TO IP MANAGEMENT IN SOCIAL FRANCHISING

Introduction

This chapter explains the significance of IP for franchising and for social franchising and outlines some of the ways in which attitudes and approaches to IP management may vary across different models of social franchising. It first traverses the structural options available for social enterprises in franchising, providing an overview of the different structures used in franchising organisations, and highlighting the differing characteristics of each structure.[1] It then considers how the organisational structure affects IP management intrinsically, as there are rights associated with franchising which involve the use of the organisation's branding, trademarks, logos and/or copyright (and in some instances, patents).

From a legal perspective franchising is a form of licensing. As a grant of a right to use property, a license can apply to real or other types of property. In franchising the focus is on IP; a franchisor grants rights to the franchisee to use IP such as trademarks, know-how, trade secrets, designs, business concept, methodologies, branding, and copyright in documents such as operational manuals and recipes. IP rights form the foundation of franchise agreements as they set out the nature and scope of licences. It is the IP of the entire system that distinguishes franchising from other types

---

[1]Spencer, Elizabeth and Cantatore, Francina, 'Models of Franchising for Social Enterprise' (2016) 23 *Journal of Marketing Channels* 23 (1–2).

of licenses. The most attractive feature of a franchise business is the right to use the valuable IP of that franchise system owned by the franchisor or a third party associate. Because franchise agreements are essentially licensing arrangements that involve the licencing of IP rights, the rights conferred may be caught by the scope of the PPSA if the transaction gives rise to a security interest, as discussed in Chapter 6. This may apply in commercial or social franchise arrangements.

The effective management of IP rights is critical to the success of the franchised business. When a franchise system is set up, asset protection is one of the areas discussed at length by the franchisor's legal and accounting advisers. If the IP is not protected, is generic or not sufficiently distinctive, competitors may be able to use the franchisor's intellectual property and thus dilute the value of the franchise system and the individual units within the system. Often a separate company owns the IP thus reducing risk to the IP in the event that the franchisor entity is sued or liquidated. Franchisees should carefully review the information provided by the franchisor to ascertain the franchisor's rights to use intellectual property and its relationship to the term of the franchise agreement, including possible renewal. Franchisees should also prepare for contingencies affecting their rights to use the IP such as franchisor insolvency. While a franchisor is usually able to terminate the franchise agreement upon the franchisee's insolvency, franchise agreements typically do not afford a franchisee an automatic right to terminate the franchise agreement in the event of franchisor insolvency.

In commercial franchising there are usually strict provisions regulating the operation of franchises, for example through a Franchising Code of Conduct.[2] An example of a typical Franchise Agreement with annexures is attached marked Appendix E. However, in relation to social franchises the waters can be muddied through a lack of definition, and result in loosely structured unregulated arrangements.

Social Franchising

Social franchising can take a variety of forms; these can sometimes be difficult to distinguish and define. Broadly, social franchising can be defined as

---

[2]In Australia the applicable Franchising Code of Conduct is included as Schedule 1 to the *Competition and Consumer (Industry Codes—Franchising) Regulation 2014*.

'an adaptation of a commercial franchise in which the developer of a successfully tested social concept (franchiser) enables others (franchisees) to replicate the model using the tested system and brand name to achieve a social benefit. The franchisee in return is obligated to comply with quality standards, report sales and service statistics, and in some cases, pay franchise fees. All service delivery points are typically identified by a recognizable brand name or logo'.[3]

An example of a well-known social franchise operation is Marie Stopes International (MSI). MSI is a registered charity in the UK that delivers healthcare to millions of poor and vulnerable women. Operating in nine countries with 1100 franchisees, MSI has 'partial franchising' model for its social franchise networks; as only some of the franchisees' services/commodities are regulated by MSI, and each network is tailored to meet local needs. Upon joining a franchise network, franchisees are required to sign a contract or make a formal agreement with MSI, and pay a nominal annual fee.[4] MSI provides ongoing coordination, technical support and advice to each franchisee. Franchisees receive high quality but reduced-price commodities from MSI that they sell to clients according to an agreed pricing structure. They also receive training on client care and relevant services.[5]

Marie Stopes is just one example, however, in a diverse landscape of social enterprise in franchising. In order to conduct research and to formulate law and policy appropriate for social franchising activity, it is necessary to identify the essential characteristics of the practice of franchising in the social enterprise context. This chapter identifies the most common social franchising models and addresses the gap in current research by contextualising and describing these models in relation to their contractual relationships and outcomes. It examines the application of these models in practice, and includes a pilot qualitative case study of a successful Australian microfranchise, providing foundational findings for future research in the nascent area of social franchising research. Drawing upon three strands of

---

[3]T. P. Koehlmoos, R. Gazi, S. S. Hossain and K. Zaman, 'The Effect of Social Franchising on Access and Quality of Health Services In Low- And Middle-Income Countries' (2009) 2 *Cochrane Database of Systematic Reviews* 1.

[4]C. Eldridge, *Social Franchising: Reaching the Undeserved*, Marie Stopes International (2011), <https://mariestopes.org/resources/>.

[5]Ibid.

scholarship and research on commercial franchising, social franchising and social enterprise, the meaning of social franchising can be distilled to two fundamental elements: one, that it uses the commercial franchising model and two, that it applies that model for a social purpose.

Again, drawing from the literature, these fundamental elements can be explained according to the four principal attributes of *commercial franchising*—the grant of a right, usually in the form of a licence; to exploit another's business model, including the system or marketing plan and trademark; typically for a fee; where there is control exercised and/or assistance provided by the franchisor—and four 'indicators' of *social enterprise* (namely, that social purpose prevails over the aim of delivering profit to shareholders; organisational culture, structure, management, processes, and less centralised resources than those of strictly commercial enterprises; imperatives to collaborate prevail over market competition; and greater complexity in the involvement and interests of stakeholders/customers).[6]

With respect to the first four principal attributes, social franchising is identical to commercial franchising. It is the social enterprise indicators that distinguish the nature of the social franchising enterprise and so the application and interpretation of law and regulation. This chapter provides a basis for discussion of franchising in the non-profit sector by modeling social franchising according the first of the four indicators of social enterprise derived from the literature, social purpose over profit. It suggests that there are three distinct models of hybrid forms of social franchising that can be identified according to the for-profit or non-profit status of the contracting parties; these are 'traditional social franchising', 'microfranchising' and 'social franchising investment'.

This chapter also considers how these models have been implemented in the Australian landscape, and provides insight into an example of the application of the microfranchising model in an Australian social enterprise.

The framework of interest here are the models of engagement in social enterprise—they include cooperatives, fair trade, community development corporations, affirmative business, microenterprise and microfinance. They may be government funded or non-governmental organisations, trusts, centers, and foundations, private non-profit or charitable. Increasingly,

---

[6]Elizabeth Crawford-Spencer, 'Deriving Meaning for "Social Franchising" from Commercial Franchising and Social Enterprise' (2015) 22(3) *Journal of Marketing Channels* 163.

social enterprise is taking varied forms that stretch even these diverse categorisations.

This widened scope of activity has led to the concept of the non-profit hybrid, in which motives, methods, goals, profitability, accountability and use of income all figure in the determination of the nature and structure of the organisation.[7] The trend in terms of the emergence of hybrid organisations is also seen as a convergence between sectors.[8] Social franchising is a term that is used to describe various types of non-profit activity and hybrid activity, but there is not a consensus about what precisely the term means.

This chapter contributes to a unifying framework for further research about franchising as a structure for social enterprise. This framework can help to ensure development of a coherent social franchising research agenda, particularly with respect to the legal implications of collaboration between for-profit and non-profit sector enterprise, such as contractual and tortious obligations, governance, and tax. Based on surveys of activity that have been labeled 'social franchising' this research generates models of social franchising according to the nature and goals of the enterprise. Having identified contracting parties as important stakeholders in social franchising, Dees' social enterprise hybrid spectrum model[9] is applied to differentiate and categorise stakeholders according to their orientation toward profit and their principal aims.[10]

This chapter also examines, through a pilot case study,[11] the effectiveness of applying a social franchising model to an Australian social enterprise in the context of microfranchising. The case study of the Buffed social franchise is described as a 'purposive sample'.[12] Buffed was identified in this context as a successful microfranchise in Australia, and an in-depth face-to-face interview with a key staff member of Buffed formed the nucleus

---

[7]Shifting stakeholder expectations of non-profit organizations to achieve larger scale social impact while also diversifying their funding has been credited as a major factor in the appearance of the "non-profit hybrid", part for-profit and part non-profit enterprises. At this intersection of business and the traditional non-profit is where the social enterprise lies (see Alter, 2010).

[8]Lyons, above n 119.

[9]Dees uses four indicators—motives, methods, goals and destination of income—to determine the nature of a social enterprise according to their philanthropic and commercial interests, and identifies a combination of the two interests as "hybrid". See Alter, above n 119, for a descriptive table of the model: J. Gregory Dees, 'Enterprising Nonprofits' (1998) 76(1) *Harvard Business Review* 54.

[10]See also Alter, above n 119.

[11]Crawford-Spencer, E. and Cantatore, F. (2015) "Building a brand culture: Franchising as a means of managing intellectual capital in Third Sector Organisations in the Asia Pacific Region", Journal of Marketing Channels, Volume 23(1).

[12]Collis and Hussey, above n 215.

of the discussion and provided data about the structure of the enterprise.[13] The data obtained from this interview illuminates issues surrounding the structure and operation of a successful microfranchise in Australia, and serve as foundational qualitative research on which to base further research into comparative social franchising models.

Generally speaking governments regulate social enterprise according to: the nature of business activities related or unrelated to organisations' missions; use or destination of earned income to mission activities or other purposes; whether the source of income is the general public, clients, third party payers (insurance, donors), government; the amount of income earned through social enterprise; or a combination of these.

The law in many countries does not make provision for or recognise the social enterprise (income-generating non-profit) as legitimate or legal. Therefore, non-profit organisations risk losing their non-profit status and associated privileges by launching a social enterprise or income-generating activity. Some countries have made special provisions in the law and tax codes for social enterprises, but the legal situation must be analyzed on a country-by-country and case-by-case basis.[14] Currently there is insufficient understanding of the regulatory frameworks and legal risks and benefits of various structures and contracting norms in social franchising.

In this context, contractual relationships are means as well as objects of regulatory intervention.[15] Analysis of the contractual relationship has yielded rich results in research in commercial franchising but has not yet been applied to a particularised understanding of the social franchise phenomenon in all its facets, including approaches to recognising, protecting and managing IP.[16] Thus, the contractual relationships between parties are an important factor to consider when characterising the type of enterprise one is dealing with.

---

[13]Norman K. Denzin and Yvonna S. Lincoln (eds), *Handbook of qualitative research* (Sage, 2nd ed, 2005); Interview with J. Gehre (Location, 23 June 2014).

[14]Janelle A. Kerlin, 'A Comparative Analysis of the Global Emergence of Social Enterprise' (2010) 2 *Voluntas* 162.

[15]Hugh Collins, *Regulating Contracts* (Oxford University Press, 1999).

[16]See, e.g., J. A. Brickley, 'Incentive Conflicts and Contractual Restraints: Evidence from Franchising' (1999) 42(2) *Journal of Law & Economics* 745; F. Lafontaine and K. L. Shaw, 'The Dynamics of Franchise Contracting: Evidence from Panel Data' (1999) 107(5) *Journal of Political Economy* 1041; J. E. L. Bercovitz, 'An Analysis of the Contract Provisions in Business-format Franchise Agreements' in J. Stanworth and D. Purdy (eds), *Proceedings of the 13th Conference of the International Society of Franchising* (1999).

Models of Social Franchising: Social Franchising and Contracting Parties

The nature of non-profit organisations and SE is diverse, making it difficult to generate and test theory in the field with consistency. Faced with this problem, this chapter adopts a similar approach to that of Alter's hybrid spectrum, which charts the motives, methods and goals of income/profit in organisations that are purely philanthropic, hybrid, and purely commercial. Noting that all hybrid organisations generate both social and economic value, Alter categorises them according to the extent of activity relating to motive (mission versus profit), accountability (stakeholder versus shareholder), and use of income (income reinvested in social programs or operational costs versus profit redistributed to shareholders).[17]

This method is consistent with that of Justo et al,[18] Nicholls,[19] and Peredo and McLean.[20] This simple approach provides significant insight into the diversity of social franchising. It does not preclude—indeed it is hoped it may facilitate—construction of further analysis using these categories as a foundation. All the models described here are based on direct franchising, though some, such as Youth to Youth, suggest elements of a master franchising model. As all of these models are types of social franchising, the general term, 'social franchising', is used as an umbrella that encompasses all of—but is not used to describe any one of—the 'sub-species', the three models described here. The first model has been labeled 'traditional non-profit franchising'; the second, 'microfranchising'; and the third, 'social franchise investment.' The attributes of each model are outlined below.

Traditional Social Franchising: Non-profit Franchising Model with Non-profit Franchisor

Many non-profit organisations operate according to a traditional franchise model, i.e. traditional non-profit franchising as depicted in Figure 5. In her

---

[17] Alter, above n 119.

[18] Siri Terjesen, Jan Lepoutre, Rachida Justo and Niels Bosma, *Report on Social Entrepreneurship Study: Methodology and Data*, Global Entrepreneurship Monitor (2009) <http://www.gemconsortium.org/assets/uploads/1325198092GEM_SE_Study_-_Methodology_and_Data.doc>.

[19] Alex Nicholls, *Social Entrepreneurship: New Models of Sustainable Change* (Oxford University Press, 2006).

[20] Ana Maria Peredo and Murdith McLean, 'Social Entrepreneurship: A Critical Review of the Concept' (2006) 41(1) *Journal of World Business* 56.

1992 and 1996 publications on franchising in the non-profit arena, Oster does not use the term, 'social franchising', but rather identifies non-profit organisations that apply the franchising model as 'non-profit franchising.'[21] She notes that two thirds of all non-profits and 90% of the largest non-profit organisations in the US operate in this way.

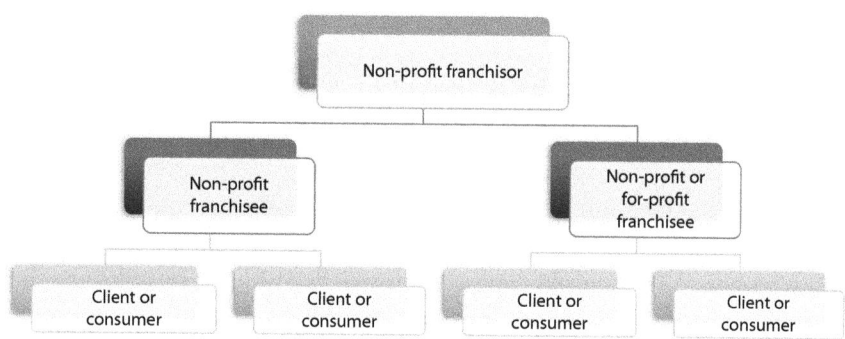

Figure 5 Traditional Non-profit Franchising.

Table 3 Non-profit Franchising—Summary of Key Characteristics.

Franchisor type	Non-profit
Franchisor objective	Pure or primary social welfare purpose for benefit of third parties/end-user client but may also wish to engender profitability of operation for franchisees
Franchisee type	The system may contract only with non-profit franchisees or with both non-profit and for-profit franchisees
Franchisee objective	Depends on profit orientation—may be principally social welfare to end user and/or to franchisee, its employees or dual purpose
End-user client/customer	The focus of the enterprise, the 'center of gravity' for the aims of the enterprise
IP management	In this model IP may be at risk in cases where the public benefit of the activities outweighs concern for management of brand, system and processes. Where the focus of the benefit is on the end-user or client, there is a particularly delicate balance to be struck between the value of the work and the value and integrity of the brand of the enterprise carrying out that work

Table 3 depicts the key characteristics of non-profit franchising models. Non-profit franchising features non-profit or for-profit franchisees in a non-profit system with a focus on the franchisor's and franchisees' shared

---

[21]S. M. Oster, 'Nonprofit Organizations as Franchise Operations' (1992) 2(3) *Nonprofit Management and Leadership* 223; S. M. Oster, 'Nonprofit Organizations and Their Local Affiliates: A Study in Organizational Forms' (1996) 30 *Journal of Economic Behavior and Organization* 83.

non-profit mission. While in most cases both franchisor and franchisees are non-profit organisations, franchisees may in some cases be for-profit (e.g. the HealthStore system), whilst the franchisor is non-profit. The principal aim of both franchisor and franchisee is to deliver social benefit; the focus is on the mission and the social benefit that is delivered to end-user clients or customers. Burand and Koch argue that this form 'may or may not draw its franchisees from the poor, but it will always aim to deliver needed products and services to the poor.'[22] However, we would widen the scope from the poor to any client of the enterprise whose improved social welfare is the objective. The non-profit franchisor achieves its objectives through contracting with non-profit or, less commonly, for-profit franchisees, for the main purpose of promoting the social goal. There may also be a secondary aim to improve the welfare of the non-profit franchisees, as, for example, in the case of Youth to Youth.

Well-suited to developed as well as developing economies and applicable in a range of social enterprise initiatives such as education, health care, energy, transportation and communication, this is the traditional non-profit franchising model that is most likely thought of in connection with social welfare projects by traditional non-profit organisations in developed countries.[23] It is also commonly used as a model for advancing social welfare initiatives in developing countries, particularly health care.

Some examples of this model with *both non-profit franchisees and franchisors* are Goodwill Industries International, which enters into franchise-like agreements with human service agencies and networks of non-profit businesses to help people with special needs overcome barriers to employment and Reach India, which is a training franchise that teaches thousands of local organisations to deliver education on health, livelihoods and family finance topics to millions of women and adolescent girls who meet in self-help groups across rural India. Reach Global, the franchisor, equips organisations to replicate and scale the delivery of life changing education to millions of very poor women and girls. The organisation is a trust, its activities funded by large foreign donations (ranging between $2 million and $8 million) with franchise fees contributing a nominal amount (about $25,000 in total) to the annual revenues.[24]

---

[22]Deborah Burand and David W. Koch, 'Microfranchising: A Business Approach to Fighting Poverty' (2010) 30(1) *Franchise Law Journal* 24, 25.
[23]Oster, 'Nonprofit Organizations and Their Local Affiliates', above n 511.
[24]http://www.globalreach.in/india/.

An example of this model with *non-profit franchisor and mixed for-profit and non-profit franchisees* is The HealthStore Foundation, a Minnesota-based s 501(c)(3) non-profit corporation, founded in 1997, with a mission to improve access to essential drugs, basic healthcare, and prevention services for children and families in the developing world, using business models that maintain standards, are geometrically scalable, and achieve economies of scale. In 2000, The HealthStore Foundation launched the CFW network, a branded business format franchise system of clinics and drug shops. The CFW network has grown to 82 clinics and drug shops owned and operated by Kenyan nurses and health workers in rural Kenya and three 'company owned' clinics in Rwanda. The CFW Business Format and Operations consists of a standardised franchise system with training and compliance programs.[25]

Microfranchising: Non-profit Franchising with a Non-profit Franchisor and For-profit Franchisees

The second model of franchising for social enterprise is microfranchising as depicted in Figure 6 below. Like non-profit franchising, microfranchising is typically characterised by a non-profit franchisor and system. Unlike traditional social franchising, however, where the franchisee carries out the mission and purpose of the franchisor to benefit a third party or social aim, in microfranchising the main social welfare aim is focused on the franchisee; the mission and purpose of the franchise is to benefit franchisees. In this model the franchisee is more likely to be for-profit.

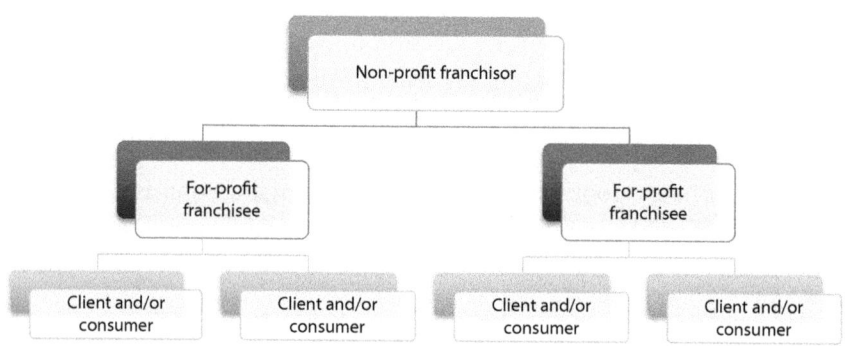

Figure 6 Microfranchising.

---

[25]The Healthstore Foundation, *Our Mission* (2014) <http://www.healthstore.org>.

Table 4 Microfranchising with Non-profit Franchisor—Summary of Key Characteristics.

Franchisor type	Non-profit or for-profit
Franchisor objective	Social welfare or dual purpose. Social welfare purpose is the financial development and empowerment of franchisees (and potentially other parties)
Franchisee type	For-profit
Franchisee objective	Profit
End-user client/customer	The focus here is more on the profitability and so empowerment of franchisees rather than on social welfare of client/consumer, though there may be an end-user social welfare element here as well
IP management	In this model the management and protection of IP should be emphasised as good practice and part of the capacity building of franchisees, as well as accruing to the benefit of the enterprise. Attention should be paid also to IP created by franchisees as fledgling business operators. Whereas franchise contracts typically provide for all IP to be owned by the franchisor in the interests of the system, there may be more complicated considerations here related to franchisee empowerment and development

Microfranchising typically features for-profit franchisees in non-profit system with a focus on opportunity creation for franchisees; it is typically comprised of a non-profit franchisor that uses profitable franchises for the purpose of achieving social goals. Table 4 sets out the key characteristics of microfranchising models with a non-profit franchisor. This model may be part of micro or tandem franchising initiatives. While there may be social welfare benefits to end-users, such as the provision of essential services and infrastructure such as telephones and water, the focus here is first on the affordability of business opportunities for franchisees, and also on the profitability of franchisees and/or on the products and services they deliver to the target market or community. Burand and Koch documented the microfranchising phenomenon in their 2010 article, observing that:

> [T]he term micro-franchise means a business model that, although adopting many of the business practices employed in mainstream commercial franchising, involves businesses that are affordable enough to be owned and operated by people living at the base of the economic pyramid …[26]

While microfranchising is most commonly applied in developing economies, it is also finding application to achieve social welfare objectives in

---

[26]Burand and Koch, above n 512, 25.

middle and higher-income developed economies. 'Social (sector) franchising typically is aimed at bringing products and services, like education and health care, to people living at the base of the economic pyramid through the use of business format franchise practices'.[27] This suggests that microfranchising can be considered a subset rather than a separate category. It is a subset in that it is aimed at bringing products and services, not only education and health care, but also business and training and entrepreneurial skills as well as confidence, initiative and empowerment, 'to people living at the base of the economic pyramid through the use of business format franchise practices'.[28] According to Fleisch & Bundesverband Deutscher Stiftungen, microfranchising fits less comfortably as a subset of:

> [A] process by which the developer of a successfully tested social concept, the franchisor, in order to scale up the coverage of target groups and the quality of products (services), enables others, the franchisees, to replicate the model, using the tested system, using the brand name, in return for social results, system development, information on the impact.[29]

The difference here is that the successfully tested social concept is the concept of free enterprise. Here a non-profit (or less commonly a for-profit) franchisor and for-profit franchisees are engaged in what is actually very much like commercial business format franchising with the primary aim to create sustainable revenue streams for the franchisees, it 'may or may not deliver goods and services to the poor, but it will always aim to build franchiseable business opportunities that are affordable for the poor'.[30] 'Tandem franchising' is another term for microfranchising that has been used in South Africa, to describe,

> a funding and mentoring programme for franchisees from previously disadvantaged backgrounds ... [the aim is to create] an

---

[27]Ibid.
[28]Ibid.
[29]H. Fleisch and Bundesverband Deutscher Stiftungen, *Social Franchising: A Way of Systematic Replication to Increase Social Impact* (2008) <http://www.stiftungen.org/fileadmin/bvds/de/Projekte/Projekttransfer/Social_Franchise_Manual_Englisch.pdf> 35.
[30]Burand and Koch, above n 512, 25.

alternative funding mechanism that enables transfer of ownership over time, in tandem with achieving skills transfer.[31]

Tandem franchising is about making franchising affordable at the base of the economic pyramid where transfer of information, skills, ownership of the franchise is gradual over time. In this type of microfranchising, the end user/consumer may not be a focus of the mission of the organisation, as the principal aim is to provide opportunity for the franchisees. This may be a point of risk, as there are cases where such ventures misjudge the market, which can cause the entire venture to fail, and cause more problems for the very franchisees it aimed to help. Compared to traditional commercial business format franchising, microfranchise networks are also still relatively few in number worldwide. As Burand and Koch note: 'Although no single repository purports to have a complete list, one source recently listed around 60 micro-franchise opportunities in twenty countries'.[32]

Examples of microfranchising, where a non-profit franchisor operates in cooperation with for-profit franchisees include VisionSpring, an organisation which loans entrepreneurs a 'Business in a Bag' micro-franchise that contains all the products and materials needed for marketing and selling eyeglasses, and running a small business. 'Vision entrepreneurs' receive training and support from local staff and they repay VisionSpring for the cost of glasses sold. VisionSpring engages with a wide variety of organisations, from microfinance institutions with large networks of borrowers to local non-profits providing services in communities;[33] and FanMilk, which is reportedly the leading distributor of dairy products in Ghana with some 8,500 micro-franchisees selling milk, ice cream, yogurt, and popsicles from carts and bicycles.[34]

Social Franchise Investment: For-profit Franchisor with Non-profit Franchisees

The third model of franchising for social enterprise is social franchise investment as depicted in Figure 7 below. While both non-profit franchising and microfranchising are characterised by a non-profit franchisor and

---

[31] Anita Du Toit, *The Financing and Mentoring of Emerging Franchisees Through Tandem Franchising* (2007) <https://emnet.univie.ac.at/fileadmin/user_upload/conf_EMNet/2007/papers/duToit.pdf> 1.
[32] Burand and Koch, above n 512, 26.
[33] Vision Spring <http://visionspring.org>.
[34] FanMilk International A/S <http://www.fanmilk.com>.

system with predominantly non-profit franchisees in the traditional model and predominantly for-profit franchisees in microfranchising, social franchise investment can be distinguished by its use of *a for-profit franchisor* (see *Fietspunt* example below), and a franchise system in which non-profit franchisees invest.

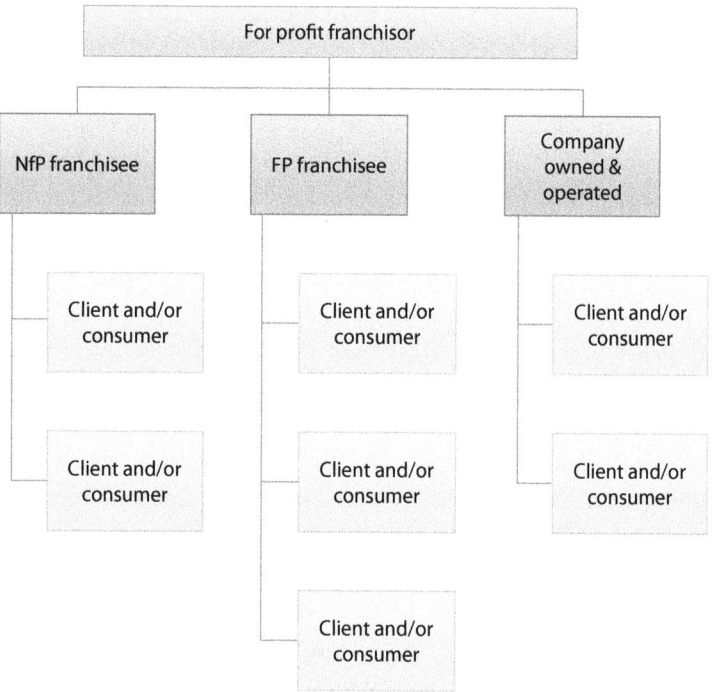

Figure 7 Social Franchise Investment.

Social franchising involves non-profit organisations that identify, acquire and operate proven and successful franchised for-profit businesses. The non-profit organisation participates as a franchisee in a for-profit franchise system to resource non-profit purposes and/or to provide employment or other social welfare benefit. The principal aim of the franchisor is profit. In this model the franchisor's system also includes for-profit and possibly also company-owned units that operate on a for-profit basis (depicted in the diagram in light grey to indicate that they do not constitute social franchising).

The principal aim of the non-profit franchisee may be either a social welfare purpose or a dual purpose, profit and social benefit. If one aim is to generate profit, the for-profit activity will need to be consistent with the non-profit mission and brand, and revenue will feed back into the operations of a non-profit organisation in compliance with local tax and regulatory requirements.

Table 5 Social Franchise Investment—Summary of Key Characteristics.

Franchisor type	For-profit
Franchisor objective	Profit only or dual purpose for franchisor, social welfare plus profit generation. If primarily profit, a franchisor still may forego some profitability for social welfare purpose, and/or to gain brand image benefits, and in the interests of corporate social responsibility
Franchisee type	Non-profit within mixed system (there are other franchisees in the Franchisor's system that are not classified as social enterprises)
Franchisee objective	Three possible aims: social welfare, profit generating or dual purpose social welfare plus profit generation
End-user client/customer	The focus of the enterprise, the 'center of gravity' for the aims of the enterprise may be employees or participants within the organisation of the franchisee rather than end-user clients or consumers of goods and/or services
IP management	In this model employees or other participants connected with the organisation of the franchisee are likely to be the primary focus of the social welfare objective, rather than end-user client or consumer of goods and/or services. Where the franchisor is for-profit, it is likely that standard practices of IP management will be in place

The for-profit franchisor may discount start-up costs and royalties for non-profit franchisees and gains the benefit of enhanced goodwill and publicity. While the franchisor system derives profit from the relationship, it may be less than with other purely commercial franchisees. Of course, the for-profit aims of franchisor or other participants do not preclude social welfare benefits to them or deriving from their activities.

Some non-profit organisations identify, acquire and operate proven and successful franchised businesses not to create profit, but rather with the aim of training, employment or other social welfare services to third parties such as employees of the franchisee. This model could include a non-profit franchisor and is likely to consist of exclusively non-profit franchisees rather than a mix, as the profit motivation is clearly secondary. The end user is not the sole focus of the enterprise; here the goal of providing employment, training, care or similar to employees of franchisee is equally or more important. A good example of this variation is Fietspunt, 'social franchising by bike', which employs disadvantaged people in bicycle shop franchises in The Netherlands.[35] Table 5 above contains a summary of the key characteristics of social franchise investment models.

The potential for the application of this model in developed economies with mature franchise sectors, such as the US and Australia, is significant; this model has been adopted with success in the US. One example is Platte River Industries in Denver. Ben and Jerry's social franchising program is another well-known example.[36]

The Use of Social Franchising in Australia

We have examined the different social franchising models and illustrated how the components of the models differ and overlap. In this part of the article we consider the application of social franchising in the context of social enterprise in Australia as depicted in Table 6 below. Based on a qualitative in-depth interview, an Australian case study provides insight into the effectiveness of applying a social franchising model in the context of microfranchising.

An early adopter of an Australian social franchising structure was the Brumby's Bakery franchise (Brumby's), now owned by listed company Retail Food Group. Brumby's commenced as a single bakery in Melbourne owned by a yoga foundation to generate income to fund its teaching work. In 1981 the foundation relocated to Warwick in Queensland to create an alternative lifestyle community based on yoga principles, with the bakery business growing to more than 100 stores and continuing to fund foundation activities.[37] However, after the foundation went into receivership, it was bought by a consortium of franchisees and management, who continued to grow the business and operate it commercially until it had nearly 300 bakeries and was sold for $46 million in 2007. While the early days of Brumby's demonstrated the characteristics of a social franchise, the subsequent insolvency of the foundation which owned it caused a complete change in the profit focus of the business. Brumby's continues to support charitable causes, but is today operated with the principal purpose of generating profits for its franchisees and shareholders.[38]

---

[35] Fietspunt B.V. <www.fietspunt.net>.
[36] Ben and Jerry's, *Partnershops* <http://www.benjerry.com/values/how-we-do-business/partnershops>.
[37] Gehre, above n 503.
[38] Ibid.

Table 6 Summary of Models of Franchising for Social Enterprise

	Non-profit franchising	**Microfranchising**	**Social franchise investment**
Non-profit or for-profit orientation of contracting parties	Non-profit franchisor and non-profit franchisees only or non-profit or for-profit franchisee within social welfare framework	Non-profit franchisor and for-profit franchisee	For-profit franchisor and non-profit and/or for-profit franchisees within mixed system
Examples	Goodwill Industries Youth to Youth ReachIndia The HealthStore	VisionSpring	Subway/TBBC Fietspunt Aunt Annie's/PRI Service Master Clean/PRI
Principal purpose	Social Welfare	Social welfare	Dual purpose Differs for franchisor and franchisee
Franchisor	Non-profit	Non-profit	For-profit
Franchisor objective	Primarily social welfare of *end-user client*, but may also wish to engender profitability of operation for franchisees	Social welfare, in the form of profitability of operation for franchisees	May be principally profit or dual purpose May be profit first for franchisor system overall. If primarily profit, may forego some profitability for social welfare purpose
Franchisee	Non-profit or for-profit	For-profit	Profit or for-profit dual purpose may be present as well
Franchisee objective	Depends on profit orientation—may be principally social welfare or dual purpose; Social welfare for benefit of third parties (but may also benefit franchisees)	Profit—the social welfare benefit is profitability and capacity building for franchisees	Social welfare or dual purpose as for-profit franchisees which may be present in franchisor's system strictly for commercial purpose and not classified as social enterprises se
End-user client/customer	The focus of the enterprise, the 'center of gravity' for the aims of the enterprise	The focus here is more on the profitability and capacity building of franchisees rather than on social welfare of client/consumer, though there may be a social welfare element here toward end-user/client as well	Employees or other participants connected with the organisation of the franchisee likely to be the primary focus of the social welfare objective, rather than end-user client or consumer of goods and/or services
Management of IP	Since the focus of the benefit of this model is first and foremost the end-user or client, there is a particularly delicate balance to be struck between the value of the work and the value and integrity of the brand of the enterprise carrying out that work	Here, the management and protection of IP should be emphasised as good practice and part of the capacity building of franchisees, as well as accruing to the benefit of the enterprise	Here also the management and protection of IP should be emphasised as good practice as well as accruing to the benefit of the enterprise

Traditional Non-profit Franchising and Social Franchise Investment: Both Under Represented in Australia

The authors' research revealed that the first two models discussed above have found limited application in Australia to date. There are many examples in other countries of the *traditional non-profit franchising model with a non-profit franchisor*.[39] The HealthStore Foundation is an example of this model with mixed for-profit and non-profit franchisees in the US. However, examples from the UK, US and Germany appear not to be widely represented in Australia. More research is needed to investigate further why this may be so.

One example of this model which has been documented in Australia is the Florence Melton Mini-School Institute of the Hebrew University of Jerusalem. The Melton School, a social franchise, forms an international network of community-based schools offering adults the opportunity to acquire Jewish literacy.[40] The non-profit franchisor, The Melton School, was established in 1980 and is based in Israel and North America. There are two franchises in Australia—one in Sydney sponsored by the University of Sydney, and the other in Melbourne sponsored by the Jewish Museum of Australia.[41] This franchise operates specifically within and for the benefit of the Jewish community by providing religious education. The two outlets appear to be directly franchised to the parent organisation, which provides the education curriculum and teaching guidelines. There are currently no other identified organisations in Australia that fit this social franchising model.[42]

As outlined in the previous section, *social franchise investment* is distinguished by its use of a for-profit franchisor and a franchise system in which the non-profit franchisee invests. The principal aim of the franchisor is profit. While the franchisor's system also includes for-profit and possibly also company-owned units that operate on a for-profit basis, the principal aim of the non-profit franchisee may be either a social welfare purpose or dual purpose, profit and social benefit. Further research will explore

---

[39] Such as Goodwill Industries International, Youth-to-Youth, Reach India, Marie Stopes International and Future Clean.
[40] The Florence Melton School of Adult Jewish Learning, *About Melton* <http://www.melton-school.org/aboutus/about-melton>.
[41] Ibid.
[42] Gehre, above n 503.

whether there are other examples that this preliminary research has not identified.

Examples of Microfranchising in the Australian Context

In *microfranchising* the franchisor is typically non-profit, as noted above, and the social welfare aim is the franchisee, i.e. the benefits of the arrangement to the franchisee. While there are not a great many instances where this model has been applied in Australia, a notable instance in which this franchising model has been implemented with great success is the Community Bank program of Bendigo Bank and Adelaide Bank.[43] Their model, however, differs from the proposed structure in this article, as the franchisor constitutes a for-profit organisation operating a 50/50 partnership with the Community Bank, which entitles it to 50% of the revenue generated by its franchisees.[44] A discussion of these types of franchise/partnership arrangements falls outside the scope of this article, as they do not subscribe to the typical social franchising structures described above. Further, the banking industry may be described as a highly regulated industry with specific rules and regulations not generally applying to social franchises operating in other industries.

A smaller but more replicable franchising model is presented by the Buffed initiative, a shoe-shining franchise with a non-profit franchisor (the Wise Foundation), where the franchisor enjoys no financial benefit but operates solely for the benefit of the franchisees with a community and social purpose. We include here a brief case study of the Buffed model. This pilot case study may be replicated in further research to compare the operation of social franchises in practice under the three different frameworks proposed here. For the purpose of this research Buffed was identified as a successful social franchise model in the Australian context, and a good example of microfranchising.

---

[43] Bendigo Bank, *About Community Banking* (2014) <http://www.bendigobank.com.au/public/community/community-banking/about-community-bank>.

[44] Mareeba Community Bank Branch & Dimbulah Community Bank Branch, *Annual Report 2013*, Bendigo Bank (2013) <http://www.bendigobank.com.au/public/__data/assets/pdf_file/0007/91780/2013-annual-report.pdf> 7; Coleraine and District Community Bank Branch, *Annual Report 2013*, Bendigo Bank (2013) <http://www.bendigobank.com.au/public/__data/assets/pdf_file/0004/90544/annual-report-201-13.pdf>.

Mini-case Study of Microfranchising: Buffed Shoe Shine

The Australian success story of 'Buffed' is the best example this research identified of an Australian microfranchise which fits the microfranchising model. Buffed is a network of shoe shine stands based in major cities across Australia. The Buffed website characterises the organisation as a social enterprise.[45] According to our model, we would further characterise Buffed as a social franchise because both fundamental elements of social franchising, i.e. that it uses the commercial franchising model and that it applies that model for a social purpose, are evident. A brief case study of Buffed will form the basis of discussion in this part of the article.

Based in Melbourne, Australia, the Wise Foundation was formed in April 2008 to further the community development and social commitments of The Body Shop Australia, the Adidem Group of companies, and the Wise family. The Wise Foundation launched Buffed in 2011 to create business opportunities for refugees, asylum seekers and people who are long term unemployed or are facing difficulties in the job market, to secure their futures through small business ownership.[46]

The Foundation enables individuals to 'purchase' Buffed shoe shine stands and operate them as their own franchise business. Buffed franchisees receive comprehensive training in the art of shoe shining, customer service skills and business training development. Buffed also provides support for franchisees through business mentorship and assists them with marketing to ensure franchisees have the best chance of creating successful businesses.[47]

Microfranchising is a novel concept in Australia and this initiative by the Wise Foundation is an example of the microfranchising model used to achieve social welfare objectives in a higher-income developed economy like Australia. The Buffed approach reflects the microfranchising model characteristics discussed above with the following characteristics:

a. The franchisor is a non-profit organisation;
b. The franchisees are for-profit enterprises which are run with the objective of making a profit;

---

[45] Buffed, *About Buffed* <http://www.buffed.org.au/about-buffed.aspx>.
[46] Interview with M. Ryan (Location, 6 March 2014).
[47] Buffed, above n 535.

c. The social welfare purpose is to provide disadvantaged franchisees with the opportunity to run their own business at a profit—they are the beneficiaries of the franchise arrangement; and

d. The end user/customer receives a reasonably priced shoe-shining service for payment—thus they obtain some benefit but the primary focus of the enterprise is to benefit franchisees.

The purpose of this enterprise is to provide disadvantaged people, e.g. refugees or unemployed unable to find employment, with an opportunity to run a profitable small business in the form of a shoe-shining and repair service franchise. The concept that franchisees are provided with the support and tools to run their franchise and receive ongoing support from the franchisor, fits the microfranchising model discussed in this article.

The Buffed model accords with the characteristics of a social franchise discussed above.[48]

- First, the grant of a right, usually in the form of a licence, applies here—franchisees have the right to operate under the Buffed trademark and no licence fee is payable;
- Franchisees exploit another's business model, including the system or marketing plan and trademark—franchisees are provided with the Buffed business plan, business training (through partner University of Queensland (UQ) Business School), set-up expenses (through Bank of Queensland (BoQ) support to the franchisor). They are assisted with marketing through franchisor marketing efforts and internet presence;
- In this case there is no 'franchise fee'. Franchisees are provided with training, support, equipment (including a specially designed chair) free of charge, although it remains the property of the franchisor. The only fee charged to the franchisee is a 'royalty fee' of $50 per month to cover insurance costs;
- There is control exercised and assistance provided by the franchisor in the form of initial and ongoing support and assistance;
- The social purpose prevails over the aim of delivering profit to shareholders—the franchisor is a non-profit foundation thus fulfilling a social purpose is the sole aim of the enterprise;

---

[48]Ryan, above n 536.

- The organisational culture, structure, management, processes, and resources are less centralised than those of strictly commercial enterprises—this is true as the franchisees operate their own businesses by means of the franchise, in a number of different locations in Melbourne, Sydney and Brisbane, and allowances are made for franchisees depending on their requirements, due to the focus on empowering disadvantaged members of the community;
- In this enterprise, imperatives to collaborate prevail over market competition—here Buffed operates with the assistance of industry partners, such as UQ and BoQ; and
- There is greater complexity in the involvement and interests of stakeholders/customers—in this case the stakeholders are the franchisees and the complexities arise as a result of their diversities, e.g. language barriers, lack of formal education etc.

From the above analysis, it is apparent that the Buffed model meets the social franchise requirements as proposed in the microfranchising model on all main points, and the focus of the enterprise is on the profitability and, consequently, empowerment of franchisees rather than on the social welfare of clients or consumers.

As further noted, the contractual framework for this microfranchising model requires a non-profit franchisor and for-profit franchisee. In the case of Buffed, this framework prevails and contractual arrangements are characterised as follows.[49]

(a) Franchisees are provided with free legal advice in relation to their franchise and contractual obligations;
(b) The franchise agreement is in the nature of 'a simplified commercial agreement';
(c) There are no restraint of trade conditions imposed upon franchisees;
(d) The agreement allows for trading at a profit to the franchisee;
(e) There is provision for a $50 monthly payment in respect of public liability insurance in respect of the franchise;
(f) Confidentiality clauses are included in the agreements;
(g) There is no franchising fee as the franchisor carries the set-up costs;

---

[49]Ibid.

(h) There are no ramifications for breach of contract as, in the view of the franchisor, it would be difficult to enforce an agreement, due to the 'nature of the franchisees'; and
(i) Essentially the contract allows the franchisee to retain all profits earned except for the $50 insurance payment.

In view of the supportive and beneficial partnerships enjoyed by the enterprise and its franchisees, the social franchise arrangement allows franchisees the best possible opportunity for success. There are significant advantages and incentives for franchisees to succeed in their venture. However, as with any business model, it must be financially sustainable for the franchisor for longevity of the enterprise.

Social Franchise: The Way Forward

As businesses and non-profit organisations increasingly turn to hybrid forms of enterprise as means to serve diverse needs and objectives, the incidence of social franchising can be expected to rise. Just as there are many forms of traditional business format franchising, this research suggests that the forms that social franchising may take are varied, a finding that could be expected due to the versatility of this business model.

This chapter has identified three models of franchising for social welfare purposes. Classifying them according to the for-profit or non-profit orientation of the franchisor and the franchisee, the three forms are distinguished as 'traditional non-profit franchising'; 'microfranchising'; and 'social franchise investment'. The microfranchising model has already been applied successfully in Australia, while traditional non-profit franchising and social franchise investment have not been taken up in any significant way in Australia.

Of the three basic forms of social franchising identified here, each has important particular characteristics. In addition to the profit making orientation of each organisation the analysis has considered the principal mission or purpose of the relationship and the attitude of each enterprise with respect to consumer or client, as well as other constituencies, stakeholders and/or beneficiaries, such as employees, investors and shareholders, and the environment. Finally, this chapter has considered how the microfranchising structure is applied in an Australian context, by way of a qualitative pilot case study.

The characteristics of these models will have implications for the nature of the relationships among the franchisor and franchisee as well as clients, end-users, providers of finance and other stakeholders. This of course includes management of IP. There are also implications for contracting processes, judicial interpretation, and regulation, including tax status. It is clear that the nature of the enterprise varies according to its principal aims, the nature of participants, and the products and services involved, and that all of these factors must be viewed in the context of cultural factors, geography, geopolitical factors, and economic conditions.

The models proposed here could be developed to reflect other considerations such as resource structures and control mechanisms. Increasing variation and complexity in social franchising can be expected as this form develops and as the pressure on non-profit enterprise increases to adapt new structures to the exigencies of resource acquisition, accountability to stakeholders the formation of networks and alliances, changing regulatory requirements, accountability to stakeholders, and so on.

Further research is needed to understand better which forms of social franchising are most successful for different purposes, to understand the risks and benefits of various models of social franchising for participants in different contexts. While the nature of the contractual relationship and the motivations of the contracting parties are highly variable, it appears that franchising which involves the non-profit sector is probably not as commonly driven by transaction costs as commercial franchising. Among the models suggested here, those that place emphasis on profit-making and brand value maximization might be explained more by transaction costs and agency theory. To the extent that the relationship is less about profit than the social welfare objective(s), the transaction cost saving is likely to be significant as a motivating factor.

Franchising in the non-profit sector may instead be more commonly driven by resource acquisition factors. Again, the calculus depends on the type of social franchising involved, but in many cases the greater consideration is not the contribution of the franchisee in financial terms. Rather the most important resource in question is the labour and commitment of the franchisee to the social welfare purpose. This could explain why there may be less stringent requirements on franchisees in social franchising applications. What is of greater concern to the franchisor is that the franchisee stays in the system, rather than strict compliance for reasons of uniformity, consistency, branding, and the associated financial returns.

Conclusion

Further research in this area would benefit from analysis of the contractual terms in each of the types of social franchising outlined here, and the nature of the parties' rights and obligations. Questions that should be addressed include: How does the franchise exercise control? What latitude does the franchisee have? What are the ramifications for breach? What are the dispute resolution provisions? What are the other regulatory, tax, liability and related legal ramifications? Not only will this and future research be useful in the context of the development and better understanding of third sector enterprise, but also, the lessons learned in the non-profit sector can have important crossover benefits for traditional commercial franchising. Additionally, the pilot case study included here on the Buffed microfranchise may serve as foundational qualitative research to establish how the proposed models in this article are applied in practice in other social enterprises.

IP is a critical, driving factor in franchising and social franchising activity. Yet, while different models of social franchising provide different features that can impact IP management, it appears that IP management considerations do not play a significant role in the choice of structure of the social enterprise. Since the focus of the benefit in non-profit franchising is first and foremost the end-user or client, there is a particularly delicate balance to be struck between the value of the work and the value and integrity of the brand of the enterprise carrying out that work. This would indicate that IP rights management should be a factor in regulating this relationship. In discussing microfranchising and social franchise investment it has been indicated that the management and protection of IP should be emphasised as good practice and part of the capacity building of franchisees, as well as accruing to the benefit of the enterprise. A structured approach to licensing arrangements, with due consideration of the types of IP rights being licenced or conferred, should be an integral part of a franchise agreement in order to protect the rights of all parties involved.

APPENDIX A

LICENCE OF INTELLECTUAL PROPERTY

THIS AGREEMENT is made the _____ day of _____, 20 ____

BETWEEN: [*Name of Company*] [*ACN if Corporation*] of [*Address*] ("the Company") of the first part

AND: [*Name of Licensee*] [*ACN if Corporation*] of [*Address*] ("the Licensee") of the second part.

RECITALS
The Company is the owner of [*trade marks, patents, trade secrets, copyright, know-how, registered designs, plant breeders rights/or other intellectual property*].

The Company has agreed to grant to the Licensee an exclusive licence [*with the right to grant sub-licences*] to [*manufacture/market/distribute/use/exploit/sell*] the intellectual property.

NOW THE PARTIES AGREE as follows:

Interpretation

1. (1) In this Agreement the following definitions apply:
    'Commencement Date' means the _____ day of _____, 20 ____ .

'**Intellectual Property**' includes but is not limited to the trade marks, patents, copyrights, processes, know-how, registered designs or other like rights, particulars of which are in Sch 1.

'**Manufacture**' includes construction, assembly, production or such other preparation for commercial use or exploitation of the product or service incorporating the Intellectual Property.

'**Net Sales Price**' means [*the selling price exclusive of freight, insurance charges, sales tax and any other like tax and after deducting allowances made for returned or defective products and/or trade discounts*].

'**Processes**' includes technologies, products, devices, processes or techniques.

'**Product**' means the products and/or processes set forth in Sch 2 which incorporate the use of the Intellectual Property.

'**Territory**' means the geographical locations set forth in Sch 3.

(2) A reference to persons includes corporations;

(3) Words including singular numbers include plural numbers and vice versa;

(4) Words including a gender include all genders.

(5) A reference in this Agreement to a statute or a section of a statute includes all amendments to that statute or section passed in substitution for the statute or section referred to and incorporating any of its provisions.

(6) Except for the purpose of identification headings and underlinings have been inserted in this Agreement for the purpose of guidance only and are not part of this Agreement.

Commencement and Term

2. This Agreement commences on the Commencement Date and continues, subject to rights of early termination provided for in cl 9, for the respective term stipulated in Sch 4.

Licence

3. (1) The Company grants to the Licensee a licence with the right to grant sub-licences to use the Intellectual Property to

[*manufacture/market/distribute/use/exploit/sell*] the product within the Territory for the Term of this Agreement.

(2) The Company will furnish the Intellectual Property to the Licensee for the purposes of this Agreement in the manner and at the times stipulated in Sch 5.

(3) The Licensee will not use the Intellectual Property to manufacture, have made, use or market the product in any location other than the Territory nor will it use the Intellectual Property for any purpose other than that permitted by the Company under cl 3(1).

(4) Where the Company has indicated to the Licensee that the whole or any part or parts of the Intellectual Property comprises confidential material the Licensee will not at any time during the Term of this Agreement or after its termination or expiration disclose such confidential material to any person or corporation without obtaining prior written consent of the Company. The Licensee will take such steps as may be necessary to ensure that any of its servants or agents do not disclose such confidential material.

Licence Fees

4. (1) During the Term of this Agreement the Licensee must pay to the Company [*number*] per cent (GST exclusive) of the Net Sales Price of [*the product sold*] by the Licensee calculated at the end of each calendar quarter and payable within thirty (30) days of the end of the quarter by cheque made out to the Company.

(2) The Licensee must notify the Company with each quarterly payment of the licence fees of:
 (a) the number of Products manufactured and/or sold during the quarter;
 (b) the Net Sales Price of each of the products sold during the quarter;
 (c) the manner in which the Net Sales Price is calculated including discounts, transportation charges, purchasing costs, insurance and taxes;

and such notification must, if required by the Company, be certified as correct by the auditor of the Licensee or if the Licensee does not have an auditor, by a person approved by the Company for this purpose.

Maintenance and Inspection of Records

5. (1) The Licensee must maintain in sufficient detail for a period of seven (7) years in a manner approved by the Company separate and accurate records and accounts of:
    (a) the manufacture and sale of Products;
    (b) the Net Sales Price at which the Products are sold; and
    (c) any other information reasonably required by the Company relevant to the Products manufactured and sold and the determination of sales price.
   (2) The Licensee must permit an accountant or auditor of the Company from time to time during ordinary business hours to inspect and verify all or any records required to be maintained by the Licensee. The Licensee must give all assistance necessary to such accountant or auditor to carry out such inspection and verification and permit such accountant or auditor to take copies of any such records.
   (3) The obligations in this clause on the Licensee to account to the Company and maintain relevant records in respect of the licence fees must apply to any amounts due to the Company from the Licensee pursuant to the terms on which the Company provides his consent to a sub-licence under subcl 3(1) above.

Non-Grant, Revocation or Expiration of Protection for any of the Intellectual Property

6. If no exclusivity exists as a consequence of the refusal to grant or the subsequent invalidity, revocation or expiration of any of the Intellectual Property licensed under this Agreement in any country comprising a significant part of the Territory and the profitability of the Licensee is significantly and materially adversely affected with regard to the manufacture, use and sale of the product; then
    (1) the licence fees payable to the Company arising from the countries so affected is reduced by fifty percent (50%) effective from the decision of the court at first instance if no party has appealed to declare the relevant Intellectual Property valid or granting the relevant Intellectual Property; and/or

(2) the parties agree a lesser proportion of licence fees to be payable to the Company from such country or countries in the event that the Licensees demonstrate good and sufficient reason for such reduction.

Loss of Exclusivity

7. (1) The Company must not during the Term of licence permit any other person except itself to manufacture, have made, use and market the product in the Territory provided the Licensee pays the Company the minimum fees set forth in Sch 7 for any twelve (12) month period.
(2) In the event the Licensee fails to pay the Company the minimum fees referred to in cl 7(1) and the Licensee's rights under this Agreement have been converted into non-exclusive rights, the Licensee continues to be bound by each and every provision of this Agreement and must continue to pay the licence fee. When the Company appoints an additional Licensee of the Intellectual Property in respect of the product in the Territory, the Company must upon signing any related Licence Agreements provide a copy of the Licence Agreement to the Licensee. The Licensee has the right to elect by notice in writing to the Company that the licence fee from that date be calculated in the same manner as set out in that Licence Agreement.

Infringement

8. (1) (a) If the Licensee learns of:
    (i) any infringement or threatened infringement of the Intellectual Property rights licensed under this agreement; or
    (ii) any common law passing-off which may cause deception or confusion to the public by a third party,

the Licensee must immediately notify the Company in writing giving particulars of the infringement.

(b) The Company must then seek the opinion of Counsel practising in the relevant Territory in Intellectual Property Rights as to the possible success of any actions.

(c) The Company must promptly institute and prosecute an action against infringement unless there is little prospect of success as determined by Counsel.

(2) The proceeds from any judgment or settlement made by the Company in any action brought by it under subcl 8(1) must be used to reimburse the Licensee or its sub-licensees for all expenses incurred by it or them in assisting the Company in prosecuting the action. Also, the proceeds must be used to pay the Company's costs and expenses. The remainder of the proceeds must be shared by the Company and the Licensee equally.

(3) If the Company fails within ninety (90) days of receiving notice to institute and prosecute an action against any infringement of the Intellectual Property then the Licensee or its sub-licensees have the right, at the Licensee's expense, to institute and prosecute such actions in the Company's name.

(4) The proceeds from any judgment or settlement made by the Licensee or its sub-licensees in any action brought by the Licensee under subcl 8(3) must be used to reimburse the Company for all expenses incurred by it in assisting the Licensee or sub-licensee's costs and expenses incurred in such prosecution and the remainder is shared by the party that prosecuted the action and the Company equally.

(5) The Licensee and the Company must each execute all documents and do all things reasonably necessary to aid and cooperate in the prosecution of any such actions brought by a party under subcll 8(1) and 8(3).

Termination

9. (1) Termination of this Agreement can be made by either party by written notice to the other party if the other party commits any breach of any provision of this Agreement and has failed to remedy such breach within thirty (30) days of receipt of written notice requiring it to do so.

(2) The Company may by notice in writing terminate this Agreement in any of the following circumstances:
   (a) upon the happening of any of the following insolvency events:
      (i) the Licensee ceases to (or is unable to) pay its creditors (or any class of them) in the ordinary course of business, or announces its intention to do so;
      (ii) a receiver, receiver and manager, administrator, liquidator or similar officer is appointed to the Licensee or any of its assets;
      (iii) the Licensee enters into, or resolves to enter into, a scheme of arrangement, compromise or composition with any class of creditors;
      (iv) a resolution is passed or an application to a court is taken for the winding up, dissolution, official management or administration of the Licensee;
      (v) anything having a substantially similar effect to any of the events specified above happens under the law of any applicable jurisdiction;
   (b) the making by the Licensee of an assignment or attempted assignment for the benefit of its creditors;
   (c) in the event that the Licensee fails to make, sell, lease, hire or distribute the Product for a period of [*number*] months after the Commencement Date.
(3) Any termination of this Agreement pursuant to subcll 9(1) or 9(2) is without prejudice to the rights of the party terminating to seek and obtain damages for any breach of this Agreement by the other party.

Effect of Termination

10. On early termination of this Agreement under cl 9:
   (1) the Licensee must deliver to the Company all documents and other materials (including all copies) in its possession relating to the Intellectual Property and do such further things as may be reasonably required by the Company to protect its right, title and interest in the Intellectual Property.

(2) all licence fees previously paid remain the property of the Company and the Licensee can make no claim in respect of them. The Licensee must further pay to the Company any licence fee accrued but unpaid as at the date of the termination or expiration.

Secrecy Obligations

11. (1) The Licensee must:
    (a) keep confidential all information and technical data disclosed by the Company to the Licensee provided that the Licensee has the right to disclose such information to its employees insofar as it is necessary for them to know the information for the use of the licences granted in this Agreement; and
    (b) not use any of the Company's disclosures or other information or technical data, except for the purposes of the licences granted herein and on the terms of this Agreement.
 (2) Notwithstanding the provisions of subcl 11(1) the Licensee may disclose information if and to the extent that:
    (a) such disclosure is forced by laws, regulations or orders;
    (b) the information is generally available in the public domain except where that is a result of a disclosure in breach of this Agreement; and
    (c) the Licensee can prove that he or she knew the information before it was disclosed to him or her by the Company.

Company's Warranties

12. (1) The Company warrants that the use of any or all of the Intellectual Property according to the terms and conditions of this Agreement will not result in the infringements of proprietary rights of third parties.
 (2) The Company indemnifies the Licensee against any losses, costs, actions, claims, demands, expenses, judgments, court orders or other liabilities arising directly or indirectly out of or in connection with any claim made or threatened, whether by legal proceedings or otherwise, against the Licensee by a third party on

the grounds that by virtue of rights to which such third party lays claim, under letters patent or copyright (whether registered as a design or not) or any other similar right or claim including (but without limitation) rights arising from the disclosure under cover of confidence, such third party is entitled to prevent or interfere with the free use of any or all of the Intellectual Property by the Licensee pursuant to this Agreement. The Company also indemnifies the Licensee against any claim by the Licensee's customers in respect of any similar loss or injury and court fees and expenses of damages and costs and loss or injury suffered by compliance with an injunction ordered on the part of such customer.

Licensee's Indemnity

13. (1) The Licensee must promptly advise the Company in writing of any actions, suits, claims, demands, proceedings, losses, damages, compensation, sums of money, costs, charges and expenses which may be brought or claimed against the Licensee or the Company or in respect of which the Licensee or the Company may become liable arising out of the promotion, sale, supply or other use of the product by the Licensee, its servants or agents.
    (2) The Licensee indemnifies the Company against any actions, suits, claims, demands, proceedings, losses, damages, compensation, sums of money, costs (including solicitor and client costs), charges and expenses arising out of the promotion, sale, supply or other use of the product by the Licensee, its servants or agents. The defence of any litigation to which this clause applies is to be under the control of the Licensee, its solicitors and counsel, and all legal costs and expenses of any such litigation is borne by the Licensee. The Company, its solicitors and counsel may participate in such litigation at the expense of the Company.

General

14. (1) *Waiver.* Any waiver in regard to the performance of this Agreement operates only if in writing and applies only to the specified

instance, and must not affect the existence and continued applicability of the terms of it thereafter.

(2) *Entire Agreement.* This Agreement embodies all the terms binding between the parties and replaces all previous representations or proposals.

(3) *Assignment.*
 (a) the Licensee must not assign all or any of its rights in this Agreement without the prior written consent of the Company, which consent the Company may grant or not in its absolute discretion;
 (b) the Company may at its discretion assign all or any of its rights under this Agreement.

(4) *Applicable law.* This Agreement must be read and construed according to the laws of the State of [*Name of State*] and the parties submit to the jurisdiction of that State and the Commonwealth of Australia.

(5) *Amendments.* This Agreement may not be varied except in writing signed by the parties.

(6) *Severability.* If any provision of this Agreement is held by a court to be unlawful, invalid, unenforceable or in conflict with any rule of law, statute, ordinance or regulation it must be severed so that the validity and enforceability of the remaining provisions are not affected.

(7) *Notices.* All notices must be in writing and be given by any one of the following means:
 (a) by delivering it to the address of the party on a business day during normal business hours;
 (b) by sending it to the address of the party by registered post [*or if registered post is not available by ordinary post*] ;
 (c) by sending it by facsimile transmission to the facsimile number of the party.

(8) A notice is deemed to be given and received:
 (a) if given in accordance with subcl 14(7)(a) on the next business day after the day of delivery in the place of delivery;
 (b) if given in accordance with subcl 14(7)(b) five (5) clear business days after the day of posting in the place of delivery;
 (c) if given in accordance with subcl 14(7)(c) on receipt of a successful transmission sheet.

(9) The address and facsimile numbers referred to in subcl 14(7) (in the absence of notice to the contrary) are set out below:

The Company:	[*Name of Company*]
Address:	[*Address*]
Facsimile:	[*Facsimile Number*]
The Licensee:	[*Name of Licensee*]
Address:	[*Address*]
Facsimile:	[*Facsimile Number*]

(10) *Further agreements*. Each party must execute such agreements, deeds and documents and do or cause to be executed or done all such acts and things as necessary to give effect to this Agreement.

(11) (a) GST means a goods and services tax as defined in A New Tax System (Goods and Services) Act 1999.

(b) In respect of a taxable supply, the Licensee must pay to the Licensor an additional amount equal to the Licence Fees plus the prevailing GST rate. The additional amount referred to in this clause is payable at the same time and in the same manner as the Licence Fees made under cl 4.

(c) All stamp duties and governmental charges arising out of or incidental to this Agreement are the responsibility of and must be paid by the Licensee.

EXECUTED as an Agreement.

Executed by _____ [*Name of Company*] _____

_____   _____
Director   Director/Company Secretary

_____   _____
Name (please print)   Name (please print)

or

Sole Director and Sole Company Secretary

Name (please print)

Executed by _____ [*Name of Licensee*] _____

| Director | Director/Company Secretary |

Name (please print)   Name (please print)

or

Sole Director and Sole Company Secretary

Name (please print)

SCHEDULE 1

The Intellectual Property

SCHEDULE 2

The Product

SCHEDULE 3

The Territory

SCHEDULE 4

Term
- In respect of a patented invention, the life of any and all patents, divisions, continuations, continuation-in-part, supplemental disclosures and reissues of the patented inventions.
- In respect of Intellectual Property protected by registration, the Term of the registration.
- In respect of Intellectual Property protected as confidential, the period of time it remains outside the public domain.
- In respect of Intellectual Property protected by law which does not require registration, the period of time prescribed by law.
- The Company acknowledges that at the expiration of the period of protection in respect of each form of Intellectual Property licensed under this Agreement the Licensee is free to use the subject matter of the previously protected Intellectual Property for any purposes.

SCHEDULE 5

Manner in which the Intellectual Property is to be supplied

SCHEDULE 6

Information to be supplied with Licensee's statement

SCHEDULE 7

Minimum Royalty

APPENDIX B

DEED OF ASSIGNMENT OF INTELLECTUAL PROPERTY RIGHTS

BY:

___[Name of Assignor]___ of ___[Address]___

IN FAVOUR OF:

___[Name of Assignee]___ of ___[Address]___

Background

A. The Assignor owns certain Intellectual Property Rights in the Assigned IP.
B. The Assignor and the Assignee have agreed that any Intellectual Property Rights which are owned by or vested in the Assignor in the Assigned IP will be assigned by the Assignor to the Assignee pursuant to this Deed.

Operative Provisions

Definitions

In this Deed,

Assigned IP means All software, source code, development notes, manuals and instructional devices associated with products that are produced by or on behalf of the Assignor and/or marketed by or on behalf of the Assignor including any release, update variation, adaptation or related property.

Intellectual Property Rights means all past, present and future intellectual and industrial property rights conferred by statute, at common law or in equity and wherever existing, including:

patents, designs, copyright, rights in circuit layouts, plant breeder's rights, trade marks, know how, brand names, domain names, inventions, product names, trade secrets and any other rights subsisting in the results of intellectual effort in any field, whether or not registered or capable of registration;

any application or right to apply for registration of any of these rights;

any registration of any of those rights or any registration of any application referred to in paragraph (b); and

all renewals and extensions of these rights; and

Moral Rights has the meaning given to that term in section 189 the *Copyright Act 1968 (Cth)*.

Release means new software that has been developed primarily to provide an extension, alteration, improvement, enhancement or additional functionality to the existing software and that once provided to users forms part of the software.

Update means new software that has been produced primarily to overcome minor non-conformance of the software with any documentation provided to users detailing the functionality and performance specifications of any software or relating to the use of the software and that once provided to users forms part of the software.

Assignment of Intellectual Property Rights

The Assignor assigns, transfers and sets over to the Assignee:

any and all legal and beneficial rights, title and interest including all Intellectual Property Rights (whether presently existing or in the future) the Assignor may own, create or develop in relation to the Assigned IP with effect from the date of ownership, creation or development in each of the Assigned IP; and all other legal and beneficial rights, title and interest including all Intellectual Property Rights relating to any works or products commissioned by, created for or developed for the Assignee by or on behalf of the Assignor either prior to the date of this Deed or in the future.

Right to Sue

The Assignor assigns, transfers and sets over to the Assignee all rights and immunities relating to, or arising from, or to arise from any of the Intellectual Property Rights subsisting in each of the Assigned IP, including all present and past rights to sue for infringement of the Intellectual Property Rights in the Assigned IP.

Moral Rights

To the extent that Moral Rights subsist in the Assigned IP, the Assignor will procure that each creator who has Moral Rights in each of the relevant Assigned IP sign a copy of the annexed Moral Rights Deed Poll.

Further Acts

The Assignor hereby appoints the Assignee as the Assignor's attorney to do all acts and execute all documents on behalf of the Assignor to the extent necessary to vest the rights in the Assignee as contemplated by this Deed; and

The Assignor agrees to execute all such further documents and do all such further acts necessary to effect the assignment of the Intellectual Property Rights in each of the Assigned IP to the Assignee under clause 2.

Warranties

The Assignor warrants and it is a condition of this Deed that:

it has good legal and beneficial title to the Assigned IP prior to the assignment;

it has the right to make the assignment under clause 2;

no other person's consent is required in respect of the assignment of the Assigned IP; and the Intellectual Property Rights in the Assigned IP under this Deed will not infringe any third party's rights (including Intellectual Property Rights).

No Further Claims

The Assignor acknowledges that consequent upon execution of this Deed the Assignor has no further rights including Intellectual Property Rights or otherwise to ownership of the Assigned IP and that the Assignor has and will make no further claim of whatsoever nature for monetary compensation or otherwise in the future against the Assignee in relation to the creation of the Assigned IP or the past or future use of the Assigned IP by the Assignee.

Indemnity

The Assignor unconditionally and irrevocably indemnifies the Assignee on demand against any claim, loss, liability or expense which the Assignee incurs, pays, or is liable for, arising directly or indirectly from any breach, act or omission of the Assignor in respect of this Deed.

General

Further Assurances

A party, at its own expense and within a reasonable time of being requested by another party to do so, must do all things and execute all documents that are reasonably necessary to give full effect to this Deed.

Governing Law and Jurisdiction

This Deed is governed by and must be construed in accordance with the laws in force in the State of Queensland.

The parties submit to the exclusive jurisdiction of the courts of that State and the Commonwealth of Australia in respect of all matters arising out of or relating to this Deed, its performance or subject matter.

Counterparts

If this Deed consists of a number of signed counterparts, each is an original and all of the counterparts together constitute the same document.

EXECUTED as a Deed

DATE: _____ 20 _____

Executed by _____ [*Name of assignor*] _____

_____
Signature

_____
Witness

Executed by [*Name of company*] in accordance with section 127(1) of the Corporations Act 2001 (Cth):

_____   _____
Signature of Director/Secretary   Signature of Director

_____   _____
Name (please print)   Name (please print)

APPENDIX C

CONTRACTOR'S SERVICE AGREEMENT WITH CONFIDENTIALITY CLAUSE

THIS AGREEMENT is made the _____ day of _____, 20___

BETWEEN: [*Name of Company*] [*ACN if Corporation*] of [*Address*] ('the Company')

AND: [*Name of Contractor*] of [*Address*] ('the Contractor').

RECITALS

The Company has requested the Contractor to provide Services to the Company.

The Contractor has agreed to provide the Services to the Company upon and subject to the following terms and conditions.

NOW THE PARTIES AGREE as follows:

Interpretation

'Commencement Date' means the _____ day of _____, 20___.

'Confidential Information' includes, but is not limited to, matters not generally known outside the company, such as developments relating to existing and future products and services marketed or used or to be marketed or used, or rejected, by the company and persons or companies dealing with the company and also information relating to the general business operations with the company including:

profit and loss statements;

balance sheets;

customer/licensee/distributor lists (of actual and proposed customer/licensee/distributors);

cost and selling price information;

trade secrets, know-how and specifications in respect of the company's products;

business and marketing plans;

third party information disclosed to the company in confidence.

'Contractor's Fee' means the fees set out in Sch 1.
'Services' means the services set out in Sch 3.
'Premises' means the premises set out in Sch 2.

Commencement and Provision of Services

2. (1) Subject to any rights of early termination contained in cl 5, this Agreement commences from the Commencement Date and continues until either party terminates this Agreement by giving to the other party [*number of*] days prior notice in writing.

    (12) The Contractor must provide the Services at the Premises or such other place or places which the Company may from time to time authorise.

Remuneration

3. In consideration for the Contractor providing the services the Contractor must receive the Contractor's Fee.

Employees

4. (1) If any of the Services to be provided by the Contractor under this Agreement are to be carried out by an employee or employees

or sub-contractor or sub-contractors of the Contractor no such employee or sub-contractor has access to any document or thing related to the Services unless approved by the Company in writing. Once approval has been obtained there must be no variation to the consent unless such variation is agreed by the Company in writing.

(13) Under no circumstances must the Contractor use in the provision of the Services any sub-contractor or employee unless prior written consent of the Company has been obtained. A request for the Company's consent must be accompanied by an assignment executed by such sub-contractor or employee in the form of Annexure A to this Agreement.

Termination

5. Notwithstanding cl 2(1) this Agreement may be terminated if:
   (14) the other party commits a breach or is in default of any warranty of this Agreement; and
   (15) the defaulting party fails to correct such breach or default within [*number of*] days of receiving notice specifying such breach or default.

Warranties and Indemnities

6. (1) The Services must be provided by the Contractor in a proper and workmanlike manner and in compliance with the reasonable direction of the Company, to any applicable Company standards.
   (16) The Contractor warrants that no literary or other works employed or created by the Contractor in the provision of the Services infringe any copyright, obligation of confidentiality, patent or other right of property belonging to or benefiting any third party.
   (17) In the event that in the provision of the Services either warranties in subcll (1) and (2) is broken by the Contractor, the Contractor, upon requests being made by the Company, resupply the Services to remedy such breach and at no charge to the Company. Such remedy to the Company is without prejudice to any other right or remedy to which the Company may be entitled, whether at law, in equity or otherwise.

(18) The Contractor indemnifies the Company from and against any costs, damages, loss or liability of any kind (including legal costs and disbursements in defending or settling the claim giving rise to same) however suffered or incurred by the Company by virtue of the provision of the Services or any breach of this Agreement by the Contractor.

(19) The indemnity contained in subcl 6(4) extends (without limiting the generality of the foregoing) to any costs, damages, loss or liability (including legal costs and disbursements in defending or settling the claim giving rise to the same) incurred by the Company by virtue of any injury or disability suffered by any employee or sub-contractor of the Contractor, arising by whatever legal theory (whether statutory, tortious or otherwise).

Inventions and Copyright Works

7. (1) Subject to subcl 7(4) the Contractor assigns to the Company:
   (b) all inventions, discoveries and novel designs whether or not registrable as designs or patents including any invention of or development or improvements to equipment, technology, methods or techniques made by the Contractor solely or jointly with others ('the Inventions'); and
   (c) the entire copyright throughout the world in all writing, art works and other copyright works ('the Works');

created by the Contractor or any sub-contractor or employee of the Contractor during and pursuant to this Agreement (whether or not in normal business hours or using the premises, the Company's Premises or equipment).

(20) In addition to disclosing the Inventions or the Works the Contractor must disclose and, if required by the Company, assign to the Company any other Inventions, discoveries, designs or copyright works authored or created by the Contractor whilst engaged by the Company which relate to the future or present business or products of the Company and its related companies.

(21) The Contractor must both during and after the period of this Agreement do all such acts and things, and sign all such documents, as the Company or its attorneys may reasonably request to secure the Company's ownership or rights in the Inventions.

(22) The Contractor acknowledges that in the event that it makes a design as defined in the Designs Act 1906 during and arising out of its Service to the Company the design is owned by the Company.

(23) The assignment of the Contractor's copyright in the Works pursuant to subcl 7(1) must not restrict the Contractor's right to utilise the general expertise and knowledge accumulated by the Contractor in the performance of its duties for the Company. The Contractor is entitled to use routine procedures developed by it in the performance of its duties PROVIDED THAT the Contractor must not make any reproduction or substantial reproduction of any of the Works without the written licence of the Company.

Confidentiality

8. (1) The Contractor agrees that during the course of this Agreement it may become acquainted with or have access to Confidential Information. The Contractor during and after the term must maintain the confidential information and prevent its unauthorised disclosure to or use by any other person, firm or company, unless prior written authorisation is obtained.

(24) The Contractor agrees that it must not:
   (a) use the Confidential Information for any purpose other than for the benefit of the Company during or after the Term;
   (b) remove the Confidential Information from the Premises of the Company without the written consent of the Company;
   (c) for whatever reason, either for itself or any third party, appropriate, copy, memorise or in any manner reproduce any of the Confidential Information.

(25) The Contractor agrees to return any or all of the Confidential Information howsoever embodied on the request of the Company.

(26) The Contractor agrees that it must not, both during or after the Term for whatever reason, make improper use of the Confidential

Information acquired by virtue of this Agreement, to gain directly or indirectly, an advantage for itself or for any other person or to cause detriment to the Company.

(27) Nothing in this Agreement imposes an obligation on the Contractor with respect to maintaining confidence regarding information which is generally known or available by publication, commercial use or otherwise than as a result of a breach by the Contractor of its obligation in this section.

Relationship of Parties

9. The Contractor's relationship with the Company is that of independent Contractor. Neither the Contractor nor the Company has (nor may it represent that it has) any power, right or authority to bind the other, or to assume or create any obligation or responsibility, express or implied, on behalf of the other or in the other's name. Nothing stated in this Agreement must be construed as constituting the Contractor and the Company as partners, or as creating the relationship of employer and employee, master and servant or principal and agent between the parties.

Return of Documentation

Upon the term of this Agreement, for any reason, the Contractor must leave with the Company all records, books, drawings, note books and other documentation and things pertaining to the Works and the Inventions and to the Confidential Information, whether prepared by the Contractor or any other person, and any equipment, tools or devices owned by the Company then in the possession of the Contractor or employee or subcontractor of the Contractor.

General

11. (1) *Notices.* All notices and consents required or permitted to be given under this Agreement must be in writing and given by personal

service, pre-paid postage, a facsimile transmission at the addresses of the parties set out in this Agreement or to such other address as either party may designate to the other by written notice.

Assignment. Neither this Agreement nor any rights or obligations of the Agreement may be assigned or otherwise transferred by either party without the prior written permission of the other.

Governing law. This Agreement is governed by the laws of [*Name of State*] and the parties submit to the jurisdiction of the courts of that State and the Commonwealth of Australia.

Amendments. This Agreement may be amended only in writing signed by duly authorised persons for both parties.

Severability. If any provision of the Agreement should be held to be invalid in any way or unenforceable, the remaining provisions must not in any way be affected or impaired. This Agreement must be construed so as to most nearly give effect to the intent of the parties as it was originally executed.

SCHEDULE 1

The Contractor's Fee: _____[*set out fee*]._____

SCHEDULE 2

The Premises: _____[*Set out Premises*]._____

SCHEDULE 3

The Services: _____[*Set out Services*]._____

EXECUTED as an Agreement.

Executed by _____ [*Name of Company*] _____

_____   _____
Director   Director/Company Secretary

_____   _____
Name (please print)   Name (please print)

Or

_____
Sole Director and Sole Company Secretary

_____
Name (please print)

SIGNED SEALED AND   )
DELIVERED by [*Name of Contractor*]   )
in the presence of:)
                                                   _____
                                                   [*Signature of Contractor*]

_____
     [*Signature of Witness*]

APPENDIX D

CONFIDENTIALITY AGREEMENT

Between

(*insert name of disclosing party*)

("Disclosing Party")

and

(*insert name of recipient party*)

("Recipient Party")

This Agreement is made on (*insert date*) in the State of (*insert State*).

Parties to the Agreement:

1. (*Insert name of disclosing party*) of (*insert address of disclosing party*)
   ("Disclosing Party")

And

2. (*Insert name of disclosing party*) of (*insert address of disclosing party*)
   ("Recipient Party")

Background to the Agreement

A. The Disclosing Party possesses the Confidential Information. The Recipient Party wishes to have access to the Confidential Information for the Specified Purpose.
B. The Disclosing Party has agreed to disclose the Confidential Information to the Recipient Party subject to the terms and conditions of this Agreement.

The Parties Agree as Follows:

1 Access

The Recipient Party acknowledges that the Recipient Party may be given access to certain Confidential Information of the Disclosing Party for the Specified Purpose.

2 Obligation of Confidentiality

In consideration of the Disclosing Party allowing the Recipient Party to have access to the Confidential Information, the Recipient Party agrees that it will keep and will ensure that its employees keep confidential the Confidential Information unless and until the parties agree that the Confidential Information is in the public domain other than by a breach of this Agreement.

3 Duties of Recipient Party

3.1 *Non-Disclosure and Use*

The Recipient Party will not and will ensure that its employees do not:

disclose any of the Confidential Information to any other person without the prior written consent of the Disclosing Party; or

use all or any of the Confidential Information otherwise than for the Specified Purpose.

3.2 Uncertainty

If the Recipient Party is uncertain as to whether any information is Confidential Information, the Recipient Party will treat the information as if it were Confidential Information and as not being in the public domain unless and until the Disclosing Party agrees in writing that the information is in the public domain.

3.3 Precautions

The Recipient Party will take all reasonable precautions to maintain the confidentiality of and to prevent the disclosure or use of the Confidential Information.

3.4 Unauthorised Disclosure or Use

The Recipient Party will immediately notify the Disclosing Party of any unauthorised disclosure or use of the Confidential Information of which the Recipient Party becomes aware and will take all steps which the Disclosing Party may reasonably require in relation to such unauthorised disclosure or use.

3.5 Return of Confidential Information

At the conclusion of the Specified Purpose or upon the written request of the Disclosing Party, at its own expense, the Recipient Party will immediately deliver to the Disclosing Party all records and materials (and copies of those records and materials) containing or embodying the Confidential Information that are in the possession of the Recipient Party, its employees and any person to whom the Recipient Party has disclosed all or any of the Confidential Information (whether or not with the consent of the Disclosing Party).

4 Exceptions

The Recipient Party will not be bound to keep confidential any information if and to the extent that:
(a) the information is, or becomes part of the public domain otherwise than by breach of this Agreement by the Recipient Party;
(b) the information is lawfully obtained by the Recipient Party from another person without any restriction as to use and disclosure;
(c) the information was in the Recipient Party's possession prior to disclosure to it by the Disclosing Party;
(d) the information is required to be disclosed by the operation of any law, stock exchange, judicial or parliamentary body or governmental agency;
(e) the Disclosing Party has authorised in writing the disclosure of the information; or
(f) the information is disclosed by the Recipient Party to its professional advisers who have agreed to keep confidential the Confidential Information.

5 Remedy

The Recipient Party acknowledges and accepts that the Disclosing Party would suffer financial and other loss and damage if the Confidential Information were disclosed to any other person or used for any purpose other than the Specified Purpose and that monetary damages would be an insufficient remedy. The Recipient Party acknowledges and accepts that, in addition to any other remedy which may be available in law or equity, the Disclosing Party is entitled to injunctive relief to prevent a breach of this Agreement and to compel specific performance of this Agreement. The Recipient Party will immediately reimburse the Disclosing Party for all costs and expenses (including legal costs and disbursements on a full indemnity basis) incurred in enforcing the obligations of the Recipient Party under this Agreement.

6 Indemnity

6.1 *Indemnity for Costs*

The Recipient Party indemnifies the Disclosing Party against all costs, expenses, actions or claims directly or indirectly incurred or suffered by the Disclosing Party as a result of any breach of this Agreement by the Recipient Party.

6.2 *Scope of Indemnity*

The indemnity in clause 6.1 extends to and includes all costs, damages and expenses incurred by the Disclosing Party in defending and/or settling any such costs, expenses, actions, suits proceedings, claims or demands (including legal costs and disbursements on a full indemnity basis).

7 Cumulative Rights

The rights arising out of this Agreement do not exclude any other rights of either party.

8 Enforceability

8.1 *Effect of Ineffectiveness on Part of the Agreement*

Any clause or part of a clause of this Agreement which is Ineffective in any jurisdiction is Ineffective only to that extent in that jurisdiction.

8.2 *Severance of Ineffective Parts of the Agreement*

Where any clause or part of a clause is Ineffective it may be severed without affecting any other part of this Agreement.

9 Waiver

9.1 *No Waiver Except by Notice in Writing*

No right under this Agreement is waived or deemed to be waived except by notice in writing signed by the party waiving the right.

9.2 *No Waiver of Subsequent Breaches*

A waiver by one party under clause 9.1 does not prejudice its rights in respect of any subsequent breach of this Agreement by the other party.

9.3 *No Waiver by Extension or Forbearance*

A party does not waive its rights under this Agreement because it grants an extension or forbearance to the other party.

10 Variation

A variation of this Agreement will be in writing and signed by the parties.

11 Governing Law and Jurisdiction

11.1 *Governing Law*

This Agreement is governed by the laws of (*insert State*).

11.2 *Jurisdiction*

The parties irrevocably submit to the non-exclusive jurisdiction of the courts of (*insert State*).

12 Definitions

In this Agreement:

"Confidential Information" means all trade secrets, ideas, know-how, concepts and information whether in writing or otherwise relating in any way to the matters described in item 1 of the Schedule, and all other information relating to the Disclosing Party and its affairs or businesses, sales, marketing or promotional information, which is not in the public domain and includes any such information in the Disclosing Party's power, possession or control concerning or belonging to any other person;

"Ineffective" means void, illegal or unenforceable; and

"Specified Purpose" means the purpose set out in item 2 of the Schedule.

13 Execution Clauses

Executed as an Agreement by the parties

Signed for and on behalf of the Disclosing Party

By (*insert name*)

who warrants by his or her

signing that he or she has

authority to sign this

Agreement.

                                              Signature

In the presence of

Witness:

Name of Witness:

                                              (please print)

Signed for and on behalf of the Recipient Party

By (*insert name*)

who warrants by his or her

signing that he or she has

authority to sign this

Agreement.

_____
Signature

    in the presence of

    Witness: _____

    Name of Witness: _____

    (please print)

SCHEDULE

Item 1 — (*Describe subject matter of Confidentiality Obligation—Clauses 1 and 12*)

Item 2 — (*Insert purpose of disclosure—Clauses 1 and 12*)

APPENDIX E

FRANCHISE AGREEMENT

THIS AGREEMENT is made on _____ day of _____ 20__

BETWEEN ("the Franchisor");

AND The person or company named as such in Item 1 of **schedule 1** ("the Franchisee")

Recitals

A The Franchisor has exclusive rights to franchise the Business in the State of Queensland and Australia.
B The Franchisor is the licensee of Intellectual Property which is used in the operation of the Business.
C The Franchisor has developed a System for the operation of the Business.
D The Franchisor makes available to its the Franchisees initial and continuing information, experience, advice, guidance and know-how with respect to shop management, operation, financing, promotion and new developments.
E The Franchisee wishes to operate a Franchise for the Business in the Territory and for that purpose has requested the Franchisor to enter into this document.

F   The Franchisee acknowledges that it is essential to the maintenance and the success of the System that the Franchisee adheres to certain uniform standards, procedures and policies described in this document.

It is Agreed

1 Interpretation

Definitions

In this document:

"**Agreement**" means the franchise agreement recorded in this document.

"**Approved Premises**" means the premises from which the Franchisee conducts the Franchise which must be located, fitted out and maintained in accordance with the Manual.

"**Approved Products and Services**" means those products and services approved by the Franchisor from time-to-time for sale, lease, hire or provision by the Franchisee.

"**Approved Suppliers**" means those suppliers from whom the Franchisee must purchase the Approved Products as advised by the Franchisor from time-to-time.

"**Business**" means the business of under the name "Proactive Therapy" in accordance with the System whether carried out by the Franchisor, the Franchisees or all of them.

"**Business Name**" means the business name specified in item 13 of **schedule 1** or such other business name as may be nominated from time to time by the Franchisor.

"**Capacity**" means any capacity whatever and whether alone or together with any other person, company, firm, partnership, trust or statutory body and whether directly or indirectly and including, but without limiting the generality of this definition, any one or more of a promoter, shareholder, partner, joint venturer, agent, consultant, adviser, trustee, lender, supplier, licensor, creator, owner or part owner.

"**Commencement Date**" means the date referred to in item 3 of **schedule 1**.

"**Confidential Information**" means all information in any form or medium whatsoever disclosed by the Franchisor to the Franchisee in relation to the Business, the System and this Agreement including but without limiting the generality of this definition:

- information forming part of the System;
- information disclosed in this document;
- the Manual; and
- details of the Franchisor's employees, agents, contractors, subcontractors, franchisees and their activities and methods, the Franchisor's corporate or commercial structure, its activities, associations or affiliations, its financial arrangements (including pricing and profits), details of suppliers, customers (existing or potential) and their respective business undertaking and any information concerning any lease, license or other agreement to which it is a party; and
- the mode of operation of the Business, its advertising, publicity, trade secrets, technical information, product catalogues, price list, training manuals, sales promotion aids, business forms, accounting procedures, marketing reports, information bulletins, inventory systems, formulae, recipes, packaging information and quality control information.

"**Franchise**" means the Business carried on by the Franchisee pursuant to this document in the Territory.

"**Franchise Fee**" means the amount set out in item 5 of **schedule 1**.

"**Franchise Renewal Fee**" means the amount set out in item 7 of **schedule 1**.

"**Franchise Sale Fee**" means an amount equal to the Franchise Sale Price multiplied by the percentage set out in item 8 of **schedule 1**.

"**The Franchise Sale Price**" means in the event of a Transfer of the Franchise by the Franchisee (other than to the Franchisor) the consideration payable by the purchaser/transferee for the Franchise, the Franchisee's stock and the Franchisee's goodwill.

"**Franchise Service Fee**" means the amount referred to in item 4 of **schedule 1**.

"**The Franchisee**" means the Franchisee and where there is more than one each Franchisee shall be jointly and severally liable to the Franchisor. Where any Franchisee is an individual the expression includes his personal representatives and in the case of a corporation includes the successors of the corporation. Where any Franchisee is a partnership the expression includes the partnership as it is constituted at the date of this document and each of its members and also the successors of the partnership whether comprising the same or a different name and each of the members of the partnership or its successors as may be constituted from time to time. Where any Franchisee is or becomes a trustee (whether or not that fact is disclosed to the Franchisor) the expression includes the Franchisee in its personal capacity as well as its capacity as a trustee.

"**The Franchisor**" means the Franchisor, its assigns, successors and shall also include every present or future corporation which now or in the future shall be deemed to be related (within the meaning of Section 50 of the Corporations Act 2001) to the Franchisor.

"**Further Term**" means the period set out in item 17 of **schedule 1** commencing on the day after the expiration of the Term subject always to the provisions for termination set out in **clause 9**.

"**GST Amount**" means the goods and services tax paid or payable if any by the Franchisee in respect of supplies of Products and Services. The GST amount is calculated before allowance for any input tax credits available to the Franchisee.

"**Intellectual Property**" means all or any of the following:

- the Marks;
- present or future copyright held by the Franchisor in material, plans, designs, or other work relating to the System;
- know-how and systems used in the System and the Business; and
- present or future designs whether or not registered or protected by copyright derived or acquired by the Franchisor and applied in the System.

"**Manager**" means the person or person named as such in item 15 of **schedule 1**.

"**Management Fee**" means the amount set out in Item 5.1 of **schedule 1**.

"**Manual**" means the Franchisor's standard operating manuals as up-dated from time to time by the Franchisor which may be provided either electronically, in hard copy or published on the Business intranet or internet.

"**Marketing Fund Contributions**" means the contributions to be paid by the Franchisee to the Franchisor for the publicity of the Business pursuant to **clause 7.12** as described in item 11 of **schedule 1**.

"**Marks**" means the trade marks which are described in item 14 of **schedule 1** or any future trade mark applications made in respect of the Business and notified to the Franchisee.

"**Products**" means those products specified in the Manual for sale or supply in the Franchise and such further products as may be approved from time to time by the Franchisor and specified in the Manual.

"**Recruitment Fee**" means the amount set out in item 10 of **schedule 1**.

"**Restraint**" means the series of combinations achieved by matching the prohibition contained in **clause 7.11(a)(ii)** with each of the Restraint Periods and then combining each of those combinations with each of the Restraint Areas.

"**Restraint Areas**" means the areas set out in item 19 of **schedule 1**.

"**Restraint Periods**" means the periods commencing on the expiration of the Term or any Further Term or the date of earlier termination of the Agreement and ending at the expiration of the periods set out in item 20 of **schedule 1**.

"**Sale Price**" means the price at which the Franchisee wishes to Transfer the Franchise to the Transferee which, for the avoidance of doubt, includes any payment for the goodwill of the Franchise.

"**Services**" means those services specified in the Manual for provision in the Franchise and such further services as may be approved from time to time by the Franchisor and specified in the Manual.

"**System**" means the operation of the Business in accordance with the Manual and this document including the use of the Intellectual Property and any system, know-how, trade secrets, methods of operating, get up and image materials, methods of advertising, style and character of equipment, insurance, finance and funding arrangements and any other matters specified in the Manual.

"**Term**" means the period set out in item 2 of **schedule 1** commencing on the Commencement Date subject always to the provisions for termination set out in clause 9.

"**Territory**" means the area set out in item 21 of **schedule 1**.

"**Total Gross Revenue**" means all the revenue derived by the Franchisee from the Franchise whether from sales for cash, credit or exchange and irrespective of whether such money has been collected by the Franchisee but excluding any GST Amount and any revenue from the sale of telephone calls.

"**Training Fee**" means the amount set out in item 9 of the **schedule 1**.

"**Transfer**" includes, sell, assign, transfer, dispose of or otherwise create any legal or beneficial interest in or otherwise deal with the Franchise.

"**Transfer Conditions**" means the conditions upon which the Franchisee will Transfer the Franchised Business to the Transferee.

"**Transfer Fee**" shall be the amount set out in item 18 of **schedule 1**.

"**Transfer Notice**" means a written notice from the Franchisee to the Franchisor expressing an intention to Transfer the Franchise and offering to sell same to the Franchisor.

"**Transferee**" means an assignee or other transferee from the Franchisee of the Franchised Business or any part of it.

"**Warranty Fund Contributions**" means the contributions to be paid by the Franchisee to the Franchisor to cover warranty claims pursuant to **clause 7.14** as described in item 12 of **schedule 1**.

Construction

Unless expressed to the contrary:

(a) words importing:
  i. the singular include the plural and vice versa;
  ii. any gender include the other genders;
  iii. if a word or phrase is defined cognate words and phrases have corresponding definitions;
(b) a reference to:
  i. a person includes a firm, unincorporated association, corporation and a government or statutory body or authority;
  ii. a person includes its legal personal representatives, successors and assigns;
  iii. a statute, ordinance, code or other law includes regulations and other statutory instruments under it and consolidations, amendments, re-enactments or replacements of any of them;
  iv. a right includes a benefit, remedy, discretion, authority or power;
  v. an obligation includes a warranty or representation and a reference to a failure to observe or perform an obligation includes a breach of warranty or representation;

vi. provisions or terms of this document or another document, agreement, understanding or arrangement include a reference to both express and implied provisions and terms;
(c) time is to local time in Brisbane in Australia;
(d) "$" or "AUD$" is a reference to the lawful currency of Australia;
(e) this or any other document includes the document as varied or replaced and notwithstanding any change in the identity of the parties;
(f) writing includes any mode of representing or reproducing words in tangible and permanently visible form, and includes facsimile transmissions;
(g) any thing (including, without limitation, any amount) is a reference to the whole or any part of it and a reference to a group of things or persons is a reference to any one or more of them; and
(h) documents and records include electronic records and data.

Headings

Headings do not affect the interpretation of this document.

2 Grant and Term, Non-exclusivity, Franchise Fee and Lease

2.1 *Grant*

The Franchisor grants to the Franchisee and the Franchisee accepts from the Franchisor the exclusive license:

(a) to operate the Franchise within the Territory; and
(b) to use the System in connection with the Franchise

for the Term commencing on the Commencement Date and upon the conditions set out in this document.

2.2 *Exclusivity*

The rights granted in clause 2.1 are exclusive in respect of the Approved Products and the Franchisor may not grant similar rights to other Franchisees or operate outlets itself within the Territory. The Franchisee may sell Products and provide Services outside the Territory as part of a single sale to one customer provided that such sale includes the provision of Products and Services both in and outside the Territory and provided that the prior consent of the Franchisor has been obtained. The allocation of revenue from such sales and the proportion of the revenue therefrom which is to be included in the Franchisee's Total Gross Revenue shall be determined in accordance with the procedures set out in the Manual.

2.3 *Franchise Fee*

In consideration of rights granted in **clause 2.1** the Franchisee shall pay the Franchisor the non-refundable Franchise Fee when the Franchisor signs this document.

3 Intellectual Property and Confidentiality

3.1 *Intellectual Property*

The Franchisee acknowledges that the Intellectual Property is the exclusive property of the company who has licensed the Franchisor to use the Intellectual Property for the purposes of licensing franchisees to carry on Proactive Therapy franchises. The Franchisee shall during or after the Term:

(a) not do anything or aid or assist any other party to do anything which would infringe upon or harm the rights of the owners of the Intellectual Property and/or the Franchisor in the whole or any part of Intellectual Property;

(b) not contest the rights of the owners of the Intellectual Property or the Franchisor in the whole or any part of the Intellectual Property;

(c) notify the Franchisor of any suspected infringement of the Intellectual Property in the Territory and take such action as the Franchisor shall direct in relation to such infringement;

(d) not use any Mark, trademark or name other than as licensed in connection with the Franchise;

(e) not use the Intellectual Property except directly in the Franchise and in accordance with the terms of this document;
(f) compensate the owners of the Intellectual Property and the Franchisor for any use by the Franchisee of the Intellectual Property otherwise than in accordance with the terms of this document;
(g) indemnify the owners of the Intellectual Property and the Franchisor for any liability incurred to third parties for any use of the Intellectual Property other than in accordance with this document;
(h) use the Intellectual Property only during the Term and in respect of the Territory; and
(i) provide to the owners of the Intellectual Property and the Franchisor all necessary details of any discovery or improvement made by the Franchisee concerning the System and the Franchisee hereby assigns to the Franchisor its full right, title and interest including any copyright, design rights, patent rights, trade mark rights or other intellectual property rights in respect of any improvement or discovery and agrees to execute any documents necessary to give full effect to such assignment.

3.2 Business Names, the Marks and Other Trade Names

(a) The Franchisee shall operate, advertise and promote the Franchise under the Business Name and authorised Marks or other trade names as set out in the Manual and shall not use and allow the use of such names with any prefix or suffix or other words, terms, designs or symbols or in any modified form.
(b) Subject to **clause 3.2(a)** the Franchisee shall not without the prior consent of the Franchisor either during or after the Term, use or allow the use of the name "Proactive Therapy" or any similar name or any of the Intellectual Property in or as part of the firm or corporate name of the Franchisee and shall, upon the demand of the Franchisor at any time, promptly discontinue or require the discontinuance of the use of any such name or words (or any confusingly similar name or words) in its firm or corporate name, and shall promptly take such steps as may be necessary or appropriate in the opinion of the Franchisor to eliminate any such name or word from the Franchisee's firm or corporate name.

(c) The Franchisee acknowledges that its right to use the word "Proactive Therapy" as part of the Business Name is derived only in part from this document and agrees that upon the termination of the Agreement, for whatever reason, or at the earlier request of the Franchisor it shall cause the Business Name to be transferred at the Franchisor's direction to the Franchisor or a nominee of the Franchisor or alternatively cause the name to be de-registered at the Franchisor's request.

(d) The Franchisee irrevocably makes, nominates, constitutes and appoints the Franchisor to be the true and lawful attorney of the Franchisee for the purposes of effecting the provisions of **clause 3.2(c)** and to execute such documents or give such directions or authorities as it shall require in this regard.

(e) The Franchisee shall display its firm or corporate name at its premises and on its business stationery in such manner as is approved by the Franchisor.

(f) The Franchisee shall conduct the Franchise as an independent proprietor in the Franchisee's own name and as its own business. At all times during the conduct of the Franchised Business the Franchisee will when requested by the Franchisor:

(g) exhibit a conspicuous sign at any Approved Premises stating that the Franchisee is the proprietor of the Franchise which is operated under a Franchise from the Franchisor; and

(h) clearly indicate on all invoices, letters, cheques and other business papers and stationery of the Franchisee and that the Franchisee is the proprietor of a franchise within the Proactive Therapy Franchise Group. The particular franchise operated by the Franchisee is not to appear on such documents.

(i) The Franchisee acknowledges that during the Term the Franchisor may add to or modify the Business Name or Marks or other trade names to be used in conjunction with the Franchised Business and the Franchisee agrees to use any such new or modified names in conjunction with the Franchise subject to the limitations contained in this **clause 3**.

(j) For better securing the objects of this **clause 3**, the Franchisee shall enter into all such agreements and sign such documents and do such acts and things as may be required, including without limitation the execution of all documents in relation to the registration of the Franchisee as a registered sub-user of the Marks and the variation or cancellation of such registrations. The Franchisee shall pay the costs of registration of any document required to be registered to secure the objects of this **clause 3**.

3.3 *Display*

The Franchisee shall display in or about any Approved Premises, and on all vehicles, advertising material, stationery, invoices, uniforms and other items used in or about or in connection with the Franchise only such distinguishing marks, symbols, colours, logos, insignia, designs, trade names, trade marks and business names (including the Marks and the Business Name) as the Franchisor specifies in the Manual or may in its absolute discretion from time to time require and shall allow the Franchisor its officers servants or agents to enter its business premises at any time for the purpose of applying, altering, covering, obliterating or deleting any of the distinguishing features to comply with the Franchisor's requirements.

3.4 *Goodwill*

The Franchisee acknowledges the Franchisor is the owner of valuable goodwill in the System and in the Intellectual Property and that all goodwill which may arise from the Franchisee's use of the Intellectual Property or the System, or from this document, is and shall at all times remain the sole and exclusive property of the Franchisor and shall endure to the sole benefit of the Franchisor. Nothing contained in the preceding sentence shall be construed to prohibit the Franchisee from receiving for a sale of the Franchise made in compliance with this document a price greater than that paid by the Franchisee for the Franchise and/or which includes payment for any goodwill belonging to the Franchisee, subject to the payment of the Transfer Fee.

3.5 *Quality Control*

The Franchisee acknowledges that it is essential to the preservation of the System, and in particular to the Franchisor's interest in maintaining its connection in the course of trade with the Marks, that the Franchisor has control over the quality and methodology used in selling, renting, installing, servicing and maintaining the Products and providing the Services provided by the Franchisee under the Marks.

The Franchisee shall at all times strictly comply with the provisions as to quality control and methodologies contained in the Manual and in this document and shall not use the Marks in respect of the supply, installation service or maintenance of any Product or in the provision of any Service which is not approved by the Franchisor.

3.6 Confidential Information

(a) The Franchisee acknowledges that the Confidential Information is the valuable property of the Franchisor.
(b) The Franchisee agrees that both during and after the Term:
  i. it will not reveal the whole or any part of the Confidential Information to any other person, firm, or entity;
  ii. it will not use the whole or any part of the Confidential Information in connection with any business or venture in which it has a direct or indirect interest, whether as proprietor, partner, joint venture, shareholder, officer director or in any other capacity whatever other than in connection with the operation of the Franchise;
  iii. it will take reasonable steps to ensure that servants or agents of the Franchisee or partners of the Franchisee or, if the Franchisee is a corporation, the officers of the Franchisee, will also observe such requirements as to secrecy and, if required by the Franchisor, shall procure from each person nominated by the Franchisor from time-to-time a deed of confidentiality in the form set out in **schedule 2** or such other form as is approved by the Franchisor from time to time;
  iv. it will indemnify and hold harmless the Franchisor against any costs, losses, claims, demands, damages or expenses arising as a result of any disclosure or use of the Confidential Information in contravention of this document by any servant, agent, partner or officer of the Franchisee.
(c) The obligations under **clause 3.6(b)** will not apply with respect to any part of the Confidential Information which:
  i. at the time of disclosure is public knowledge; or

    ii. after disclosure is published or otherwise becomes public knowledge other than by the action of the Franchisee; or
    iii. was in its possession at the time of disclosure and was not acquired directly or indirectly from the Franchisor; or
    iv. is the subject of written notice from the Franchisor which expressly states that such Confidential Information is no longer to be kept confidential the onus of proving which shall lie with the Franchisee.
(d) The Franchisee shall properly and securely use, keep and store the Confidential Information in such a manner as will keep it confidential at all times.
(e) The Franchisee agrees that all documents containing or embodying the Confidential Information shall be and remain the property of the Franchisor and upon determination of this document shall:
    i. deliver up to the Franchisor all of the Confidential Information in material form (including any copies and any source or object code) which is in its power, possession, custody or control; and
    ii. erase all electronic databases and computer records comprising the Confidential Information and certify to the Franchisor that it has done so, PROVIDED THAT the return or erasure does not release the Franchisee from its obligations under this document.
(f) The Franchisor hereby agrees to maintain the confidential nature of all information provided by the Franchisee with respect to the operation of the Franchised Business including, but without limiting the generality of the foregoing, all information provided to the Franchisor pursuant to clause 5.7 hereof.
(g) The obligations contained in this **clause 3.6** shall survive the expiration or determination of this Agreement.

4 Continuing Obligations of the Franchisor

4.1 *Continuing Obligations*

The Franchisor agrees that it will perform the following continuing services for the benefit of the Franchisee:

(a) from time to time the Franchisor may, at its option, provide a training program or programs in or such other City as the Franchisor nominates to the Franchisee and such of its employees as the Franchisor may reasonably designate (including the Manager) and the Franchisee agrees to attend and cause all such designated employees to attend such training program or programs. All travel, lodging, meals and other living expenses, incurred by the Franchisee and such employees in attending such initial or subsequent program or programs shall be paid for by the Franchisee;

(b) The Franchisor agrees to make available to the Franchisee from time to time all improvements and additions to the System, to the same extent and in the same manner as they are made available to the Franchisor's franchisees generally;

(c) The Franchisor agrees to counsel and assist the Franchisee on a continuing basis with respect to the management and operation of the Franchise and to make available to the Franchisee the benefits of the Franchisor's information, experience, advice, guidance, and know-how in connection with the Business;

(d) The Franchisor shall provide the Franchisee with the Manual and any updates or amendments made from time to time.

5 Fees

5.1 *Franchise Fee*

Subject to the provisions of **clause 15.3** the Franchisee shall pay to the Franchisor the Franchisee Fee in consideration of the licenses referred to in clause 2.1 in the amount set out in item 5 of **schedule 1** in the manner provided for in item 6 of **schedule 1**. Subject to the provisions of Clause 15.3 the Franchisee shall pay to the Management Company the Management Fee as set out in Item 7 of Schedule 1 in the manner provided for in Item 8 of Schedule 1. Payments of the Franchise Fee and the Management Fee shall be effected by transfer of funds into a bank accounts (nominated by the Franchisor to the Franchisee in writing) and by the Management Company (nominated in writing by the Franchisor to the Franchisee) ("the Franchisor's bank account" and "the Management Company's bank account" respectively) in accordance with the terms hereof. Notwithstanding any agreement by the Franchisor or the Management Company to defer the payment of all or any part of the Franchise Fee or the Management Fee or to accept payment of the Franchise Fee or the Management Fee in installments upon the termination or expiration of this Agreement for any reason whatsoever any unpaid balance of the Franchise Fee or the Management Fee shall become due and payable on demand by the Franchisor or the Management Company.

5.2 Franchise Service Fees

Subject to the provisions of **clause 15.3** the Franchisee shall pay to the Franchisor the Franchise Service Fees set out in item 4 of **schedule 1**. This payment shall be effected by transfer of funds into the Franchisor's Bank Account within 2 days of the end of each week (measured from the commencement of the Term) during the Term and any Further Term or by such other method as the Franchisor may prescribe from time-to-time.

5.3 Franchise Renewal Fee

Subject to the provisions of **clause 15.3** if the Further Term is granted to the Franchisee the Franchisee must pay to the Franchisor the Franchise Renewal Fee in consideration of the granting of the Further Term. This payment shall be effected by the transfer of an amount equal to the Franchise Renewal Fee into the Franchisor's bank account within seven (7) days of the commencement of the Further Term.

5.4 Franchise Sale Fee

Subject to the provisions of **clause 15.3** if the Franchisee Transfers the Franchise (other than to the Franchisor) the Franchisee must pay to the Franchisor the Franchise Sale Fee. Payment of the Franchise Sale Fee shall be effected by the transfer of funds into the Franchisor's bank account before the completion of the Transfer of the Franchise. The Franchisee agrees that no transfer of the Franchise will be completed unless and until the Franchise Sale Fee has been paid.

5.5 Training Fee

Subject to the provisions of **clause 15.3** and in consideration for the training to be provided by the Franchisor to the Franchisee the Franchisee shall pay to the Franchisor the Training Fee on the day this Agreement is signed.

5.6 Recruitment Fee

Subject to the provisions of **clause 15.3** and in consideration for the time, cost and expense expended by the Franchisor in recruiting and selecting the Franchisee the Franchisee shall pay to the Franchisor the Recruitment Fee on the day this Agreement is signed.

5.7 Reports and Records

(a) The Franchisee shall submit to the Franchisor with and at the time payment of the Franchise Service Fees is made as required pursuant to **clause 5.3** a true, correct and complete statement of Total Gross Revenue, and Federal or State taxes paid, and all other information relating to the operation of the Franchise and this document as may be reasonably required by the Franchisor, on forms prescribed by the Franchisor, containing all information called for by such forms and certified correct by the Franchisee.

(b) Within 30 days after the close of the Franchisee's financial year the Franchisee shall at the request of the Franchisor furnish the Franchisor with a statement for the preceding year, on forms prescribed by the Franchisor, containing all the information requested on such forms, certified correct by the Franchisee and by a authorized public, certified or chartered accountant, showing the Total Gross Revenue and all revenue of the Franchise and all amounts due to the Franchisor under this Agreement for the preceding financial year as finally adjusted and reconciled after the closing and review of the Franchisee's books and records for such financial year.

(c) The Franchisee shall submit to the Franchisor within twenty one (21) days for the quarters ending 30 September, 31 December, 31 March and 30 June a performance report in the format prescribed by the

Franchisor detailing sales revenue, cost of products sold and services provided, expenses and wage costs for the quarter.

(d) All books and records shall be preserved for a period of not less than 5 years after the close of the Franchisee's financial year to which they relate and shall be open at all reasonable times to inspection and verification by the Franchisor or any or its representatives. The Franchisor shall be entitled at such reasonable times and at such reasonable intervals to access to all of the Franchisee's books and records and to have the Franchisee's books and records examined or audited at the Franchisee's expense and the Franchisee shall co-operate fully with the party or parties making such examination or audit on behalf of the Franchisor.

(e) Interest shall be payable by the Franchisee on any overdue amount at the rate then being charged by the Franchisor's bank (on the Franchisor's trading account) PLUS % per annum or such lesser rate as the Franchisor may prescribe from the date on which payment was due up to the date when payment is made.

(f) The Franchisee hereby authorizes the Franchisor to obtain from the Franchisee's suppliers and customers all information which those suppliers and customers have provided to the Franchisee or which they would or be compelled to supply to the Franchisee or to which the Franchisee would have access.

5.8 The Franchisee May Not Withhold Payments Due

The Franchisee agrees that he shall not have the right to withhold any payment or payments of any amounts due by reason of any goods purchased from the Franchisor, rents, if applicable, or any other amounts or sums due and owing to the Franchisor by reason of any set-off based on the grounds of any alleged non-performance by the Franchisor of any of its obligations.

6 Warranties and Guarantees

6.1 Exclusion of Warranties and Guarantees for Products Services

(a) The Franchisor makes no warranties or guarantees, expressed or implied to the Franchisee or its customers with respect to the Products or

Services, except as expressly set forth in this document. The Franchisee shall make no warranties or guarantees to its customers with respect to the Products or Services except as expressly set forth in this document or the Manual.

(b) Nothing contained in this document shall be taken to exclude restrict or modify or to purport to exclude restrict or modify the application of any enactment the exercise of any of the rights conferred by any such enactment or the liability of the Franchisor for breach of any warranty or condition implied by such enactment which is incapable of being excluded or modified.

7 Agreement by the Franchisee with Respect to Operation of Franchise Business

7.1 *Approved Products and Services*

(a) The Franchisee shall only offer for provision to the public the Approved Products and Services and other products and services specified in the Manual or approved by the Franchisor for sale or provision by the Franchisee from time-to-time.

(b) The Franchisee shall only purchase Approved Products for provision to the public from the Approved Suppliers.

(c) The Franchisee shall not and shall not allow the offer for sale or provision to the public of products or services other than Approved Products and Services without the prior written consent of the Franchisor.

7.2 *Pricing*

The Franchisor may recommend suggested prices for which its franchisees will provide the Products and Services to the public PROVIDED ALSO THAT the Franchisor may from time to time recommend suggested prices for particular Products or Services.

7.3 *Managerial Responsibility*

(a) The Franchisee shall appoint the Manager and subject to the provisions of this clause 7 at all times during the Term the Manager shall:

    i. devote his or her full time and effort to the active management and operation of the Franchise;
    ii. irrespective of any delegation of authority not inconsistent with clause 7.3(a)(i), reserve and exercise ultimate authority and responsibility with respect to the management and operation of the Franchise; and
    iii. represent and act on behalf of the Franchisee in all dealings with the Franchisor.
(b) In the event of the resignation, disability, incapacity or death of the Manager or in the event that the Manager is absent from the Business for a period in excess of 14 days (save for planned absences which the Franchisor has given prior approval) the Franchisee shall, as soon as possible, nominate an alternate Manager for approval by the Franchisor. In the event that the Franchisee makes no such nomination or the Franchisor (acting reasonably) does not approve an alternate Manager within 7 days after the resignation, disability, incapacity, death or absence of the original Manager then the Franchisor may, at the cost of the Franchisee appoint a person to be Manager on such reasonable terms as the Franchisor deems necessary. If no alternate Manager is approved or appointed within 21 days after the resignation, disability, incapacity, death or absence of the original Manager then the provisions of clause 8 shall apply.

7.4 Standards of Operation

The Franchisee will at all times give prompt, courteous and efficient service to the public and the Franchisee's customers and clients, will perform work competently and in a workmanlike manner and in all business dealings with members of the public and with clients will be governed by the highest standards of honesty, integrity, fair dealing and ethical conduct. The Franchisee will do nothing which would tend to discredit, dishonour, reflect adversely upon or in any manner injure the reputation of the Franchisor, the System, the Franchisee, or any of the Franchisor's other franchisees.

7.5 Liability for Loss or Damage

(a) The Franchisee shall be solely responsible for all loss or damage arising out of or relating to the operation of the Franchise or arising out of

the acts or omissions of the Franchisee or any of its agents, servants or contractors in connection with the sale, installation service or maintenance of Products or the provision of Services by the Franchisee and for all claims for damage to property or for injury or death of any persons directly or indirectly resulting from the provision of Services.
(b) The Franchisee shall indemnify and hold the Franchisor harmless against and from any and all claims, losses and damages referred to in **clause 7.5(a)**, including all costs and legal fees (on a solicitor and client basis).

7.6 Payment of Accounts

(a) The Franchisee shall pay all invoices rendered by the Franchisor in strict accordance with applicable payment and credit terms.
(b) Any amount not paid when due shall bear interest from the date when payment falls due at the rate referred to in **clause 5.7(e)** until paid, but the payment of such interest does not excuse any delay in payment of such invoices or other amounts.
(c) The Franchisee shall pay when due all accounts and other amounts owed to third parties whether or not under any purchasing arrangement in which the Franchisor may be involved. Under no circumstances shall the Franchisor become liable to any such third party by virtue of any failure of the Franchisee to make such payment.

7.7 Compliance with Laws

The Franchisee shall comply with all statutes, laws, ordinances, regulations, rules or orders of any governmental or quasi-governmental entity, body, agency, commission, board or official applicable to the Franchise. Nothing in this document shall prevent the Franchisee from engaging in a bona fide contest of the validity or applicability of any such laws in any manner permitted by law.

7.8 The Franchisee not Agent of the Franchisor

Nothing in this document shall create any relationship of partnership, joint venture, sub-contract, master and servant or employment between the parties and the Franchisee shall not act or attempt to act, or represent itself, directly or by implication, as an agent, partner, joint venturer, subcontractor, servant, employee or legal representative of the Franchisor or of any company related to the Franchisor or of any of the Franchisor's other Franchisees. The Franchisee shall not in any manner assume or create or attempt to assume or create any obligation on behalf of or in the name of the Franchisor or of any company related to the Franchisor or of any other franchisee of the Franchisor.

7.9 Incorporation of the Manual

All the provisions of the Manual (as amended or revised by the Franchisor from time to time) or any new edition of it are incorporated into and form part of this document as though fully set out in this document and in the event of any conflict between a provision of this document itself and a provision of the Manual this document itself shall prevail.

7.10 Right to Inspect

The Franchisor, through its authorised representatives, may at all reasonable times, visit the premises and residence of the Franchisee and any Approved Premises for the purpose of inspecting the merchandise and equipment on hand, use of Intellectual Property and advertising material, the nature and quality of Products and Services provided, examining and auditing the Franchisee's books and records and observing the manner and method of operating the Franchise. If any of the Franchisee's books, records or inventory are located outside any Approved Premises, the Franchisor shall have similar rights with regard to that other location. The Franchisee shall deliver all such items to the Approved Premises on demand by the Franchisor.

7.11 Non-competition

(a) The Franchisee covenants and agrees that it will not in any Capacity:
    i. during the Term and any Further Term of the Agreement; and

ii. during the Restraint Period and in respect of the Restraint Area, (except with the prior written consent of the Franchisor) carry on any business as a supplier of products or services advertised, promoted, marketed or provided by the Business during the Term or any Further Term or at the date upon which the Franchisee ceased to carry on the Franchised Business.
(b) The Restraints imposed by **clause 7.11(a)** are separate distinct and severable from each other so that the unenforceability of any Restraint shall in no way prejudice or affect the enforceability of the other Restraints.
(c) The Franchisee acknowledges that each of the Restraints is fair and reasonable and that the Franchisor has received full consideration for the Restraints, by the Franchisor agreeing to enter into this Agreement.
(d) This **clause 7.11** shall survive the expiration or termination of this Agreement.
(e) The Franchisee shall upon request of the Franchisor procure the execution of a deed in like terms to that set out in **schedule 3** from any director, shareholder, employee, agent or interested person nominated by the Franchisor.

7.12 *Marketing Fund*

Subject to the provisions of clause 15.3;

(a) The Franchisee shall pay to the Franchisor the Marketing Fund Contribution. The Franchisor shall maintain a separate ledger for each of its franchisee's contributions made in accordance with Franchise Agreements.
(b) The Franchisor shall be solely responsible for all advertising, marketing research, media production, and administration of the marketing fund, marketing and promotion of the Business in the Territory and shall expend the Marketing Fund solely on advertising and media costs, commissions and fees, consultancy fees as the Franchisor shall in its sole discretion deem appropriate, production costs and other costs (including salaries and wages) as a consequence of promoting and administering the Business.
(c) The Franchisor shall purchase and place from time to time advertising or enter commercial arrangements promoting the Business, the Products and the Services generally provided by the Business.

(d) All decisions regarding whether to authorise national, regional, or local advertising, or some combination thereof, and regarding selection of the particular media and advertising content, shall be within the sole discretion of the Franchisor and such agencies or others as it may appoint.
(e) The Franchisor may from time to time in its discretion supply promotional material to the Franchisee for use in promoting the Business in the Territory. The Franchisee shall not be obliged to use such material unless specified by the Franchisor. If it is used, it shall be used in the manner directed by the Franchisor at the cost of the Franchisee.

7.13 Approved Premises

The Franchisee agrees that any Approved Premises approved by the Franchisor shall be decorated, equipped and maintained in strict accordance with the relevant provisions contained in the Manual from time to time.

7.14 Warranty Fund

Subject to the provisions of clause 15.3;

(a) The Franchisee shall pay to the Franchisor the Warranty Fund Contribution. The Franchisor shall maintain a separate ledger for each of its franchisee's contributions to the warranty fund made in accordance with Franchise Agreements.
(b) The Franchisee shall be responsible for all warranty claims made in respect of goods or services provided by or procured by the Franchisee to customers of the Business.
(c) The Franchisor may apply all or part of the amount deposited into the warranty fund to fund the satisfaction of warranty claims which a franchisee fails or refuses to satisfy or which, for any other reason (including, without limitation, the death or illness of any Franchisee, Manager or employee of the Franchisee) to the reasonable satisfaction of the Franchisor. The Franchisee acknowledges that its contributions to the warranty fund may be used by the Franchisor to satisfy warranty claims made in respect of goods or services supplied by other franchisees of the Franchisor. The Franchisee acknowledges and agrees that nothing in the foregoing provisions of this clause shall operate so

as to relieve, excuse or temper the Franchisee's primary obligation to satisfy warranty claims in respect of products or services supplied by the Franchisee.

7.15 *Insurances*

Subject to any provision in any agreement between the Franchisor and the Franchisee to the contrary, the Franchisee agrees to obtain and maintain at the Franchisee's sole expense such insurance policies protecting the Franchise and other assets as are specified in the Manual (for such limits of liability as are from time to time specified in the Manual), including but not limited to:

(a) General third party liability (public risk) insurance;
(b) Professional indemnity insurance;
(c) Liability on account of accident or injury to employees and independent contractors;
(d) Property damage;
(e) Loss of income;
(f) Loss or theft of cash; and
(g) Key person coverage on the Manager.

The Franchisor shall be named as an additional insured in all such policies (worker's compensation excepted). Such policies of insurance shall expressly protect both the Franchisor and the Franchisee and shall require the insurer to defend both parties in any such action. The Franchisee shall furnish to the Franchisor a certificate with respect to each insurance policy, evidencing coverage as set out above in the names of both parties and providing that such policies shall not be cancelled, modified or amended except upon 10 days' prior written notice to the Franchisor. If the Franchisee fails to maintain insurance or to furnish the certificate the Franchisor may in addition to all other remedies it may have obtain such insurance and the Franchisee will reimburse promptly the Franchisor for any premiums paid by the Franchisor for such insurance. The Franchisor shall upon the due date for payment provide the Franchisor with a copy receipt for the payment of premiums due.

7.16 *Computer System*

(a) The Franchisee agrees that the Franchisor may at any time introduce certain computer or other electronic facilities into the System which facilities the Franchisee will be required to use in the Franchise. Without limiting the generality of the foregoing, the Franchisor may introduce:
   i. electronic cash registers;
   ii. direct debit system whereby amounts due by the Franchisee to the Franchisor are automatically debited to the Franchisee's bank account and credited to the Franchisor's bank account;
   iii. a system for the electronic transfer of customer's funds to the Franchisee's bank account;
   iv. a system for the transmission of data in either direction between the Franchisor and the Franchisee; and/or
   v. a business support system incorporating a centralised management and accounting function.
(b) The Franchisee shall co-operate with the Franchisor to implement any such facility and shall comply with the terms and conditions reasonably determined by the Franchisor in respect of the use of any such facility. Without limiting the generality of the foregoing, the Franchisor shall have access to the facility and the Franchisee shall not divulge to anyone the contents of any software program used in connection therewith. Any equipment used in connection with the facility shall be provided by the Franchisor in consideration of which the Franchisee shall pay to the Franchisor a fee to be reasonably determined by the Franchisor. The Franchisee shall be responsible for the costs of installing and maintaining any such equipment.

7.17 *Illness of the Franchisee*

If the Franchisee or the Manager becomes incapable or unable to conduct the Franchise through accident, ill-health or any other reason for a period in excess of 5 continuous working days or such longer period as the Franchisor may in its unfettered discretion select then the Franchisor (itself or through its agents) may at its option for such period as such incapability or inability continues but without prejudice to any right or remedy the Franchisor may have against the Franchisee pursuant to this document enter into and service the Franchise for and on behalf of and as the agent of the Franchisee to continue the efficient running of the Franchise during such absence of the Franchisee. The Franchisee shall pay to the Franchisor such reasonable fees prescribed by the Franchisor from time to time for so continuing to carry on the Franchise together with any travelling accommodation or sundry expenses.

7.18 *Airtime*

The Franchisee acknowledges and agrees that the percentage of airtime calls which it may offer to customers of the Business as discounts shall not exceed the percentage set out in item 23 of **schedule 1**. The Franchisee further agrees to comply with the requirements of the Manual with respect to issues concerning airtime.

7.19 *Commencement of Trade*

The Franchisee must commence the operation of the Business within 30 days of the date of this Agreement.

8 Transferability

8.1 *General*

Subject to the provisions of this document the Franchisee shall not make or allow any assignment of the Agreement or of any rights or interest under the Agreement. Any assignment of the Agreement made in contravention of this clause shall constitute a breach of the Agreement and shall be a basis for termination under clause 9.1, and shall confer no rights or interest whatever under the Agreement upon any other party. Each of the following shall be deemed to be an assignment of the Agreement:

(a) any sale, transfer, mortgage, pledge, assignment or relinquishment or any rights conferred on the Franchisee by this document;

(b) the passing by operation of law to any other party or parties of the Franchisee's interest in this Agreement or any part of this Agreement;
(c) if the Franchisee is a corporation:
   i. any change in or appointment of directors of the Franchisee PROVIDED THAT where:
      A. despite such change or appointment the directors as at the date of this Agreement would continue to exercise not less than 51% of the voting power of the Board of Directors of the Franchisee; and
      B. The Franchisor agrees by notice in writing that it does not reasonably consider such change or appointment contrary to its interests, then such change or appointment shall not be deemed an assignment of the Agreement; and
   ii. any allotment of shares or approval of transfer of shares in the Franchisee unless the Franchisor agrees by notice in writing that it does not reasonably consider such allotment or approval of transfer reasonably contrary to its interests, in which case such allotment or approval of transfer of shares shall not be deemed an assignment of the Agreement;
(d) if the Franchisee is a partnership, any change in the members of such partnership: or
(e) if the Franchisee purports to declare or acknowledge that all or any part of the assets of the Franchise are held upon trust for another party.

8.2 Sale of Franchise

(a) If at any time the Franchisee wishes to Transfer the Franchise or any part of it, the Franchisee shall first give a Transfer Notice to the Franchisor.
(b) The Transfer Notice shall state:
   i. the Transfer Conditions;
   ii. the Sale Price;
   iii. the name of the proposed Transferee; and
   iv. that if the Franchisor does not give a notice in writing to the Franchisee ("**Acquisition Notice**") within 14 days from receipt of the Transfer Notice the Franchisor shall be deemed to have declined to acquire the Franchise.

(c) If the Franchisor gives an Acquisition Notice:
   i. The Franchisee shall be bound to Transfer the Franchise to the Franchisor; and
   ii. The Franchisor shall be bound to pay the Sale Price in accordance with such of the terms of the Transfer Conditions as shall be applicable.
(d) Upon the Transfer by the Franchisee of any part of the Franchise the rights of the Franchisee insofar as they relate to the Franchise so disposed of shall terminate without prejudice to the existing and/or continuing obligations of the Franchisee.
(e) If within 14 days of receipt of the Transfer Notice the Franchisor has not given to the Franchisee an Acquisition Notice, the Franchisee shall be free within 90 days of the date of the Transfer Notice to Transfer the Franchise or any part of it at a price equal to or greater than the Sale Price on the same terms as the Transfer Conditions to the proposed transferee and upon the Franchisor consenting to the assignment of the Agreement pursuant to **clause 8.3**. If the Franchise is not Transferred within that 90 day period all preceding provision of this clause shall again become applicable.

8.3 *Transfer of Franchise*

Subject to the Franchisor not having exercised its rights under **clause 8.2** to take a Transfer of the Franchise, the Franchisee shall not Transfer, assign, charge or otherwise deal with the Franchise, its assets or the Agreement in any way without the prior written consent of the Franchisor, which consent shall not be unreasonably withheld PROVIDED THAT:

(a) The Franchisee shall first notify the Franchisor in writing of such proposed sale, assignment, transfer or other action, setting forth in detail:
   i. the nature of the item, interest or share to be sold, assigned, transferred, or otherwise acted upon;
   ii. the name and address of the proposed Transferee or party acquiring any such item, interest or share; and
   iii. the consideration, if any;
(b) the proposed Transferee is a respectable, competent and financially responsible person and possesses the business experience and capability,

credit standing and financial resources necessary to successfully operate the Franchise in accordance with the terms of this document. If the proposed Transferee is a corporation or partnership the provision of the preceding sentence shall apply to the individuals who are to own the shares in such corporation or constitute the members of such partnership. The onus of proving such things to the satisfaction of the Franchisor shall be on The Franchisee. The Franchisee shall cooperate with the Franchisor in making available such information as the Franchisor may require to make the above determinations;

(c) the person who is to be substituted for the Manager shall have been approved by the Franchisor and shall have successfully completed the training course then in effect for The Franchisor's franchisees. Upon completion of the assignment the Agreement shall be deemed amended by the insertion of the name of such person in item 15 of **schedule 1**;

(d) The Franchisee shall pay to the Franchisor all moneys due to the Franchisee up to the date of such assignment, pursuant to the Agreement;

(e) there is not any existing unremedied breach of the terms, covenants, conditions and restrictions on the part of the Franchisee contained in this document (except in circumstances where **clause 8.4** applies);

(f) the proposed Transferee covenants by deed with the Franchisor to observe, perform and fulfill the terms, covenants, conditions and restrictions on the part of the Franchisee expressed or implied in this document. Such deed or deeds shall be prepared by the Franchisor's solicitors at the expense of the Franchisee. The Franchisor may, in its absolute discretion, require the Transferee to enter into a franchise agreement for the balance of the Term or Further Term on the same terms, covenants, conditions and restrictions as this document or on the same terms, covenants, conditions and restrictions contained in the then standard Franchise agreement of the Franchisor. At the time the Franchisor advises the Franchisee that its consent is given to an assignment, the Franchisor shall advise the Franchisee which of the abovenamed documents the Transferee shall be required to enter into;

(g) if the Transferee is a corporation, its directors and shareholders thereof shall execute and deliver to the Franchisor a joint and several guarantee, in a form acceptable to the Franchisor, of the performance by the corporation of its obligations under this Agreement;

(h) in the case of any party who is to acquire an interest or shareholding in the Franchisee in the event that the Franchisee is a corporation or partnership, such party shall execute and deliver to the Franchisor a guarantee and covenant in the form set out in **schedule 4**;

(i) The Franchisee shall have executed and delivered to the Franchisor a general release in a form acceptable to the Franchisor of any and all claims and cause of action against the Franchisor and, its officers, agents and employees;

(j) The Franchisee shall pay the Franchisor all the Franchisor's reasonable costs incidental to the sale of the Franchise and the Transfer Fee.

(k) the proposed Transferee enter into a Power of Attorney as specified under **clause 3.2(d)**;

(l) Deeds of confidentiality and deeds of restraint in the forms set out in **schedule 2** and **3** respectively or such other forms as the Franchisor may require be entered into by such persons on behalf of the proposed Transferee as the Franchisor may require;

(m) The Franchisee shall have made to the proposed Transferee not less than 7 days prior to the execution of the contract of sale or the agreement referred to in **clause 8.3(f)** (whichever is the earlier) full disclosure of financial information pertaining to the Franchise including (but not limited to) copies of the three preceding financial year's trading/profit and loss statements (or as applicable) of the Franchise including the accountant's or auditor's reports, as the case may be, in respect of each year's statements;

(n) representative of the proposed Transferee and it's proposed manager successfully complete all requirements of the Franchisor with respect to training and the payment of any training fees.

8.4 *Assignability by the Franchisor*

(a) Subject to **clause 8.4(b)**, the Agreement may be assigned by the Franchisor or by any successor, to any corporation which may succeed to the business of the Franchisor or of such successor whether by purchase of assets or shares or upon merger, reconstruction or amalgamation.

(b) If the Franchisor wishes to sell, assign or otherwise dispose of the whole of its interest under this Agreement, the Franchisor must give the Franchisee not less than 2 months notice in writing of the Franchisor's intentions, in order to give the Franchisee an opportunity to negotiate with the Franchisor with a view to disposing of the

Franchisee's interests in the Agreement, as part of such sale, transfer or assignment. Nothing contained in this **clause 8.4(b)** shall prevent the Franchisor from proceeding with such sale, transfer or assignment irrespective of whether or not such negotiations can be concluded provided that the Franchisor has negotiated with the Franchisee in good faith and provided further that the person to whom the Franchisor sells, transfers or assigns is bound by the same obligations as those which bind the Franchisor under this Agreement. This subclause shall not apply to any assignment by the Franchisor to any master or area franchisee of the Franchisor.

9 Default and Termination

9.1 *Termination*

(a) If the Franchisee
   i. fails to make any payment of money owed to the Franchisor when due under this or any other arrangement made between the Franchisor and the Franchisee;
   ii. fails to submit to the Franchisor when due any report required by this document;
   iii. fails to commence business when agreed;
   iv. fails to comply strictly with the provision of the Agreement as to quality control; or
   v. fails to make any payment of money owed to a supplier,
   vi. fails to satisfy the Franchisor's requirements as to training; and
   such default (where capable of doing so) is not remedied within 14 days after the Franchisor giving written notice of such default to the Franchisee then the Franchisor may terminate the Agreement at any time by giving written notice of such termination to the Franchisee.
(b) Subject to **clause 9.1(c)** if the Franchisee fails to perform any obligation imposed upon the Franchisee by the Agreement, other than those referred to in **clause 9.1(a)** and such default it not remedied within 14 days after the Franchisor gives written notice of such default to the Franchisee, then the Franchisor may terminate the Agreement at any time by giving notice of such termination to the Franchisee.

(c) If the default under **clause 9.1(b)** is of such nature that it is not capable of being remedied with reasonable diligence by the Franchisee within the 14 day period specified then the Agreement shall not be terminated by the Franchisor if:
  i. The Franchisee can show that it has commenced immediately upon receipt of such notice, to exercise reasonable diligence to remedy such default;
  ii. The Franchisee continues to be diligently engaged in remedying such default upon the expiration of the 14 day period; and
  iii. the remedying of the default is completed as soon after the 14 day period is reasonably practicable.
(d) If:
  i. The Franchisee has been given written notice of default by the Franchisor three times within any period of twelve consecutive months pursuant to **clauses 9.1(a)** or **(b)** (or both); and
  ii. in each of such prior instances the Franchisee has cured the default within the time permitted, then if the Franchisee again fails within the twelve month period to perform any obligation referred to in **clauses 9.1(a)** or **(b)** (or both) the Franchisor may at any time after the default terminate the Agreement by notice in writing to the Franchisee forthwith without giving prior notice of the default and without affording the Franchisee any period in which to remedy the default.

9.2 Automatic Termination

(a) Notwithstanding any other rights the Franchisor has at law or in equity the Franchisor may terminate this Agreement by notice in writing to the Franchisee immediately upon the occurrence of any of the following events:
  i. any wilful and material falsification by the Franchisee of any report, statement, or other written data furnished to the Franchisor;
  ii. any wilful and repeated deception of the Franchisor, other franchisees or customers by the Franchisee relating to the source, nature or quality of the Services;
  iii. any attempted or purported assignment of the Agreement in contravention of **clause 8**;

iv. if any execution is levied against any assets of the Franchisee or if any assets of the Franchisee are taken or sold by an encumbrancer or if the Franchisee ceases to carry on the Franchise or fails to make payment to any creditors when such payments are due;

v. if the Franchisee (being a corporation) grants an equitable or floating charge over the whole or any part of the Franchisee without the prior written consent of the Franchisor, which consent cannot unreasonably be withheld if such charge serves a fixed advance or advances from time to time for the ordinary commercial purposes of carrying on the Franchise;

vi. if the Franchisee:
   A. being a corporation goes into liquidation otherwise than for the purpose of reconstruction or a meeting is called for the purpose of considering liquidation or a provisional liquidator is appointed;
   B. has a receiver or a receiver and manager appointed over any of its property;
   C. proposes or enters into any scheme or arrangement or a composition with its creditors; or
   D. being a corporation has an official manager, administrator, inspector or similar external administrator appointed pursuant to the provisions of the Corporations Law or such similar law in the Territory; or
   E. suffers any event similar to that described above (but which may be differently described in the Territory);

vii. The Franchisee violates any law, ordinance, rule or regulation of any governmental authority in connection with the operation of the Franchise and does not correct such violation within 7 days after receipt of notification thereof from any source unless there is a bona fide dispute as to the violation or status of such law, rule or regulation and the Franchisee contests the fact of the violation, law, rule or regulation within 7 days of notification of the violation by commencing the appropriate court or administrative proceedings;

viii. The Franchisee ceases or threatens to cease to carry on its business or a substantial part of it or fails to maintain normal and continuous operation of the Franchise for a period of 7 days;

ix. breaches or fails to comply with any obligation in this document dealing with confidentiality, the protection of Intellectual Property, Confidential Information or non-competition; or

x. makes any Transfer which the Franchisor reasonably considers (whether before or after the Transfer takes effect) to be against the best interests of the Franchisor.

(b) If the Franchisor does not elect to exercise its right to terminate the Agreement pursuant to this **clause 9.2(a)(iii)**:
   i. such inaction shall not be deemed to constitute a consent to such assignment described in **clause 9.2(a)(iii)** nor to confer any rights of interest whatever upon the purported assignee; and
   ii. the Agreement shall remain binding and in full force and effect as between the Franchisor and the Franchisee unless and until the Franchisor elects to terminate the Agreement.

(c) Any act or omission described in **clauses 9.2(a)(i)** and **(ii)** above shall be conclusively deemed to be wilful and repeated if it occurs after written notice from the Franchisor to cease and desist but nothing in this provision shall be construed to mean that acts or omissions described in said clauses may not be considered to be wilful and repeated in the absence of such notice from the Franchisor.

(d) Any notice of termination given by the Franchisor pursuant to this **clause 9.2** shall be fully effective and the Agreement shall be terminated:
   i. notwithstanding that the Franchisee may have ceased engaging in, or may not at the time of such notice be engaged in, any of the acts which give rise to such notice;
   ii. notwithstanding, that the Franchisee may have taken steps to counteract the effects of any such acts;
   iii. without any requirement on the part of the Franchisor to conduct a detailed enquiry into the circumstances giving rise to the event or events of default; and
   iv. without the need to comply with **clause 12** provided that there is no legitimate dispute as to the interpretation of the meaning of the events referred to in **clause 9.2** or factors giving rise to such events.

9.3 Obligations Upon and After Termination

(a) Upon termination of the Agreement whether by lapse of time, by termination pursuant to any provision of this clause, by mutual consent of the parties, by operation of law or in any other manner, the Franchisee shall cease to be an authorised franchisee of the Franchisor as to any Services whatever and the Franchisee and all persons directly or indirectly having any interest or shares in the Franchisee or in any way associated with or related to the Franchisee shall:

i. within 7 days of the date of termination or expiration of the Agreement cause the Franchisee to pay the Franchisor all liquidated or ascertainable sums owing from the Franchisee to the Franchisor without set-off or other diminution on account of unliquidated claims;

ii. within 7 days of the date of termination or expiration of the Agreement pay all the Franchisee's trade and other creditors which are unpaid;

iii. immediately and permanently discontinue the use of the Intellectual Property, or any marks, names or indicia which in the opinion of the Franchisor are confusingly similar thereto or any other materials which may in any way indicate or tend to indicate that the Franchisee is or was an authorised franchisee of the Franchisor or is or was in any way associated with the Franchisor;

iv. promptly surrender to the Franchisor the Manual and all copies of the Manual, all stationery, letterheads, forms, printed matter, promotional displays and advertising containing any of the Intellectual Property or other things the use of which is prohibited by **clause 9.3(c)**, including any Confidential Information (which shall be dealt with strictly in accordance with **clause 3.6(e)**);

v. immediately and permanently discontinue all advertising placed by the Franchisee as an authorised franchisee of the Franchisor or which contains or makes reference to any of the marks, names, indicia or other things the use of which is prohibited by **clause 9.3(c)** and cancel all such advertising already placed or contracted for which would otherwise be published, broadcast, displayed or disseminated after the date of termination or expiration of the Agreement;

vi. immediately and permanently discontinue any use of the word and logo's "Proactive Therapy" or any words which are confusingly similar in the Franchisee's firm name, corporate name, or trade name and take such steps as may be necessary to appropriate in the opinion of the Franchisor to change such names to eliminate the words "Proactive" and "Therapy" or any words which are confusingly similar including the execution of such documents as may be required under **clause 3.2**;

vii. refrain from doing anything which would (directly or indirectly) indicate that the Franchisee is or was an authorised franchisee of the Franchisor or is or was in any way associated with the Franchisor; and

viii. do all such things including executing any documents required to give effect to any assignment of Franchises to the Franchisor or any third party nominated by the Franchisor; and

ix. pay all amounts (if any) owing in respect of the Franchise.

9.4 General Provisions Regarding Termination

(a) Termination of the Agreement under any circumstances shall not abrogate, impair, release, or extinguish any debt, obligation or liability of the Franchisee to the Franchisor which may have accrued under this Agreement including without limitation any debt, obligation or liability which was the cause of termination or arose out of such cause.

(b) All covenants and agreements of the Franchisee which by their terms or by reasonable implication are to be performed in whole or in part after the termination of the Agreement shall survive termination.

(c) Upon termination or expiration of this Agreement, the Franchisor shall have the right (exercisable by written notice to the Franchisee) to purchase all or part of the Franchisee's physical assets used in the Franchise. The purchase price for such assets shall be the fair market value and in the event that the Franchisor and the Franchisee cannot agree on the purchase price for the assets which the Franchisor wishes to purchase pursuant to this **clause 9.4(c)**, the value shall be determined by an independent registered valuer appointed by the President from time to time of the Law Society of Queensland and his or her decision shall be final and binding and there shall be no appeal from that decision. The cost of such valuation shall be borne equally by the parties. The Franchisor shall be entitled to set off against the purchase price for the assets any amounts then owed by the Franchisee to the Franchisor.

(d) For the purposes of this Agreement any act or omission by any director officer or shareholder of any Franchisee shall be deemed to be an act or omission of the Franchisee notwithstanding that such director, officer or shareholder may have at the relevant time been acting (or refraining from acting) in a capacity other than as a director, officer or shareholder of the Franchisee.

9.5 Termination for failure to meet training requirements

In the event that this Agreement is terminated because the Franchisee has failed to meet the Franchisor's training requirements then;

(a) the Training Fee shall be forfeited to the Franchisor;
(b) the Franchisee shall pay to the Franchisor on demand all costs incurred by the Franchisor for goods or services purchased for use in the Franchise which cannot be reasonable put to use in another franchise;
(c) all other fees paid to the Franchisor by the Franchisee shall be refunded save for an amount equal to 10% of all such fees which shall be retained by the Franchisor.

10 Further Term

10.1 *Notice*

On or before the date 6 months prior to the expiration of the Term, time which shall be of the essence, the Franchisee shall notify the Franchisor in writing whether the Franchisee wishes to continue the Franchise for the Further Term.

10.2 *Grounds for Refusal or Imposition of Special Conditions*

(a) The Franchisor with good cause may refuse to grant the Further Term or impose in addition to the terms of this document special conditions on the granting of the Further Term. If the Franchisor refuses to grant the Further Term or imposes any special conditions the Franchisor shall give written details of the nature of the grounds of refusal or of such special conditions and in the case of the special conditions the time period within which such special conditions must be met (if applicable).

(b) For the purposes of **clause 10.2(a)** "good cause" includes by way of illustration, but without limitation, any of the following:
  i. the failure by the Franchisee through act or omission to achieve and maintain those standards reasonably or usually required by the Franchisor to authorise the provision of Services or to preserve the goodwill of the Franchisor's indicia and the System;
  ii. repeated late payment of sums due by the Franchisee to the Franchisor;
  iii. failure to devote sufficient time to the Franchise;
  iv. poor relationships with other franchisees or customers;
  v. poor control over employees;
  vi. failure to promote the Business;
  vii. repeated breach of the terms of this Agreement which may have been grounds for termination of the Agreement if repeated or if not cured within any time period allowed; and
  viii. failure by the Franchisee to adhere to the Manual, and includes conduct by the Franchisee which would not necessarily constitute grounds for termination of the Agreement pursuant to **clause 9**.
(c) The "special conditions" which The Franchisor may impose pursuant to **clause 10** include, by way of illustration but without limitation, such conditions which are necessary to provide for changes in the Franchise which the Franchisor reasonably requires to maximise the sale of Products and the provision of the Services by the Franchisee and to preserve the goodwill of the Franchisor in the Marks and the System.

10.3 Conditions of Further Term

Upon the commencement date of the Further Term if granted to the Franchisee, the Franchisee shall:

(a) enter into the Franchisor's then current franchise agreement (including such special conditions as may be required by the Franchisor pursuant to **clause 10.2**);
(b) execute any other documentation the Franchisor then requires its franchisees generally to enter into;
(c) execute the Franchisor's then current general release pursuant to which the Franchisee shall release the Franchisor from all claims which the

Franchisee may have against the Franchisor at the commencement date of the Further Term and

(d) procure the execution of deeds of guarantee and indemnity, non-competition and confidentiality by such interested persons as the Franchisor may nominate (acting reasonably).

10.4 Sale of Franchise

If the Franchisor notifies the Franchisee that the Further Term will not be granted or that the Further Term will be granted only upon the Franchisee's compliance with special conditions, the Franchisee may at its option, sell its interest in the Franchise and the Franchisor shall grant the Transferee a licence to operate the Franchise for a term the same as the Further Term subject to:

(a) the Franchisee not then being in default of this Agreement;
(b) the Franchisee satisfying the terms of **clause 8**;
(c) the Transferee complying with such special conditions as are notified to the Franchisee by the Franchisor;
(d) the Transferee entering into the Franchisor's then current Franchise Agreement and any other documentation which the Franchisor then requires to be executed by a the Franchisee of the Business;
(e) The Franchisee executing the Franchisor's then current general release document pursuant to which the Franchisee shall release the Franchisor from all claims which the Franchisee may have against the Franchisor; and
(f) The Franchisee securing the payment to the Franchisor by the Transferee of a franchise fee being equal to that customarily charged to the Franchisor's franchisees at or about the time of such sale by one payment on the commencement date of the new franchise agreement.

11 Standard of Conduct

The Franchisee acknowledges that the Agreement accords with general franchise business practice and that its provisions are only those which are reasonably necessary for the protection of the legitimate business interests of the parties, the Business and the System.

12 Dispute Resolution

12.1 *Procedure*

(a) The parties will comply with the following dispute resolution procedure:
   i. Where a dispute arises between the Franchisor and the Franchisee (**"Parties"**), the complainant will set out in writing the nature of the dispute.
   ii. Both Parties will make every effort to resolve the dispute by mutual negotiation. In doing so, each party agrees to use its best endeavors to:
   iii. clearly communicate the background facts leading to or causing the dispute;
   iv. set out clearly what action is required to settle the dispute;
   v. select a way of resolving the dispute and explain why that way of resolving the dispute can be said to be a fair resolution of the dispute; and
   vi. discuss specific means of avoiding such disputes arising in the future.
(b) In the event that the Parties are unable to reach a resolution of the dispute, either Party may by notice in writing advise the other Party that it seeks to have the dispute resolved by conciliation.
(c) Within 21 days, the Parties may refer the matter to a mutually agreed conciliator. In the event that no agreement can be reached on an appropriate conciliator, the dispute will be referred to a conciliation or mediator (**"Conciliator"**) nominated by the President from time to time of the Law Society of Queensland.
(d) The Conciliator will have the right to determine procedures and may or may not allow the appearance of lawyers on behalf of the Parties and may co-opt other expert assistance.
(e) The Conciliator is to be satisfied that both Parties have made a determined and genuine effort to resolve the dispute and have co-operated with the Conciliator.
(f) Proceedings of the Conciliator will be as informal as is consistent with the proper conduct of the matter and shall allow the Conciliator to communicate privately with the Parties or with their lawyers.

(g) The Parties to the conciliation will agree that:
   i. everything that occurs before the Conciliator will be in confidence and in closed session and held in Brisbane or at such other location as the Franchisor sees fit.
   ii. all discussions will be without prejudice; and
   iii. no documents brought into existence specifically for the purpose of conciliation process will be called into evidence in any subsequent litigation by either Party.
(h) It will be the role of the Conciliator to act fairly, in good faith and without bias with the purpose of seeking a resolution of the dispute and will treat all matters in confidence.
(i) Each Party will have the opportunity to adequately present their case.
(j) The Conciliator will have regard to the fairness and reasonableness of any matters pertaining to a dispute and the need for The Franchisor to maintain the integrity of the Business and the System.
(k) The Conciliator will deal with any matter as expeditiously as possible but not later than 14 days after referral to the Conciliator.
(l) The Parties to the conciliation will bear the conciliation costs on an equal basis and grant immunity from liability to the Conciliator.
(m) The Parties will report back to the Conciliator within 14 days on actions taken, based on the outcome of the Conciliation.

12.2 Injunctive Relief

Nothing contained in the dispute resolution procedures above will deny any party the right to seek injunctive relief from an appropriate court, where failure to obtain such relief would cause irreparable damage to the party concerned or the Business or System. Further, such dispute resolution procedures will not apply to events giving rise to the immediate termination of the Agreement under clause 9.2, where there is not legitimate dispute as to the interpretation of their meaning or factors giving rise to such events.

13 Guarantee

If the Franchisee is a corporation or if the Franchisee consists of more than 1 person and one or more of them is a corporation, the directors and shareholders of such corporation existing as at the date of this document, their spouses and any additional director or shareholder of the Franchisee subsequently appointed and any other interested person nominated by the Franchisor (acting reasonably) shall forthwith execute a Deed of Guarantee and Indemnity in favor of the Franchisor against any default by the Franchisee under this document and in the form of **schedule 4**, or in such other form as the Franchisor may require from time to time.

14 Notices

14.1 *General*

A notice, demand, certification, process or other communication relating to this document shall be written in English and may be given by an authorised representative of the sender.

14.2 *Method of Service*

In addition to any other lawful means, a communication may be given by:

(a) being personally served on a party;
(b) being left at the party's current address for service;
(c) facsimile to the party's current number for service;
(d) email to the party's current email address.

14.3 *Address for Service*

The particulars for service are initially those set out in item 16 of **Schedule 1**.

14.4 *Service*

If a communication is given by facsimile or email and the sender's machine does not produce a report or message indicating that the transmission was unsuccessful, the absence of such report will be prima facie evidence that the facsimile or email (as the case may be) was received by the addressee.

15 Miscellaneous

15.1 *Stamp Duty*

The Franchisee shall, as between the parties, indemnify the Franchisor in respect of all stamp duty (including any fine or penalty except where it arises from default by the other party) on or relating to this document and any document executed under it.

15.2 *Legal Costs*

The Franchisee shall pay to the franchisor on demand all reasonable legal costs incurred by the Franchisee in the preparation, negotiation and execution of this Agreement and any other agreement or deed relating to the Franchise. The Franchisee shall also pay all costs incurred by the Franchisor arising out of or in any way connected with any breach by the Franchisee of any of the terms or conditions set out in this Agreement.

15.3 *Goods and Services Tax*

(a) All Fees and Contributions referred to in Schedule 1 ("Fees") and any other monies payable pursuant to or by virtue of this document ("amounts payable") are expressed and have been calculated exclusive of Goods and Services Tax ("GST"). All Fees and amounts payable shall be the relevant Fee and/or amount payable increased by an amount equal to the full amount of GST payable by the Franchisor in respect of any Fee or amount payable.
(b) Each party confirms that it is agreed and it is their intent and the intent of this document that the Franchise Service Fee and the Marketing Fund Contributions and the Warranty Fund Contributions be determined on the GST exclusive value of Total Gross Revenue.
(c) Each party confirms that it is agreed and it is their intent and the intent of this document that GST should have no effect on the profitability of either the Franchisor or the Franchisee.

15.4 *Amendment*

This document may only be varied or replaced by a document duly executed by the parties.

15.5 Further Assurance

Each party shall promptly execute all documents and do all things that any other party from time to time reasonably requires of it to effect, perfect or complete the provisions of this document and any transaction contemplated by it.

15.6 Computation of Time

Where time is to be reckoned by reference to a day or event, that day or the day of that event shall be excluded.

15.7 Governing Law and Jurisdiction

This document is governed by and is to be construed in accordance with the laws in force in *[Jurisdiction]*

Each party irrevocably and unconditionally submits to the non-exclusive jurisdiction of the courts of *[Jurisdiction]* and any courts which have jurisdiction to hear appeals from any of those courts and waives any right to object to any proceedings being brought in those courts.

15.8 Joint and Several Liability

An obligation of two or more persons binds them jointly and severally.

15.9 Entire Understanding

(a) This document embodies the entire understanding and agreement between the parties as to the subject matter of this document.
(b) All previous negotiations, understandings, representations, warranties, memoranda or commitments in relation to, or in any way affecting, the subject matter of this document are merged in and superseded by this document and shall be of no force or effect whatever and no party shall be liable to any other party in respect of those matters.

(c) No oral explanation or information provided by any party to another shall:
   i. affect the meaning or interpretation of this document, or
   ii. constitute any collateral agreement, warranty or understanding between any of the parties.

16 Future Regulation

The parties agree that if during the term of the agreement either:

(a) any applicable legislation is enacted prescribing further requirements for or otherwise affecting the agreement; or
(b) a relevant authority publishes or issues a statement or statements of further requirements governing franchises or franchise agreements;

and the effect of same in the reasonable opinion of the Franchisor would be that non-compliance would render or be likely to render the Agreement invalid, voidable or unenforceable, then the parties shall forthwith amend the Agreement (and shall sign all documents as may be necessary to effect such amendment) so far as is necessary in the reasonable opinion of the Franchisor or its solicitors to avoid the Agreement being invalid, voidable or unenforceable.

The **COMMON SEAL** is affixed)
in accordance with its constitution)
in the presence of:)
)

_____

Secretary/Director

_____

Name of Secretary/Director (print)

SIGNED for and on behalf of)
and is affixed in accordance with)
its constitution in the presence of:)
)

_____ _____
Secretary/Director   Secretary/Director

_____ _____
Name of Secretary/Director   Name of Secretary/Director
(print)   (print)

Schedule 1

1	Franchisee:
2	Term:
3	Commencement Date:
4	Franchise Service Fee:
5	Franchise Fee:
5.1	Management Fee
6	Manner of payment of Franchise Fee
7	Franchise Renewal Fee:
8	Franchise Sale Fee:
9	Training Fee:
10	Recruitment Fee:
11	Marketing Fund Contributions
12	Warranty Fund Contribution
13	Business Name:
14	Marks:
15	The Manager:
16	Address for Notices:

Franchisor
- Address
- Facsimile
- Email

Franchisee
- Address
- Facsimile
- Email

Guarantor
- Address
- Facsimile
- Email

17	Further Term:
18	Transfer Fee:
19	Restraint Areas:
20	Restraint Periods:
21	Territory:
22	Approved Premises:

Schedule 2

Deed of Confidentiality

THIS DEED is made on

BETWEEN ("**the Franchisor**");

AND and the person(s) named in item 1 of the **schedule** annexed to this schedule 2 of the address set forth in item 2 of the **schedule** ("**the Covenantor(s)**")

Recitals

A The Franchisee and the Franchisor are parties to a franchise agreement executed on the date set out in item 3 of the **schedule** ("**Agreement**").
B Pursuant to the Agreement, the Franchisor will make available to the Franchisee Confidential Information.
C The Franchisor wishes to maintain the confidentiality of the Confidential Information and, under the terms of the Agreement the Franchisee is entitled to require that certain persons execute a deed in the terms of this Deed.
D The Franchisee and the Franchisor require the Covenantor to enter into this Deed and the Covenantor has agreed to do so.

It is Agreed

Operative Provisions

1 Definitions

In this document (including the recitals):

"**Business**" means the business of the sale, rental, installation, service and maintenance of telecommunications hardware and software (and other products approved by the Franchisor for sale from time-to-time) under the name "_____" in accordance with the System whether carried out by the Franchisor, the Franchisor's principal, the Franchisee or its other franchisees, or all of them.

"**Confidential Information**" means all information in any form or medium whatsoever disclosed by the Franchisor to the Franchisee in relation to the Business, the System and this Agreement including but without limiting the generality of this definition:

(a) information forming part of the System;
(b) information disclosed in the Agreement;
(c) the Manual; and
(d) details of the Franchisor's employees, agents, contractors, subcontractors, franchisees, master franchisors, its corporate or commercial structure, its activities, associations or affiliations, its financial arrangements (including pricing and profits), details of suppliers, customers (existing or potential) and their respective business undertaking and any information concerning all lease, license or other agreement to which it is a party; and
(e) the mode of operation of the Business, its advertising, publicity, trade secrets, technical information, product catalogues, price list, training manuals, sales promotion aids, business forms, accounting procedures, marketing reports, information bulletins, inventory systems, formulae, know-how and methods, packaging information and quality control information.

"**Franchise**" means the Business carried on by the Franchisee pursuant to the Agreement.

"**The Franchisee**" means the party set out in item 4 of the **schedule**.

"**System**" means the operation of the Business in accordance with manual supplied under the Agreement and in accordance with the Agreement.

2 Confidential Information

(a) The Covenantor acknowledges that the Confidential Information is the valuable property of the Franchisor.
(b) The Covenantor agrees that:
   (i) it will not reveal the whole or any part of the Confidential Information to any other person, firm, or entity; and

(ii) it will not use the whole or any part of the Confidential Information in connection with any business or venture in which it has a direct or indirect interest, whether as proprietor, partner, joint venture, shareholder, officer, director or in any other capacity whatever other than in connection with the operation of the Franchise.

(c) The obligations under **clause 2(b)** will not apply with respect to any part of the Confidential Information which:
  (i) at the time of disclosure is public knowledge; or
  (ii) after disclosure is published or otherwise becomes public knowledge other than by the action of the Franchisee; or
  (iii) was in his possession at the time of disclosure and was not acquired directly or indirectly from the Franchisor; or
  (iv) is the subject of written notice from the Franchisor which expressly states that such confidential information is no longer to be kept confidential; or
  (v) has been disclosed to a franchisee for the purposes of a Franchise Agreement (subject to the franchisee complying with all requirements as to confidentiality as may be required by the Franchisor. The onus of proving which shall lie with the Covenantor.

(d) The Covenantor shall properly and securely use, handle, keep and store the Confidential Information in such a manner as will keep it confidential at all times;

(e) The Covenantor agrees that all documents containing or embodying the Confidential Information shall be and remains the property of the Franchisor and at any time upon notice the Covenantor shall:
  (i) deliver up to the Franchisor all of the Confidential Information in material form (including any copies and any source or object code) which is in its power, possession, custody or control; and
  (ii) erase all electronic databases and computer records comprising the Confidential Information and certify to the Franchisor that it has done so

PROVIDED THAT the return or erasure does not release the Covenantor from its obligations under this Deed.

3 Miscellaneous

3.1 Stamp Duty

The Franchisee shall, as between the parties, be liable for and duly pay all stamp duty (including any fine or penalty except where it arises from default by the other party) on or relating to this document and any document executed under it.

3.2 Legal Costs

Subject to any express provision in this document to the contrary, each party shall bear its own legal and other costs and expenses relating directly or indirectly to the preparation of, and performance of its obligations under this document.

3.3 Amendment

This document may only be varied or replaced by a document duly executed by the parties.

3.4 Further Assurance

Each party shall promptly execute all documents and do all things that any other party from time to time reasonably requires of it to effect, perfect or complete the provisions of this document and any transaction contemplated by it.

3.5 Computation of Time

Where time is to be reckoned by reference to a day or event, that day or the day of that event shall be excluded.

3.6 Governing Law and Jurisdiction

(a) This document is governed by and is to be construed in accordance with the laws in force in Queensland.
(b) Each party irrevocably and unconditionally submits to the non-exclusive jurisdiction of the courts of Queensland and any courts which have jurisdiction to hear appeals from any of those courts and waives any right to object to any proceedings being brought in those courts.

3.7 Joint and Several Liability

An obligation of two or more persons binds them jointly and severally.

3.8 Entire Understanding

(a) This document and the documents specifically incorporated into it embodies the entire understanding and agreement between the parties as to the subject matter of this document.
(b) All previous negotiations, understandings, representations, warranties, memoranda or commitments in relation to, or in any way affecting, the subject matter of this document are merged in and superseded by this document and shall be of no force or effect whatever and no party shall be liable to any other party in respect of those matters.
(c) No oral explanation or information provided by any party to another shall:
   (i) affect the meaning or interpretation of this document, or
   (ii) constitute any collateral agreement, warranty or understanding between any of the parties.

Schedule

Item 1   Name of Covenantor:
Item 2   Address of Covenantor:
Item 3   Date of execution of Agreement:
Item 4   Name of the Franchisee:

EXECUTED as a deed.

The **COMMON SEAL** of is affixed in accordance with its constitution in the presence of:)
)
)

_____

Secretary/Director

_____

Name of Secretary/Director (print)

SIGNED SEALED AND DELIVERED

by

in the presence of:

Schedule 3

Deed of Non-competition

THIS DEED is made on   20__

BETWEEN   ("**the Franchisor**");

AND   and the person(s) named in item 1 of the **schedule** annexed to this schedule 3 of the address set forth in item 2 of the **schedule** ("**the Covenantor(s)**")

Recital

A The Franchisor has entered into a franchise agreement (the "**Agreement**") with the Franchisee executed on the date set forth in item 3 of the **schedule**.
B Pursuant to the terms of the Agreement, the Franchisee is entitled to require that various persons nominated by the Franchisor from time to time execute a deed in the terms of this Deed.
C The Franchisor and the Franchisee require the Covenantor to enter into this Deed and the Covenantor has agreed to do so.

It is Agreed

Operative Provisions

1 Definitions

In this Deed:

"**Capacity**" means any capacity whatever and whether alone or together with any other person, company, firm, partnership, trust or statutory body and whether directly or indirectly and including without derogating from the generality of the foregoing any one or more of a promoter, shareholder, partner, joint venturer, agent, consultant, adviser, trustee, lender, supplier, licensor, creator, owner or part owner.

"**The Franchisee**" means the party set forth in item 4 of the **schedule**.

"**Restraint Area**" means each of the areas set out in item 5 of the **schedule**.

"**Restraint Period**" means each of the periods commencing on the date that the Agreement is terminated or expires (for any reason whatsoever) or the Covenantor's association with the Franchisee terminates (whichever is the earlier) and ending at the expiration of each of the periods set out in item 6 of the **schedule**.

2 Covenantor's Covenants

2.1   The Covenantor covenants and agrees that he or she will not in any Capacity during the Restraint Period and in respect of the Restraint Area (except with the prior written consent of the Franchisor) carry on or be in any way involved with a business dealing in products sold or supplied by the Franchisee or its franchisees or goods or services of the nature sold or supplied by the Franchisee during the term of the Agreement.

2.2   **Clause 2.1** shall be construed and have effect as if it were a number of clauses resulting from the combination of the prohibition contained in **clause 2.1** with each Restraint Period and combining each such combination with each Restraint Area (the "**Restraints**"). The Restraints will be regarded as separate distinct and severable from each other so that the unenforceability of any Restraint shall in no way prejudice or affect the enforceability of any of the other restraints.

2.3   The Covenantor acknowledges that each of the Restraints is both fair and reasonable.

3 Miscellaneous

3.1 *Stamp Duty*

The Franchisee shall, as between the parties, be liable for and duly pay all stamp duty (including any fine or penalty except where it arises from default by the other party) on or relating to this document and any document executed under it.

3.2 Legal Costs

Subject to any express provision in this document to the contrary, each party shall bear its own legal and other costs and expenses relating directly or indirectly to the preparation of, and performance of its obligations under this document.

3.3 Amendment

This document may only be varied or replaced by a document duly executed by the parties.

3.4 Further Assurance

Each party shall promptly execute all documents and do all things that any other party from time to time reasonably requires of it to effect, perfect or complete the provisions of this document and any transaction contemplated by it.

3.5 Computation of Time

Where time is to be reckoned by reference to a day or event, that day or the day of that event shall be excluded.

3.6 Governing Law and Jurisdiction

(a) This document is governed by and is to be construed in accordance with the laws in force in _____

(b) Each party irrevocably and unconditionally submits to the non-exclusive jurisdiction of the courts of _____ and any courts which have jurisdiction to hear appeals from any of those courts and waives any right to object to any proceedings being brought in those courts.

3.7 Joint and Several Liability

An obligation of two or more persons binds them jointly and severally.

3.8 Entire Understanding

(a) This document embodies the entire understanding and agreement between the parties as to the subject matter of this document.
(b) All previous negotiations, understandings, representations, warranties, memoranda or commitments in relation to, or in any way affecting, the subject matter of this document are merged in and superseded by this document and shall be of no force or effect whatever and no party shall be liable to any other party in respect of those matters.
(c) No oral explanation or information provided by any party to another shall:
   (i) affect the meaning or interpretation of this document, or
   (ii) constitute any collateral agreement, warranty or understanding between any of the parties.

Schedule

Item 1 Name of Covenantor(s):
Item 2 Address of Covenantor(s):
Item 3 Date of execution of the Agreement:
Item 4 Name of the Franchisee
Item 5 Restraint Area: The Territory

The Territory plus an of _____ klm around the boundaries of the Territory

The Territory plus an area of _____ klm around the boundaries of the Territory

The Territory plus an area of _____ klm around the Territory

The Territory plus an area of _____ klm around the Territory

The City of _____

The State of _____

Item 6 Restraint Period:
2 years
18 months

12 months
6 months
3 months

EXECUTED as a Deed.

The **COMMON SEAL** of is affixed in accordance)
with its constitution in the presence of:)
)

_____

Secretary/Director

_____

Name of Secretary/Director (print)

SIGNED SEALED AND DELIVERED

by

in the presence of:

Schedule 4

Guarantee and Indemnity

TO:

of

WE, the undersigned Directors of *XXX* (hereinafter called "**the Franchisee**") **IN CONSIDERATION** of you entering into a Franchise agreement (hereinafter called the "**Agreement**") to which this form of Guarantee and Covenant is the annexure at our request **HEREBY COVENANT** jointly and severally for ourselves and our respective Executors and Administrators with you and your successors and assigns as follows:

1. We **HEREBY GUARANTEE** the performance and observance of the terms and conditions in the agreement contained and on the part of the Franchisee to be performed and observed and we hereby specifically agree and declare that this Guarantee shall be a continuing guarantee and shall in no way be avoided released or affected and shall remain in full force and effect notwithstanding any time or indulgence given or allowed to the Franchisee by you or any variation of the Agreement irrespective of whether we have consented to or received notice of any such time indulgence or variation.
2. We **HEREBY INDEMNIFY** you against all losses costs and expenses or otherwise (including but not limited to any legal costs and disbursements on a solicitor and own client basis) which may be incurred by you by reason of any default on the part of the Franchisee in the performance and observance of the agreements and conditions on the Franchisee's part contained in the Agreement.
3. This Guarantee shall be enforceable against us by you notwithstanding any action that you may take against the Franchisee in pursuance of your rights under the Agreement.
4. You may at any time grant to the Franchisee any time or indulgence and may compound or compromise with or release the Franchisee without releasing discharging or affecting the liability of us under this

Guarantee irrespective of whether we have consented to or received notice of any such act matter or thing.

5. You may act as though we were the Franchisee and we hereby waive any and all of our rights as surety which may at any time be inconsistent with the provisions of the Guarantee herein contained.
6. We undertake to exercise our powers as directors or shareholders of the Franchisee as the case may be to ensure its compliance with the provisions of the Agreement.
7. Any claim or right that you may have against the Franchisee shall in all respects take priority over any similar or competing right that we may have against the Franchisee under the Agreement or otherwise howsoever arising.

EXECUTED by the parties

SIGNED by)
XXX)
in the presence of:) _____

_____
Witness

_____
Name of Witness (print)

SIGNED by)
XXX)
in the presence of:) _____

_____
Witness

_____
Name of Witness (print)

Lightning Source UK Ltd.
Milton Keynes UK
UKHW020632110222
398546UK00009B/343